AGRICULTURE AND FOOD IN INDIA

Centre de Sciences Humaines (Centre for Social Sciences and Humanities): Created in 1990 and based in New Delhi, the CSH is part of the network of research centres of the French Ministry of Foreign Affairs. The Centre's research work is primarily oriented towards the study of issues concerning the contemporary dynamics of development in India and South Asia. The activities of the Centre are focused on four main themes, namely: Economic growth and sustainable development, International and regional relations, Institutional structures and political constructions of identity and Urban dynamics.

Centre de Sciences Humaines, 2, Aurangzeb Road, New Delhi-110011, India, Tel: (91) 11 3041 00 70, Fax: (91) 11 3041 00 79, E-mail: infos@csh-delhi.com
Website: http://www.csh-delhi.com

Institut Français de Pondichéry (French Institute of Pondicherry): Created in 1955, the IFP is a multidisciplinary research and advanced educational institute. Major research works are focusing on Sanskrit and Tamil Languages and literatures—in close collaboration with the Ecole Française d'Extrême-Orient—ecosystems, biodiversity and sustainability, dynamics of population and socio-economic development.

Institut Français de Pondichéry, 11, Saint Louis Street, PB 33
Pondicherry 605001, Tel: (91) 413 2334 168
Fax: (91) 413 2339 534
E-mail: ifpdir@ifpindia.org

Éditions Quae is a single publishing house covering four French research organizations: *Cemagref*, *Cirad*, *Ifremer* and *Inra*. Its catalogue includes over 1000 works covering life and earth sciences, natural landscapes, the environment, agriculture and crop production, forests and silviculture, animal rearing and products, fishing, aquatic and aquacultural resources, food and human nutrition, and society. The authors are recognized specialists in their respective fields, from both France and abroad.

AGRICULTURE AND FOOD IN INDIA

A Half-century Review, from Independence to Globalization

BRUNO DORIN
FRÉDÉRIC LANDY

QUAE

CSH
2009

MANOHAR

First published in French 2002
First published in English 2009

Translated from French by Helen Burford

ISBN 978-81-7304-812-8

Published by
Ajay Kumar Jain *for*
Manohar Publishers & Distributors
4753/23 Ansari Road, Daryaganj
New Delhi 110 002

Typeset at
Digigrafics
New Delhi 110 049

Printed at
Salasar Imaging Systems
Delhi 110035

Contents

List of Maps 8
List of Tables 9
List of Figures 10
List of Abbreviations 13
Preface 17
Introduction 19

1. THE NATURAL AND CULTURAL HERITAGE 23
   - Nature: From Sandy Desert to Evergreen Forest 23
   - Population: A Melting Pot 29
   - Government: Between Centralism and Decentralization 33
   - Land: A Focus for Reform and Conflict 36
   - Food: A Cultural Issue 41

2. THE TROPICAL PLANTATIONS 44
   - Spices and Nuts: A Taste of Ancient India 44
   - Tea, Coffee, Tobacco: Colonial Plantations under State Boards 47
   - Cotton: Between Agriculture and Industry 56
   - Sugar Cane: A Green Revolution Flavour 59

3. THE GREEN (CEREALS) REVOLUTION 66
   - The Motive: To Assert the Independence of a Young Nation 66
     - Hunger in British India 66
     - Agriculture or Industry? 68
     - The Decisive Crisis 70
   - The Technical Solution: A 'Package' of Three Ingredients 71
     - High-Yielding Seeds (HYV) 71
     - Chemical fertilizers 74
     - Irrigation 78
   - The Economic Solution: Procurement and Redistribution 83

- Procuring Goods with Attractive Farm Prices 83
- Redistributing Stocks to Consumers at Low Prices 85
- Collecting and Distributing Savings More Efficiently 89
• The Reward: Cereal Self-sufficiency 93

4. THE ANAND WHITE AND YELLOW FLOODS 101
• The White Revolution of Milk: Recycling Food Aid 101
- Getting up Steam 101
- The Liberalization Circuit Breakers 106
• The Yellow Revolution of Oilseeds: An Impossible Mission? 109
- The Workings of the Scandal 109
- Sam's Oilcan 112
- Business as Usual 115

5. THE RESURGENCE OF VITAMINS AND PROTEINS 121
• Horticulture: A Growing Nursery 121
- A Garden for Middlemen 121
- A Slow Process 125
- A Political Ground 129
• Animal Protein: Hatcheries and Hindrances 132
- Cattle Meat: A World Apart 132
- Aviculture: Soaring over Cities 137
- Fish and Shellfish: Fishing for Currency 143

6. THE FAILURE TO ERADICATE POVERTY 149
• A Multitude of Poverty Alleviation Programmes 149
• Centralization, Bureaucracy and Corruption 155
• Chronic Poverty and Under-nutrition 161

7. THE SACKING OF NATURAL RESOURCES 171
• The Water War 171
• Environmental Damages 179
• Endangered Biodiversity 185

8. MARKET LIBERALIZATION 198
• The Jump into Free-market Economy (1991) 198

- The GATT Agreements on Agriculture (1994) and after 206
  - Domestic Support: A Missed Opportunity for Domestic Reform 207
  - Export Support: On the Offensive 215
  - Market Access: A Comfortable Reform 219
- A Huge Market to Satisfy (up to 2030) 225

9. CONCLUSION 231

APPENDICES

Appendix 1. Two Indian Villages after the Green Revolution 239

Appendix 2. Exchange Rates, GDP and Production Indices 250

Appendix 3. Botanical Glossary 252

Appendix 4. Maps of Principal Crops (1980–2) 258

Bibliography 269

Index 277

Maps

1.	Precipitation and geological structure	24
2.	Agro-ecological regions	24
3.	Irrigated areas by canals (*c.* 1990)	27
4.	Crop values (1990-3)	28
5.	Rural population densities (1991)	30
6.	Tractor densities (2003)	31
7.	States and districts	34
8.	Wheat and rice procurement and central allocation (2004-5)	87
9.	Cattle and buffaloes density (2003) and milk production (2003-4)	104
10.	Falling water tables (2003)	178
	Maps of principal crops (1980-2): See Appendix 4	258

Tables

1. Food grain area, yield and availability (1950-1 to 2000-1) 96
2. Main seasons and regions for fruit and vegetable production (1995-6) 127
3. Infant mortality, life expectancy and literacy (1951 to 2001) 163
4. Agro-nutritional profiles (1999) 165
5. Nutritional availability and recommendations (1999) 168
6. Water consumption per sector (1997-8) and forecast (2025) 172
7. Compliance with TRIPS obligations (January 2000) 195
8. The major agricultural policy phases (1940 to 2000) 200
9. Aggregate Measure of Support as percentage of production value (1987 to 2000) 208
10. Official domestic support of agriculture (1995-6) 208
11. Price competitiveness in world market (1980-1 to 1994-5) 211
12. Input subsidies per cultivated hectare (1980-1 to 1995-6) 213
13. Input subsidies per cultivator (1980-1 to 1995-6) 214
14. Agricultural product imports by the European and Indian Unions (1991 to 1997) 220
15. Non-tariff import barrier regimes (1999) 221
16. Import duty regimes (1999-2000) 221
17. Summary of binding rates for agricultural products (1994) 224
18. Food market access (1991 to 1996) 226
19. Exchange rate of Rupee *vis-à-vis* selected currencies (1980-1 to 2004-5) 250

Figures

1. Population and agricultural workers (1951 to 2001) 37
2. Agricultural land distribution according to farm size (1953, 1970, 1995) 39
3. Spices and condiments production (1974-5 to 1997-8) 45
4. Tea production (1950-1 to 1997-8) 49
5. Coffee production (1950-1 to 1998-9) 53
6. Tobacco production (1950-1 to 1999-2000) 55
7. Cotton production (1950-1 to 1999-2000) 57
8. Sugar cane production (1950-1 to 1999-2000) 60
9. Sugar cane commodity chain and government controls (*c.* 1998) 61
10. Fertilizers production and import (1955-6 to 1999-2000) 76
11. Net irrigated area source-wise (1950-1 to 1994-5) 81
12. Food grains production, import, procurement and distribution (1951 to 2000) 86
13. An ideal view of the public food system 88
14. Rural credit official organization (1997-8) 93
15. Food grain area and production (1950-1 to 1999-2000) 97
16. Pulse area and production (1950-1 to 1999-2000) 98
17. Milk production (1950-1 to 1999-2000) 105
18. Milk procurement and processing (1997-8) 105
19. Oilseed area and production (1950-1 to 1999-2000) 116
20. Vegetable oil production and import (1980-1 to 1998-9) 117
21. Vegetable oil commodity chain 119
22. Fruit and vegetable production (1998-9) 122
23. The growing importance of livestock (1980-1 to 1995-6) 132
24. Livestock populations (1951 to 1997 censuses) 133
25. Meat production (1961 to 1999) 135

26. Egg production (1950-1 to 1999-2000) 139
27. Fish and shellfish production (1950-1 to 1999-2000) 143
28. Expenditures on 'Social services' by the central government (1998-9) 151
29. The vicious circle of food subsidies (1998-2003) 159
30. Population below absolute poverty line (1973-4 to 1999-2000) 162
31. Soil degradation (1950 to 1997) 180
32. Monthly wholesale price indices (April 1982 to March 2001) 204
33. Agricultural input subsidies (1980-1 to 1995-6) 212
34. Imports, exports and trade balance (1950-1 to 2000-1) 216
35. Agricultural main imports and exports (1960-1 to 2001-2) 216
36. Projections of the demand for food (2000, 2015, 2030) 227
37. Cumulated surpluses over 15 years (1980-1 to 1995-6) 228
38. Cumulated advantages over 15 years (1980-1 to 1995-6) 229
39. Growth Domestic Product (1950-1 to 1999-2000) 251
40. Agricultural and industrial production indices (1950-1 to 1999-2000) 251

Abbreviations

The acronyms below appear in the book without explanation of their meaning. For others, see the general index.

ASEAN	Association of South-East Asian Nations
BPL	Below Poverty Line
CBD	Convention on Biological Diversity of the United Nations
CIF	Cost, Insurance and Freight (included in an import or export value)
CIRAD	*Centre de coopération Internationale en Recherche Agronomique pour le Développement* (French agricultural research centre for international development)
CIS	Confederation of Independent States: created in December 1991 by 12 republics of the former USSR
FAO	Food and Agriculture Organization of the United Nations
FOB	Free On Board (opposed to CIF)
FPS	Fair Price Shops: PDS ration shops
GATT	General Agreement on Tariffs and Trade: negotiated and extended since 1947 after several successive rounds of international trade negotiations, now organized by the Word Trade Organization (WTO) created in 1995
GDP	Gross Domestic Product
HYV	High Yield Variety
ICAR	Indian Council of Agricultural Research
IMF	International Monetary Fund
INRA	*Institut National de la Recherche Agronomique*: French national institute of agricultural research
IRD	*Institut de Recherche pour le Dévelopement*: French research institute for development (ex-ORSTOM)
IRDP	Integrated Rural Development Programme. It became SGSY in 1999

MERCOSUR	Mercado Común del Sur: Common Market of South America
NAFTA	North American Free Trade Agreement
NGO	Non-Governmental Organization
PACS	Primary Agricultural Cooperative Society: Provides credit and agricultural inputs at the village level (funded mainly by the government)
PDS	Public Distribution System: provides mostly wheat, rice, sugar, cooking oil and kerosene at subsidized prices
RSS	Rashtriya Swayamsevak Sangh: Association of National Volunteers (Hindu nationalist organization created in 1925)
SDR	Special Drawing Rights: artificial basket of currencies used by the IMF for internal accounting since 1969. The SDR is also used by some countries as a peg for their own currency, and is used as an international reserve asset
SSI	Small-Scale Industries: industries which cannot invest above a ceiling (Rs. 50 million) but enjoy a monopoly of production for certain Indian industrial goods
TRIPS	Trade-Related Intellectual Property Rights
EU	European Union
UNDP	United Nations Development Programme
UPOV	*Union pour la Protection des Obtentions Végétales*: International Union for the Protection of New Varieties of Plants
URAA	Uruguay Round Agreement on Agriculture (1994): First international trade agreement on agriculture negotiated during the eighth and last round of the GATT (1986-94)
USA	United States of America
USSR	Union of Soviet Socialist Republics
WTO	World Trade Organization: Created in 1995 to replace the GATT negotiations

Some other terms not explained in the index need the following explanations:

Gross cropped area	Net sown area multiplied by the number of crops per year
Input	Good used in a production process (seed, water, fertilizer, pesticide, etc.)
Kharif	South-west monsoon crop.
Organized sector	As a matter of statistical definition, the organized sector in India according to the National Accounts Statistics of India comprises employment in the public sector and recognized educational institutions, and employment in enterprises with less than 10 employees registered under the Indian Factories, Bidi and Cigar Workers, Co-operative Societies and Provident Fund Acts. For statistical purposes, the remainder of the workforce is classified as being in the unorganized sector. Informal sector workers dominate the Indian labour market and represent some 90 per cent of the total Indian workforce.
Paddy	Non-husked rice (1 kg of paddy gives about 0.68 kg of rice)
Photoperiodism	Response by an animal or plant to changes in daily, seasonal, or yearly cycles of light and darkness
Precambrian basement	Eroded block (more than 570 million years old)
Rabi	Dry season in India
Rainfall	Any water fall including rain, snow, dew, hail
Swadeshi	Literally 'from one's own country': protectionist nationalist movement of Gandhian origin
Tariff line	Line of a nomenclature defining more or less precisely a commodity (4, 6, 8, 10, 12 digits...) subject to a possible custom duty
Tertiary fold belt	Recent mountain range (less than 65 million years old)
Trapps	Thick lava layers providing fertile soils

Preface

This book sets out to provide a unique overview of the agricultural and food economy of a young Republic that accounts for a sixth of the world's population. The original French version (Inra Editions, 2002), as well as this updated one translated from French to English by Helen Burford (Cirad), also had a second objective: to provide non-Indian readers with sufficiently specialized information to enable them to follow the articles, analyses and debates that punctuate daily life in India.

In other words, we did not aim at writing one more book on Indian agriculture full of research details, tables, footnotes and references, but rather a general introduction to Indian agriculture in the form of a scientifically-based synopsis reviewing almost six decades of changes and revolutions. Since these changes are complex and multidimensional, we have addressed and crossbred as far as possible various approaches (technical, economical, spatial, political, cultural) during a rather long historical span. In spite of this, the size of the book has been kept minimal, with an internal design as attractive as possible (small paragraphs and index on specific issues like in a textbook, almost no tables but graphs and maps summarizing thousands of statistics). Hence not only scholars, but also students, decision makers and businessmen should easily find precise (but short) information on a specific topic before going more into detail with other materials available in the market or on the Web (see also our bibliography). All in all, our endeavour focused here on synthesis, not on analysis, within the framework of a system approach trying to bring and link together various teachings mainly drawn from numerous compartmentalized scholarly literature, besides other materials including our own field experience in India.

The book thus has a broad target readership (diplomats, entrepreneurs, engineers, researchers, teachers, students, any world citizen concerned about food and agricultural issues), which has its drawbacks: some will find it too technical, others not sufficiently scientific. We merely hope that the attempted compromise will satisfy the majority.

The statistics were compiled and the corresponding figures produced by Bruno Dorin (Cirad, Montpellier), while the maps (except for those in the annex) were designed by Frédéric Landy and mostly drawn by Anne-Marie Barthélémy (University of Paris X-Nanterre).

Lastly, it goes without saying that the book would never have seen the light of day without the help of many people, most of them Indian, from Dalit farmers to ministers of the Union. We would like to express our heartfelt thanks to all of them.

Our thanks also go to the Indian researchers and French specialists of India from whom we have borrowed certain conclusions or estimates: their names are not quoted in the text but at the end of the book, in the bibliography. We hope that they will forgive us for opting to free our text from the quotations and references generally included in scientific literature.

Last but not least, we also hope that great Indian organizations such as the BAIF Development Research Foundation based near Pune (www.baif.org.in) will forgive us for not having mentioned their name along with few lines on their work: their past and present actions in favour of rural communities deserve in fact an entire book.

August 2006

BRUNO DORIN
FRÉDÉRIC LANDY

Introduction

India has over a billion mouths to feed, but it is no longer plagued by famine like it was prior to Independence in 1947. In a good year, it even manages to export cereals. Has it shown other countries the way in terms of agricultural and food policy?

Apparently not. The Green Revolution it has implemented is very similar to those adopted by other countries in the 1960s, in Asia (e.g. the Indonesian BIMAS programme) or elsewhere (e.g. the European Union's Common Agricultural Policy). Time and again, the priority has been self-sufficiency, based on State-funded agricultural intensification. It has also introduced a subsidized food distribution programme, like many other countries ranging from Egypt, Zambia and Pakistan to the United States, since the idea is also to guarantee 'food security' to poor consumers, or in other words, to provide 'access by all people at all times to enough food for an active and healthy life' (World Bank, 1986).

Any food policy has indeed to appreciate the most appropriate means to provide each and every citizen with a diet that is satisfactory in terms of nutrition, i.e. sufficiently rich in carbohydrates, proteins, fats, vitamins, iron and other micronutrients. This goes far beyond merely guaranteeing a minimum calorie intake, primarily from cereals. However, in 2001, when India apparently had no idea what to do with its 60 million-tonne State wheat and rice stockpile, 300 million Indians were still below the absolute poverty line, with many women and children suffering from severe nutritional deficiencies. That figure is almost equivalent to the total population of the fifteen European Union countries at the time. How can we explain these figures, except as the result of a serious lack of governance and of an important gap between agricultural policy and local requirements in a federation that nevertheless claims to be the world's largest democracy?

Likewise, how can we fail to assume that with an ever-growing population, the subcontinent will become increasingly reliant on the global food market? In this respect, it is strange to note that the alarmist concerns about China, whose future imports are said to be likely to destabilize prices and global cereal supplies, have not been repeated in the case of India until 2006. Some observers even claim that on the contrary, India is set to become a major exporter. It is true that in 1996—which it has to be said was an exceptional year—the country already exported over five million tonnes of rice, i.e. almost a third of the total global volume of transactions. India seems also to make a name for itself on the international seafood and oilcake markets, besides being already a world leader of IT services, a founder signatory of the GATT, and the world's largest producer of pulses, milk, mangoes and many other foods.

In fact, given its limited financial resources, in an area as heavily loaded with inhabitants as with history, India has undoubtedly followed a very original path in the field of food and agriculture. We shall attempt to demonstrate this by focusing on five crucial and hectic decades (from the Independence in 1947 to a WTO settlement in 2001) that have raised both hopes and concerns for the twenty-first century.

Chapter 1 begins by setting the scene: high population densities leading to high land pressure and a large agricultural proletariat; a federation that still sees itself as 'socialist' and where decentralization policies do not prevent the country from a high degree of centralism; and lastly, primarily Hindu cultural systems that have an impact on eating patterns.

In certain respects, the remainder of the book is chronological. Chapter 2 first reports on the maintenance of India's colonial heritage, tropical plantations (nuts and spices; tea, coffee and tobacco; sugar cane), often farmed by small holders and always under State control, albeit increasingly tempered by the current liberalization. Chapter 3 looks at the famous Green (cereals) Revolution launched during the 1960s. The system set up at the time, which is still in operation, relies on both inputs intensification (high-yielding seeds, irrigation, chemical fertilizers) and price guarantees for farmers when they come to sell their products. Once the country was more or less self-sufficient in terms of cereals, other 'revolutions' saw the light of day, with the 'white (dairy) revolution' and then the 'yellow (oils and oilseeds) revolution' (Chapter 4). However, the current trend is no more for large-scale State operations, but for cooperatives or even the private sector, as confirmed in Chapter 5 focusing on the recent revival of horticulture and animal productions (especially aviculture and aquaculture).

In short, these first Chapters paint a rather flattering picture of Indian agriculture. The remainder of the book sets out to describe the shortfalls and weaknesses, so as to pinpoint all the issues for this century. In fact, basic resources and services are still limited, as is the Indian population's buying power. These various handicaps are set out in Chapters 6 and 7, which successively highlight two of the stalemates that could not be broken by centralized development: continued severe poverty despite efforts to eradicate it, and the worrying erosion of the country's natural heritage (water, soil, biodiversity) even though the survival of the coming generations depends on it. This is combined with the marked disparities and inequalities[1] that the unprecedented economic liberalization of the 1990s has thrust into the spotlight (Chapter 8). This liberalization that marked the end of the twentieth century in India was driven as much from inside as from outside the country, with the emergence of a middle class keen to consume, the failure of the mixed economy model, the 1991 Structural Adjustment Plan and the signature in 1994 of the GATT agreement on agriculture.

Is it now really better to have dollars in one's pocket than grain in one's warehouse, as a Secretary of State for Agriculture once mused? This is the dilemma of food security. Gaining a foothold in the global market is no easier than satisfying by oneself a huge domestic market, especially when the latter has very limited financial resources and wants to diversify its food basket (increasing urbanization and rise of the consumer society). For the time being, India has refused to choose between one path or another. This is perhaps the wisest option, in order to make way for new, even more sweeping revolutions than the ones we will now describe in this book.

NOTE

1. Two 'spotlights', on a relatively wealthy village in Haryana and another much poorer one in Jharkhand (Appendix 1) give a practical illustration of current contrasts in the Indian agricultural landscape. The other

annexures contain economic indicators (including rupee to euro and rupee to dollar exchange rates), a lexicon of plant names (English, Latin, French and Hindi) and maps of the main crops at the start of the 1980s.

1. The Natural and Cultural Heritage

India has a wide range of natural environments in which water availability is still a crucial factor for agriculture. Its society, which has always been relatively segmented and hierarchical as a result of regional cultures, religions and the caste system, has nevertheless morphed into a centralized parliamentary democracy, in the form of a federal union of twenty-eight states and seven union territories. However, under its constitution, it is the states that are responsible for policy relating to land, water and agriculture. As a result, the various land reforms have had mixed results, although they have on the whole been conservative and have failed to relieve the strong pressure on the available land, which has in fact been exacerbated by unprecedented population growth since the mid-twentieth century: the population rose from 360 million in 1950 to one billion in 2000, with almost three quarters living and working in rural areas.

NATURE: FROM SANDY DESERT TO EVERGREEN FOREST

Geography

India straddles the Tropic of Cancer, and is not as large as one might think. Its southern tip does not stretch as far as the equator, and with its 2.97 million km² land mass (329 million-hectare geographical area, including water bodies), it is barely a third of the size of China or Brazil, to which it is often compared. However, it stretches over 3,000 km from east to west and almost as far from north to south, with an impressive range of environments, from the poplars of Kashmir to the coconut palms of Kerala. A distinction is generally made between three main zones (Map 1) in the country, which includes 20 major agro-ecological regions (Map 2): in the north, the Himalaya, with peaks of over 8,000 m, but whose foothills and valleys are populated; in the south, the vast Deccan Peninsula; and between the two, the Indo-Gangetic Plain. These last two zones include the main part of the 140 million ha of net sown area (190 million ha of 'gross

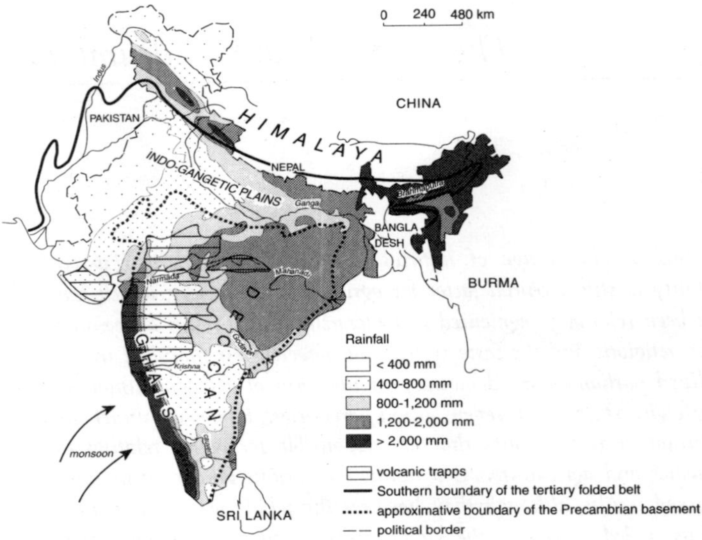

Source: Based on Racine, 1985; Spate and Learmonth, 1967.

MAP 1: PRECIPITATION AND GEOLOGICAL STRUCTURE

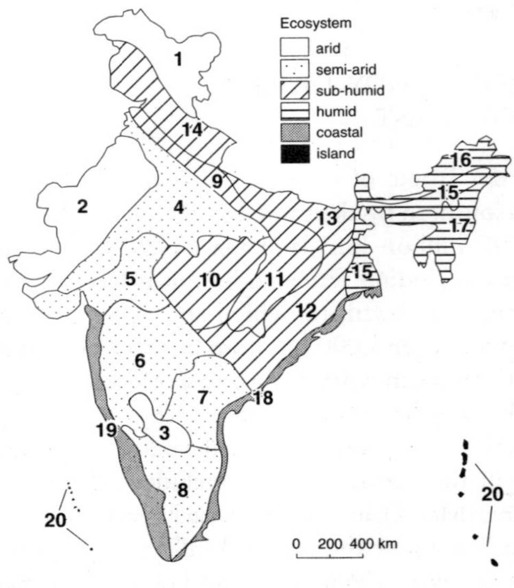

Source: Indian Council of Agricultural Research, 1992.

MAP 2: AGRO-ECOLOGICAL REGIONS

Ecosystem		*Regions*	*Climate*	*Soils*	*Growing period (days)*
Arid	1	Western Himalayas	Cold Arid	Skeletal	< 90
	2	Kutch, plains of western Rajasthan	Hot Arid	Saline, Sandy	< 90
	3	Deccan Plateau	Hot Arid	Red and Black	< 90
Semi-arid	4	Northern plain and Aravallis	Hot Semi-arid	Alluvium Derived	90-150
	5	Malwa, Kathiawar, etc.	Hot Semi-arid	Black, Often Deep	90-150
	6	Deccan Plateau	Hot Semi-arid	Black, Often Shallow	90-150
	7	Telangana, Eastern Ghats	Hot Semi-arid	Red and Black	90-150
	8	Eastern Ghats, Tamil Nadu highlands, South Karnataka	Hot Semi-arid	Red	90-150
Sub-humid	9	Northern plain	Hot Sub-humid	Alluvium derived	150-180
	10	Central highlands (Malwa, Bundelkhand, Satpura)	Hot Sub-humid	Black and Red	150-180 (210)
	11	Eastern Plateau (Chhattisgarh)	Hot Sub-humid	Red and Yellow	150-180
	12	Eastern Plateau (Chhotanagpur), Eastern Ghats	Hot Sub-humid	Red and Lateritic	150-180 (210)
	13	Eastern Plain	Hot (Sub)humid	Alluvium-Derived	180-210
	14	Western Himalayas	Hot (Sub)humid	Brown Forest and Podzolic	180-210 and more
Humid-perhumid	15	Bengal, Assam Plain	Sub-humid to Per-humid, Hot	Alluvium-derived	> 210
	16	Eastern Himalayas	Perhumid, Hot	Brown and Red Hill	> 270
	17	North-eastern Himalayas (Purvanchal)	Perhumid, Hot	Red and Lateritic	> 210
Coastal	18	Coromandel Plain	Sub-humid to Semi-arid, Hot	Coastal Alluvium-Derived	90-210
	19	Western Ghats, Malabar Plain	(Per)humid, Hot	Red, Lateritic, or Alluvium-derived	> 270
Insular	20	Andaman and Nicobar, Lakshadweep	(Per)humid, Hot	Red Loamy or Sandy	> 210

Note: Numbers 1 to 20 correspond to the regions on Map 2.

cropped area' in 2003-4 counting plots sown more than once a year).

The Indo-Gangetic Plain

The Indo-Gangetic Plain has been a hive of human activity for centuries. With its fine alluvial deposits, dense hydrographic network (Map 3) and relatively abundant groundwater, it is an ideal site for agriculture. However, since 1947, it has been deprived of most of the Indus Basin (now in Pakistan) to the west, and the most active part of the lower delta valley where the Ganges and the Brahmaputra meet (now in Bangladesh). This situation does not make relations between India and its neighbours any easier, except when they manage to sign water-sharing agreements, for instance with Bangladesh in 1996.

Peninsular India

The second major agricultural area is peninsular India, a platform of ancient, massive, mainly crystalline rock known as the Deccan Plateau. It is crossed by several large, fertile valleys whose rivers (Narmada, Godavari, Krishna, Kaveri) have their source in the Western Ghats. Elsewhere, the landscape is characterized by vast, monotonous plateaux ranging in colour from grey to brownish-red or green depending on the season and the soil type, sloping gently down to the coastal plains and deltas of the Bay of Bengal to the east. This mosaic of 'red fersiallitic' soil (Alfisols-Ustalfs, with a relatively low organic matter content and poor water retention capacity) and 'black soil', also known as 'cotton soil' (rich in clay minerals capable of swelling with water during the rainy season) forms a complex equilibrium with the parent rock, relief, vegetation and climate.

Climate

India is affected to varying degrees by the famous monsoon, which corresponds to the rainy season experienced throughout the intertropical zone, but is unusual in that in this case, it concerns very northerly latitudes: Kolkata is level with the Sahara. The southwesterly trade winds reach India from the end of May onwards (and Delhi by early July), but their actual impact depends on the relief: the Himalayas and the Western Ghats receive abundant rainfall (> 2000 mm/year), while the central part of Deccan, in the lee of the Ghats, has a semi-arid climate (500-1000 mm/year) and part of Rajasthan is actually desert. The north-eastern monsoon, in winter, is much more limited

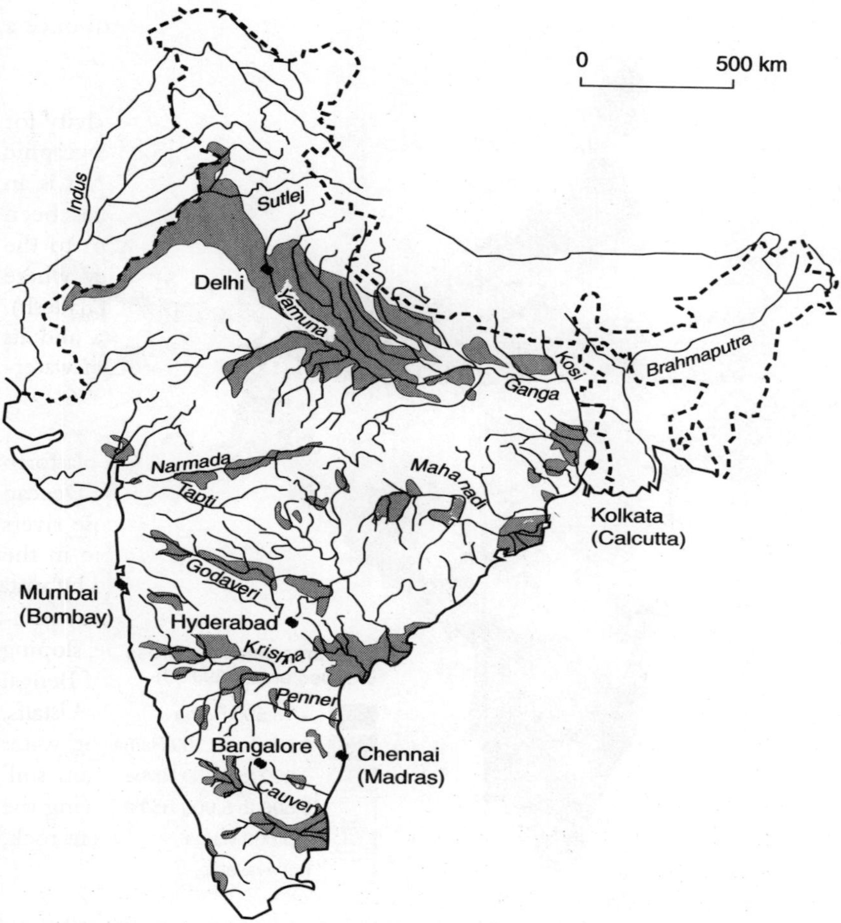

Source: Based on Land Resource Atlas of India, 1996.

MAP 3: IRRIGATED AREAS BY CANALS (*c.* 1990)

and localized. The annual mean temperature is over 20 °C, but temperature varies less than rainfall, which is thus the main factor characterizing the different regions and also the seasons.

Kharif and Rabi Seasons

The agricultural year is generally split into two seasons, with *kharif* crops grown during the rainy season (sown after the first showers in June or July and harvested four to six months later),

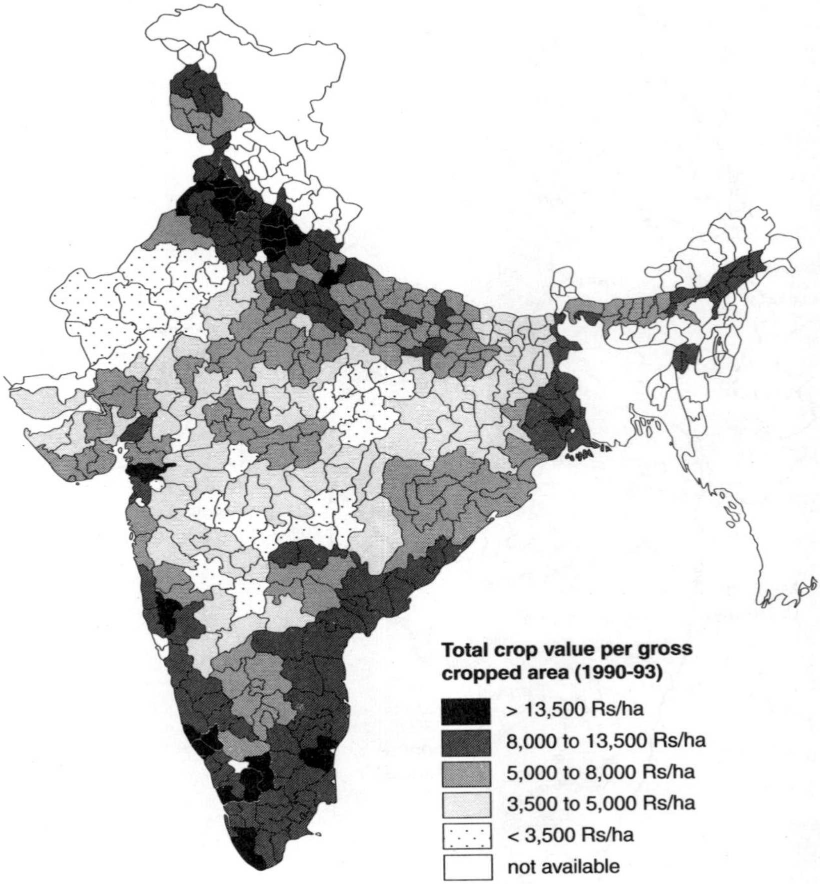

Source: © G.S. Bhalla and G. Singh, 2001 (All rights reserved. By permission of Sage Publ. India Pvt. Ltd., New Delhi).

MAP 4: CROP VALUES (1990–3)

and *rabi* crops, which generally have to be irrigated as they stretch into autumn and winter (and are harvested at the start of the hot, dry season that prevents any crop growth). However, the situation is actually much more complex, and in many regions, most of the rainfall does not in fact come from the summer monsoon. Nevertheless, generally speaking, zones with over

1,200 mm of rainfall per year can grow rice without irrigation, provided the climate is not too cold: this means the coast and the eastern quarter of the country. Below that figure, agricultural rotations are dominated by 'millets' (sorghum, finger millet, pearl millet, and so on), pulses (peas and lentils) and oilseeds (groundnut, rapeseed, mustardseed, and so on), as in central Deccan. Wheat, a temperate crop, can only be grown in winter, which is the dry season; it is thus generally irrigated, and followed by a maize or rice crop in the rainy season. Two or three crops can therefore be grown each year (shortening crop cycles and expanding double-cropping is a priority for Indian agricultural research), but only in regions with irrigation or with sufficient, evenly distributed rainfall (Map 4). This unfortunately is not the case in the arid or semi-arid regions that cover over a third of the country (Map 7).

Flora and Fauna

From the Himalayas in the east to the Ghats in the west, India's broad longitudinal stretch makes it a significant biodiversity reserve. It has over 45,000 plant species (a third of them endemic) and 81,000 animal species. This represents 8 per cent of the total world resource (1.6 million recorded species), although the country accounts for just 2.4 per cent of the total land mass. There are 97 national parks and over 400 senctuaries working to protect this flora and fauna, which are under threat from population growth, agriculture, industrialization and urbanization. Less than 20 per cent of the country is now covered in 'forest', and a part of that is steppe-type vegetation that serves as low-grade pasture for animals, and to provide household fuel.

POPULATION: A MELTING POT

Population

With a population that had doubled in the 30 years since Independence and a current annual growth rate of around 1.7 per cent (an increase equivalent to the total population of Australia each year), India had 1.027 billion inhabitants in 2001, according to the latest ten-yearly census. (One person in three is illiterate and the sex ratio is 933 women per 1,000 men.) At this rate, the population could outstrip that of China by 2030. In any event, population pressure on land and environment is increasing. The population density is almost three times that of France, and while in 1991 there were an average of 267 inhabitants per km², or 219 in rural areas, the figure was over 800 in the Ganges Valley, Kerala or the deltas (Map 5). Moreover, despite megalopolises such as Mumbai (Bombay) and Delhi, which now have about 20 million inhabitants, the Indian

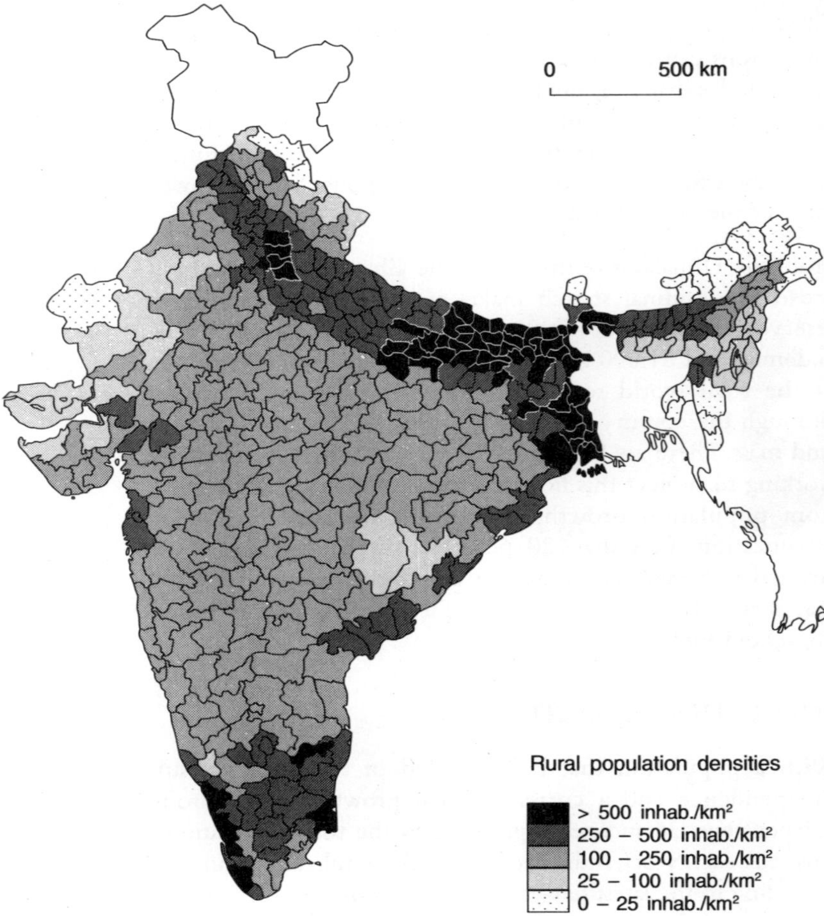

Source: Based on Census of India, 2001.

MAP 5: RURAL POPULATION DENSITIES (1991)

population is still largely rural (72 per cent in 2001). This means a huge number of farms (over 100 million), with very small amounts of land (1.3 ha on average in 2000–1, albeit with substantial variations). Per capita cultivable land availability (including forest) fell from 0.48 ha in 1950 to 0.15 in 2000. This physical fragmentation of the agricultural production system, which accounts for the low rate of mechanization (Map 6) is combined with a similar fragmentation of the country's population into a multitude of communities.

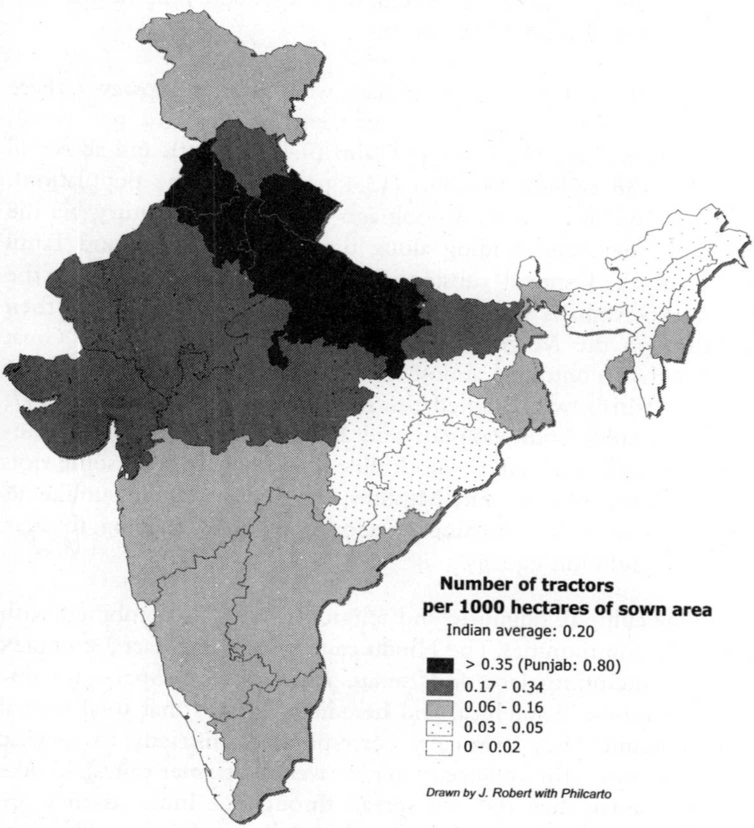

Source: Based on Ministry of Agriculture (www.indiaagristat.com).

MAP 6: TRACTOR DENSITIES (2003)

Aryans and Dravidians

The history of the Indian population is a political hot potato in contemporary India. The descendants of the *Adivasis*, the negroid 'first inhabitants' who came from South-East Asia, now make up often very poor tribes living in isolated areas. The Dravidians, whose languages—which include Tamil, Telugu, Kannada and Malayalam—are spoken in southern India, once spread as far as Afghanistan. Groups from the north who speak Indo-European languages inherited from Sanskrit, such as Hindi, Urdu, Punjabi, Bengali, Gujarati and Rajasthani, mostly descend from the Aryans who came from the north-west around 1,500 years BC. It is these groups who brought with them the Vedic religion that was in time to become Hinduism.

Hindus and Muslims

In 2001, 80.4 per cent of Indians were Hindus. However, there were also Christians (2.3 per cent), Sikhs (1.9 per cent), Buddhists (0.8 per cent) and Jains (0.4 per cent), and above all over 138 million Muslims (13.4 per cent of the population). Islam was introduced as long ago as the eighth century, via the Arab merchants trading along the coasts of Kerala and Tamil Nadu, and spread substantially overland, firstly through the Turko-Afghans from the eleventh century onwards, and then through the Mughal Empire from 1526 to 1858. The 'Great Mughals' controlled almost all of India until it was colonized by the British, who unified the subcontinent. However, in 1947, India split from Pakistan and Bangladesh and gained independence, albeit after considerable bloodshed. Despite some riots involving Hindus and Muslims, the Indian Union, unlike its neighbours, has remained a secular republic, striving to treat every religion equally.

Castes, Varnas and Jatis (Brahmins, Dalits)

This cultural, linguistic and religious mosaic is combined with caste communities. The Hindu caste system is in fact a complex one including *jatis* and *varnas*. *Jatis*—castes proper—are endogamous, hierarchical and hereditary groups that total several thousand. They originally corresponded unstrictly to specific professions (for instance potter, weaver and farmer castes). Unlike the *varnas*, they did not spread throughout India, as they are associated with specific cultural and linguistic areas. The four *varnas*, for their part, are defined in the sacred Hindu texts according to their degree of purity, which corresponds to their social function: in decreasing order, a priestly function for

Brahmins, a royal and military role for Kshatriyas and a trading, craft or agricultural role for Vaishyas, with Shudras serving the higher *varnas*. At the very bottom of the scale, scorned by the system (which nevertheless cannot function without them) are the various 'outcaste' groups who have successively been called Untouchables, Harijans and now Dalits (or Scheduled Castes–SCs) in administrative jargon). The natives ('tribals', *Adivasis*, or Scheduled Tribes–STs), who were not originally Hindus, are often similarly scorned.

Affirmative Action, Reservations

Discrimination on the grounds of caste was officially outlawed in the 1950 Constitution. The increasing modernization of contemporary India has also meant that the 'system' is dying out, with a decline in the interdependence of the various *jatis*. However, at the same time, the structure has become a political issue, with the introduction of compulsory entry quotas (reservations for the civil service, universities, etc.), which the Constitution originally intended as a temporary measure restricted to the SCs and STs, but which have since been confirmed and extended to cover Other Backward Classes (OBC), following the implemention of the Mandal Report recommendations in 1989. This has both revived and transformed the different groups. The age-old caste culture thus lives on in various forms, particularly in villages, where it was generally considered that the different *jatis* coexist in a hierarchical system based on a notion of purity (Louis Dumont's *Homo hierarchicus*). These complex relations, in which the dominant land-owning groups may or may not be castes with an agricultural tradition (like the Jats in the north-west, the Patidars in Gujarat, the Kammas and Reddis in Andhra Pradesh, the Ahirs, Sainis, Kurmis, Patels, Gounders, etc.), have an undeniable influence on the diet, habitat, economy, politics and government in India.

GOVERNMENT: BETWEEN CENTRALISM AND DECENTRALIZATION

Centre and States

The British gave India a model of parliamentary democracy and government that rapidly became well-rooted, particularly as it had been foreshadowed in some of the political units of pre-colonial India. Nowadays, the prime minister has much more power than the president, as he or she represents the political majority in the national assembly (Lok Sabha), whose 545 Members of Parliament (MPs) are elected by universal suffrage. The 245 members of the Upper House (Rajya Sabha), for their part, are mostly elected by indirect suffrage, by the assemblies of the states (twelve are appointed by the president). The 'Sovereign Democratic Republic' of India was officially founded on 26 January 1950, with one of the longest constitutions in the world, and is also and above all a union of twenty-eight states and seven territories (including Delhi, which is virtually a state in its own right).

States and Districts Each of the states (Map 7) operates as a scale model of central government, and is headed by a chief minister and local

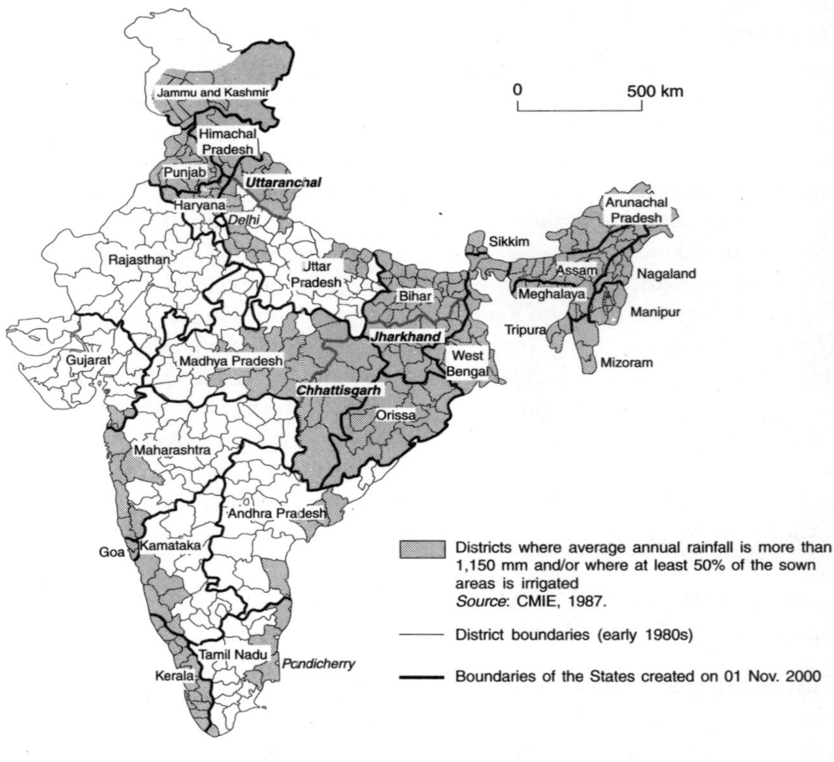

MAP 7: STATES AND DISTRICTS

Members of Legislative Assembly (MLAs), who are elected by universal suffrage. Alongside this state government and its ministries, there is also a governor appointed by the president to represent the central government. The governor may temporarily take power if he or she feels that the state government is no longer legitimate (President's Rule, Article 356 of the Constitution). Lower down the scale, revenue matters are handled by the districts (each headed by a collector), *tahsils* or *taluks*, and villages, with the village accountant. This complex system means that there are some 5,000 top-level civil servants throughout India, working in either central government or state government structures, who belong to the Indian Administrative Service (IAS), one of the main two Indian Civil Services (ICS), the other being the Indian Police Service (IPS). These civil servants work with a much larger number in each state (State Administrative Service).

Panchayats and Development Authorities (Mandals, Blocks...)

Lastly, the institutions of the Panchayati Raj are local assemblies whose members are elected by universal suffrage every five years, to form three levels of councils identified by the development authorities: villages (Gram Panchayats), medium rungs (Mandal or Block Panchayats) and districts (Zilla Parishads). These institutions are a legacy of the disappointing attempts at decentralization in the late 1950s (elections were never held in some states), and were strengthened in 1992 by the introduction of the 73rd and 74th Constitutional Amendments, applying to rural and urban zones respectively. They now have greater power, particularly to draft and implement economic development programmes. Another important resolution under the new Panchayati Raj has been the introduction of a quota of 33 per cent for women (in addition to the seats traditionally set aside for tribes, Dalits and other lower castes): this means almost 8,25,000 women on these so-called 'self-government' councils. However, in practice, apart from many success stories (particularly in Kerala), decentralization has proved to be a disappointment in many regions. The states are reluctant to delegate their powers, or the local authorities lack resources (finance, skills), or the weaknesses of civil society and the deep-rooted agrarian inequalities in the country have prevented the poorest groups from benefiting from this revival of the 'world's largest democracy'.

Agricultural Authorities (ICAR, KVKs...)

Within this democracy, annex 7 to the Constitution specifies that the states have sole responsibility for policy, legislation and taxation concerning land, water and agriculture. However, since as long ago as 1955, with the Essential Commodities Act, the central government has had overall control over food distribution, which inevitably affects upstream operations. The Centre may also recommend certain policies (for instance land reforms), provide various incentives (loans, grants, controls, infrastructures, border controls on trade, etc.) or act as an arbitrator in the event of disputes between states (particularly concerning water use). Lastly, via the Department of Agricultural Research and Education (DARE), set up in 1973, the Union Ministry of Agriculture provides the major share of the funds allocated to the Indian Council of Agricultural Research (ICAR), which draws up, funds and manages the main public agricultural research, training and development programmes. To this end, throughout the country, which it has split into 120 agro-climatic zones, the ICAR has a network of 45 institutes, 30 national research centres and 86 national programmes (All India Coordinated Research Projects) implemented by the 200 research stations run by the 29 state agricultural universities. These universities also had 79 agricultural colleges (including 18 for girls), 30 veterinary colleges and almost 55 other colleges in various fields (engineering, forestry, fish farming, dairy production, horticulture, etc.) in 1996. In addition, the *Krishi Vigyan Kendras* (KVK) or agricultural science centres manage over 200 ICAR-integrated programmes aimed at transferring research results to farmers. There are eight trainers' training centres for staff from these centres.

LAND: A FOCUS FOR REFORM AND CONFLICT

Zamindars and Ryots

With 47 per cent of its land mass used for crops at least once a year (an estimated 142 million ha in 1997–8, in addition to 69 of forest, 11 of rangeland and 82 of mountains, developed land, wasteland and other land types), India has an advantage over China (of which only 10 per cent is cultivated). However, land pressure is still considerable: the rural population density is high, and 73 per cent of workers in rural areas are still farmers (Figure 1). Immediately prior to Independence, the cultivated land was still owned by a small number of people, often from the higher castes. These owners were either zamindars, inamdars, etc. (Uttar Pradesh, Bihar, Bengal, Orissa, Hyderabad, etc.), i.e. they had rights similar to those in fiefdoms and could levy taxes, or traders, moneylenders and usurers in those regions where farmers were taxed directly (*ryots*). There could be anywhere between ten and twenty middlemen between the landlord and the actual tiller.

Land Reforms

The states were asked to implement a series of land reforms following Independence, to adjust land distribution in the hope of ensuring social justice and economic efficiency. Depending on the region, these reforms successively included the abolition of *zamindari*, an obligation to cultivate any land owned,

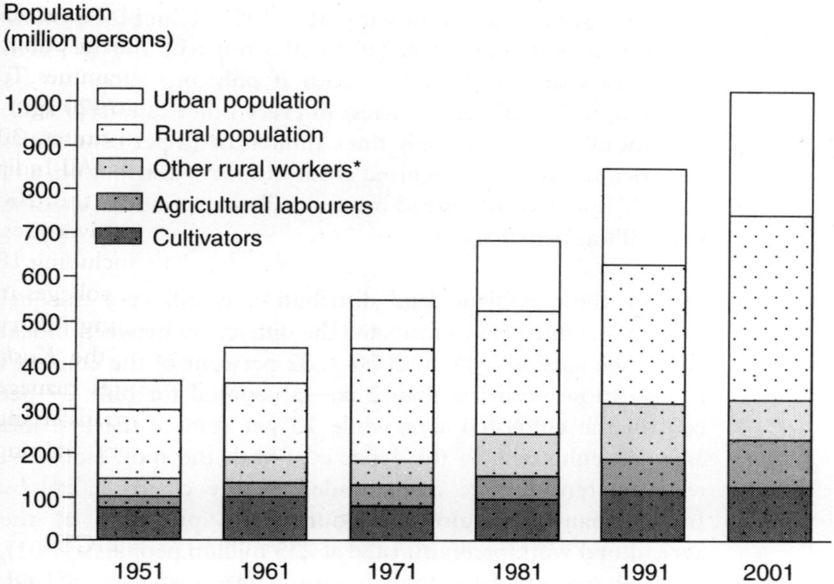

The urban agricultural workers (about 7.2 million persons in 2001) are recorded in the urban population.
* including "marginal agricultural workers" in 1981 and 1991.

Source: Based on Registrar General of India, 2001.

FIGURE 1 : POPULATION AND AGRICULTURAL WORKERS (1951 TO 2001)

Note: A 'cultivator' is defined in India as someone who spends most of the working days in a year on his own land, while an 'agricultural labourer' is employed by other farmers for most of the year.

restrictions on land purchases and the number of labourers employed, secure tenancies at reasonable rates, assisted purchase arrangements for tenants, incentives for production cooperatives, confiscation of land and its reallocation to landless farmers, the construction of houses for farmers, redistribution of state-owned wasteland, and so on. However, these laws and incentives were not applied with the same care or determination everywhere. In Bihar, for instance, until the reforms were relaunched in 1995 by a government with members drawn from the lower castes, some properties covered over a thousand ha. Likewise, the land ownership thresholds laid down in Kerala in 1959, West Bengal in 1977 (when the Communists came to power) and Karnataka in 1974 have not been strictly respected, and neither have been those recommended following the 1972 Chief Ministers' Conference: 4.05 to 7.28 ha (10 to 18 acres) with two irrigated crops per year, 10.93 ha (27 acres) if only one crop can be irrigated, and 21.85 ha (54 acres) in every other case (arid land, plantations, etc.). Lastly, only three million ha (2 per cent of the net sown area) were recognized as surplus for redistribution, and in 1995, only two-thirds had been actually redistributed, to some five million beneficiaries.

Farms

Despite these reforms, land distribution is still very unequal (Figure 2), which has exacerbated the differences between Indian farms (see appendix 1). In 2000-1, 82 per cent of the country's farms—those with less than 2 ha—accounted for only 39 per cent of the cultivated area, while 13 per cent of the available area was cultivated by the 1 per cent with the most land. The resulting tensions are compounded by the claims staked by India's many agricultural labourers (46 per cent of the agricultural workforce, estimated at 235 million people in 2001), although some of them do themselves own a small piece of land. The large landowners still hold considerable power, since the marginal farmers, labourers, lower castes or Dalits depend on them in many ways: for work, credit, seed, irrigation, marketing operations, etc. Likewise, the reforms have failed to halt the break-up of farms as a result of population growth and the sharing of inherited land between sons. The average farm size fell from 2.5 ha in 1953-4 to 1.13 ha in 2000-1. However, as even 'large' farms are still relatively small, radical land redistribution to all claimants would barely give each farmer

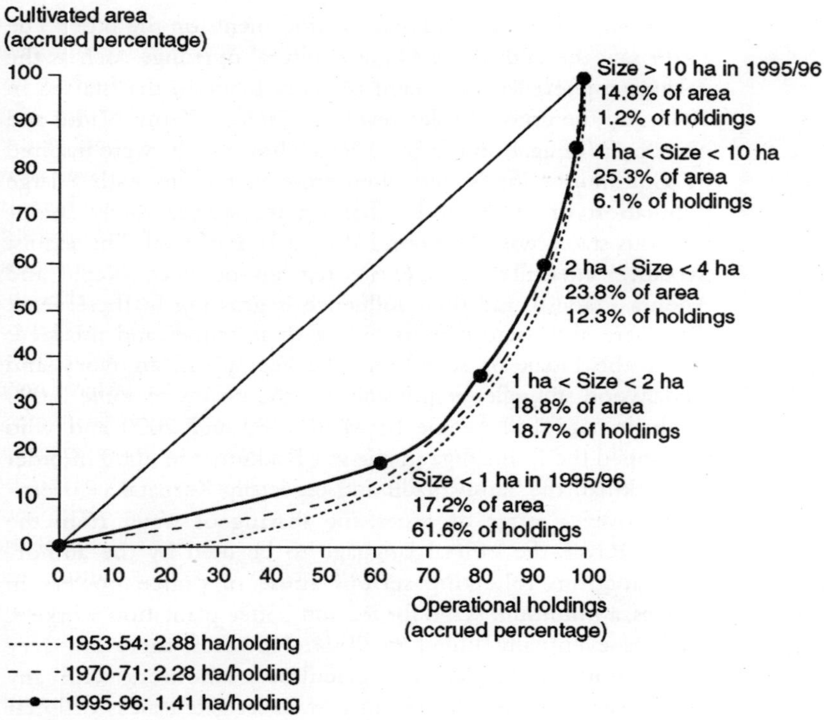

Source: Based on Centre for Monitoring Indian Economy, 1999.

FIGURE 2: AGRICULTURAL LAND DISTRIBUTION ACCORDING TO FARM SIZE (1953, 1970, 1995)

enough land to live on, leaving little room for progress. Lastly, despite their inadequacies and limitations, these reforms have served to reaffirm the rural middle classes' commitment to farming. Combined with a policy of effective land consolidation, particularly in the north-west of the country, the attention paid to agricultural land ownership by Nehru before the launch of the green revolution played a part in its success, by reinforcing a class of medium farmers able to invest in the new agricultural technology. In turn, the revolution modified the nature of the farmers' claims.

Farmers' Movements

Farmers' movements in India, which may or may not be unions, can be split into two groups: agricultural labourers' movements on the one hand, and landowners' movements on the other. The 1970s saw the end of the old agricultural uprisings, such as the Telangana guerrilla movement (Andhra Pradesh) that started in 1946, and the untouchables' revolts in Tanjore (Tamil Nadu) and Naxalbari (Bengal) in the late 1960s. These revolts were inspired by Communist ideals, and often arose in regions with a large population of Dalits and tribal groups whose lowly socio-religious status was compounded by a lack of land. The maoist 'naxalite' guerrillas hold entire regions between Nepal and Andhra Pradesh, and their influence is growing in these areas. There are also mere bandits hiding their crimes and misdeeds under the cloak of socialism, like Veerappan, an ivory and sandalwood smuggler responsible for the deaths of some 2,000 elephants and 140 people between 1989 and 2000 and who kidnapped the Kannadiga movie star Rajkumar in 2000 in order to blackmail the Tamil Nadu and especially Karnataka governments over a range of issues: the sharing of water from the Kaveri River, the official language to be used by the authorities, sanctions following serious abuse of police powers in villages, a minimum wage for tea and coffee plantation workers. He was eventually killed in 2004. However, there are very few unions of *mazdurs* or agricultural labourers with any real power nowadays, except in certain irrigated areas of Uttar Pradesh, Kerala or Tamil Nadu. They have been somewhat supplanted by the so-called 'new farmers' movements' that have taken centrestage since the 1980s. The issue is no longer land redistribution, but paddy, wheat and sugar prices.

Trade Unions (BKU, KRRS...)

Union members are primarily middle-class and wealthy farmers, the very ones who have benefited from the land reforms of the 1950s and the Green Revolution. These *kulaks* or 'bullock capitalists' as they have often been called, belong to locally dominant Shudra farming castes, who often not only have agricultural claims to stake, but also political ones, by virtue of their proclaimed status as backward classes. Each of the unions {Karnataka Rajya Raitha Sangha (KRRS) in Karnataka, Bharatiya Kisan Union (BKU) in Uttar Pradesh, Tamil Nadu Agriculturists' Association (TNAA) in Tamil Nadu, etc.} claims to have several million members, and they are all calling for higher agricultural prices and higher input subsidies. Year after year, they put pressure on the government—generally with some success—to increase the guaranteed prices set by the Commission for Agricultural Costs and Prices, and their demonstrations (blockades and sometimes calls for general strikes) have so far succeeded in keeping urea (a chemical fertilizer) supplies at a fixed, subsidized price. There is one exception to the rule: the Shetkari Sanghatana, founded in Maharashtra by Sharad Joshi, is calling for increased free trade. It wants to see prices brought into line with those on the global market, has denounced discrimination against rural areas by towns and cities, and is critical of the worsening terms of trade between agriculture and industry, which it sees as a mark of Indian policy. On the global stage, it is generally the BKU and the KRRS that receive the most publicity: they are members ofVia Campesina, the international smallholders' and agricultural labourers' movement that, strangely enough, includes somewhat big Indian cereal and sugar cane growers who may be Jats (Uttar Pradesh) or Vokkaligas (Karnataka), alongside the Brazilian Landless Workers Movement and the French Confédération paysanne. They have no qualms about using slogans calling for protection for the environment, women and agricultural labourers, whereas within India itself, it is generally a very different story. At home they are in favour of economic productivism and are socially conservative. Their only true common ground with Via Campesina is their nationalism, which prompts them to fight against the intrusion of multinationals into Indian farming (viz., the sacking of Cargill facilities in Karnataka in 1992), GMOs and American-style diets.

FOOD: A CULTURAL ISSUE

Chapattis, Dal and Rice

The Indian diet is above all a local affair, since it centres on plants and recipes specific to each region. However, to generalize, in the north-west, it centres on flat wheat bread (*chapattis*, with more or less sophisticated variations such as *naans, rotis, rumali rotis*, and so on), whilst in the south and north-east, rice is the staple. In central India, it is sorghum and finger millet that are most popular. In addition to the fact that food is eaten with the fingers of the right hand (the left being used to wash after defecation), the main common features are that cereals dominate the diet, vegetables are of secondary importance, meat is rarely eaten, and lentil *dal* is thus an important source of protein.

Vegetarianism

Diet is also a matter of religion. Muslims do not eat pork, and insist upon *halal* meat. Hindus do not have any common restrictions, not even the taboo about cows, which does not exist among the Dalits, since generally Hindu culture is defined more by caste than by religion. As a result, only a minority of Hindus (may be around 20 per cent)—the highest castes—are vegetarian for religious reasons. The remainder may eat chicken, goat and mutton often, without restriction. However, only Dalits eat beef, or sometimes pork, like tribals and Christians. Each caste thus has its own values and restrictions: in villages the rules of commensality are still extremely strict, and a person cannot theoretically take food but from someone of a higher or equal caste. At least, this is the situation in terms of the status of each group within the system, but there are major variations. Some people choose to respect the taboos observed by the higher castes, in the hope of moving up the scale of purity (sanskritization). The very poor, on the other hand, sometimes eat forbidden meat, since they can only afford beef and pork (even so, a kilo of beef costs more than the daily wage of an agricultural labourer). Lastly, as a result of westernization, young Brahmins may agree to eat meat at an outsider's home, provided there are no local witnesses. The world of English-speaking upper class has anyway a specific set of codes and behaviours.

Sacred Cows

Hindus revere five cow products that serve to purify the body and soul: milk, *ghee* (clarified butter), whey, dung and urine. Many also believe that drinking cow urine cures some serious diseases. However, these convictions have a relatively limited economic impact. While some believe that there are too many cows, resulting in over-grazing and low productivity, they forget that producing meat is far from negligible, despite the taboo: 2.9 million tonnes of bovine meat produced in 2004 and 2.6 eaten locally, according to the FAO. Above all, cows can provide draught to pull a plough, almost as well as oxen or buffalo, although the latter are more robust. They also provide dung, which is still a major fertilizer in India and is also used as fuel, particularly in heavily deforested areas. Lastly, in addition to producing milk, cows are a way for farmers to capitalize on their savings and generate a return by producing calves. The fact that India has 16 per cent of the world's cows and oxen is thus far from due to religious convictions alone, although the recommendations laid down in the Constitution, which have been hammered home even further by Hindu extremist groups such as the RSS, have led most states to impose a ban on killing cows. When all is said and done, Hindu farmers are still farmers first and foremost: they beat animals that refuse to pull a plough, and only rarely allow them to die of old age on their farm.

Hot and Cold Foods

Meat consumption is thus often limited to just one meal a week, sometimes less among the rural poor, for religious and price reasons, but also due to its perceived health implications. Traditional Ayurvedic medicine links three elements in the universe (wind, fire and water) to three elements in the human body: air, bile and phlegm (the *tridosha* theory of the three humours). Disrupting the balance of these three elements is believed to cause disease. It is therefore important not to consume excessive amounts of 'hot' foods (such as meat or chillies), 'cold' foods (such as white rice or coconut), or 'air' foods (such as peas), but to strike a balance, allowing for the temperature on the day in question and the person's general physical and psychological condition. These beliefs are widespread in India, although very few people know much about the philosophical and scientific reasoning behind them, and despite the fact that on a local level, a given variety of tomato may be considered 'hot' in one village and 'cold' in another.

2. The Tropical Plantations

Plantation crops in India date back to colonial and pre-colonial times. Even in ancient times, Indian spices were traded via complex circuits, and during British rule, they were encouraged, along with other commercial crops (tea, coffee, tobacco, sugar cane). In view of the revenue they generate, India did not dismiss plantation crops after Independence, despite placing the emphasis on food crops. However, it did place them under state control, with a sector dominated by small holders (except in the case of the tea estates in the north) and controlled through state boards (tea, coffee, rubber, spices, tobacco) or a legislative structure placing the entire commodity chain under public control (sugar cane). However, with the current move towards liberalization, growing foreign currency requirements are increasingly making low cost supplies to Indian consumers a secondary concern. Packaging and quality, which were long overlooked in favour of optimizing production, are also becoming increasingly important in the drive to capture market share and generate revenue in export markets.

SPICES AND NUTS: A TASTE OF ANCIENT INDIA

Spices and Condiments

The history of Indian spices dates back more than 7,000 years, but spice trade really took off at the very end of the fifteenth century: on 18 May 1498, Vasco da Gama landed in Calicut (Kerala) and four years later, after taking the island of Diu (off the southern tip of Gujarat), the Portuguese bombarded this port on the coast of Malabar with a view to taking control of it and diverting the European spice trade (pepper, cinnamon, cloves, ginger and so on) via Lisbon, whereas it had hitherto been the preserve of Arab traders. India is now both the leading producer (approximately 3 million tonnes in 1997–8, Figure 3), the leading consumer (everyone knows how spicy its cuisine is, partly for health reasons), and the leading exporter (almost 50 per cent of global supplies, although it exports less than a tenth of what it produces) of spices: production peaked at 5.1 million tonnes in 2004–5. Barks, buds, flowers, fruit, leaves,

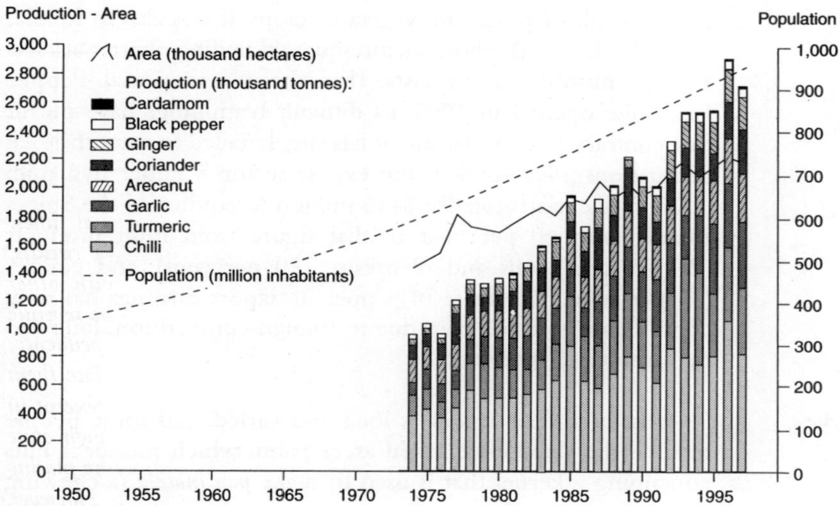

Source: Based on data from Centre for Monitoring Indian Economy.

FIGURE 3: SPICES AND CONDIMENTS PRODUCTION (1974-5 TO 1997-8)

rhizomes, roots, seeds, stigmas, styles and sometimes whole plants may be used fresh, dried, crushed, ground or distilled, in numerous culinary, medicinal and cosmetic preparations. The Indian Institute of Spices Research has the largest gene bank in the world for pepper, cardamom, ginger and turmeric (Indian saffron). However, it is not enough to be the world's leading producer of coriander, cumin, black pepper, cardamom, ginger or chilli: as with other plantation crops, the official buzzword now is quality improvement. The Spices Board, founded in 1987 by the Ministry of Commerce and Industry, manages numerous programmes that subsidize new varieties and better storage methods, and awards certificates or special logos to the best exporters, who are also listed on its website. There is also a drive to promote high added value products. The main obstacle is the production structures typical of the farming systems in Kerala state, the birthplace of pepper, where most spices and condiments are produced. Few plantations are monocultures: micro-farms grow a random mixture of coconut palms or areca trees, which serve as stakes for pepper plants, banana, cashew, nutmeg, cinnamon or clove trees, and a lower storey of chilli and turmeric, plus tapioca and vegetable crops. It was also in Kerala, in Kochi (Cochin) whose picturesque old trading quarter attracts a large number of tourists, that the International Pepper Exchange opened in 1997; its difficult beginnings have meant that contrary to expectations, it has largely failed to smooth price fluctuations. Nevertheless, the export sector is rather dynamic: in 2003–4, exports totalled $415 million (according to the Spices Board) with 60 per cent of that figure from mint products (21 per cent), oils and oleoresins (20 per cent), and chillies (19 per cent). The share of pepper in export earnings has now come down to 8 per cent due to foreign competition, followed by turmeric (7 per cent).

Areca

The list of Indian 'spices' is long and varied, and some people include the slender-stemmed areca palm, which produces nuts containing a kernel that is used to make *pan masala* (a chewing mixture made of areca, lime and a varying range of other ingredients, wrapped in betel leaves) and *supari* (flavoured nut pieces, which are sucked), both of which are very popular in India, despite the risks of mouth cancer. Areca production and the *gutka* industry have therefore not been encouraged by the state since 1971–2, and the Central Arecanut and Cocoa Marketing and Processing Cooperative (CAMPCO) research centre in Mangalore is trying to find other outlets for areca, in the event of the Union carrying out its threat to ban these products. In the meantime, areca nut production—primarily in Karnataka, Kerala and Assam—is thriving, with a record 3,79,000 tonnes being produced in 2000–1 (1,41,000 tonnes in 1970–1), on 3,13,000 ha.

Cashew

The outlets for cashew nuts, which are produced in even greater quantities than areca nuts (5,35,000 tonnes in 2003–4, on 6,83,000 ha) are very different from those for areca. Cashew originated in South America, and was introduced into India by the Portuguese in the sixteenth century, as it grows well on coastal sands or lateritic soils and thus serves to control erosion. It was not until the 1980s that people realized that the 2,81,000 ha planted with cashew were actually producing a nut that could generate considerable export revenue. Under a World Bank project, cashew nut production and processing operations, which require a considerable amount of female labour, have since been organized in various states. As a result, India is the world's leading producer (85 per cent of the global total in 1996-7 came from Kerala, Maharashtra, Andhra Pradesh, Karnataka and Orissa), processor (over 1,000 units, including 400 in Kerala, 300 in Tamil Nadu and 100 in Karnataka) and exporter (over 200 exporters are registered with the Cashew Export Promotion Council of India). However, over half the trees are now old and/or no longer harvested (including 90,000 ha belonging to State Forestry Departments), and India has also become the world's leading importer of unprocessed nuts (from Tanzania, Guinea Bissau, Indonesia, Ivory Coast, etc.). Nevertheless, the operation is still highly profitable: in 1998-9, 1,81,000 tonnes were imported at a cost of $165 million, while in the same year, after processing (sun-drying, cleaning, humification, storage, roasting, shelling, sorting and packing), 77,000 tonnes of kernels (the equivalent of around 3,08,000 tonnes of unprocessed nuts) were exported to over 50 countries (led by the United States), for over twice their original value ($383 million dollars). This is without counting the revenue generated by a growing number of by-products (syrup, confectionery, jams, pickles and the alcohol *feni*, made from cashew apples; and polymers made from a liquid extracted from the shell). However, this export revenue is now under serious threat due to demand on the Indian domestic market, which may also be about to become the world's largest (it is currently in second place).

TEA, COFFEE, TOBACCO: COLONIAL PLANTATIONS UNDER STATE BOARDS

Plantations

Under the term 'plantations', India includes tea, coffee, cocoa, rubber, cardamom, areca nut and coconut, which in all but the last two cases are concentrated in the Ghats and eastern Himalayas, i.e. near the former colonial ports. These tropical estate crops stand out in that they were generally encouraged by the colonial authorities, and even now count for a third of the country's agricultural exports. It is also significant that this sector falls under the Ministry of Commerce and Industry rather than the Ministry of Agriculture. Lastly, and this is crucial to an understanding of what is meant by 'plantations' in India, unlike seasonal crops and orchards, they are not subject to Land Ceiling Acts. On the other hand, to protect small-scale producers and reduce land concentration, the sector is closely controlled by the state (agricultural research, marketing, exports, and so on), through five boards created by the central government (tea, coffee, rubber, spices and tobacco). In spite of growing liberalization, some support is still provided: a Price Stabilization Fund Scheme was launched in 2003 for the benefit of small growers (less than 4 ha) of tea, coffee, rubber and tobacco. As a result, large estates are no longer dominant: in the case of rubber, for instance, the average plantation size—less than 0.5 ha—bears witness to how scattered the production structures are. However, these plantations are supervised by the Rubber Board, which manages in some years to make India self-sufficient (in 2004–5 synthetic rubber accounted for just 20 per cent of domestic consumption). Yields (1,705 kg/ha in 2004–5) and output are growing, notably because of the attractive prices offered to growers and because of the effective marketing structure. In all, natural rubber production in India amounted to 7,50,000 tonnes in 2004–5, making it the world's fourth largest producer, with 92 per cent of that figure coming from Kerala.

Tea Tea is also produced in Kerala and in Tamil Nadu and Karnataka, in the mountainous regions of these states (generally between 1,400 and 2,000 m above sea level) with sufficient rainfall (the ideal figure is between 1,750 and 2,000 millimetres a year). However, for agro-climatic, historic and economic reasons, three quarters of the tea produced in India come from two states in the far north-east of the country: Assam and West Bengal (Figure 4). Tea cultivation is highly labour-intensive (around 700 man-days per ha per year) and directly employs almost a million people in India, with a further million involved in related activities: the proximity of these two states to Bihar and its abundance of cheap labour (men to prune the buds and terminal leaves and women to harvest the crop) is a significant asset. It was also in the north-east that the British chose to develop the crop from 1840 onwards (compared to 1863 in southern India), having lost their monopoly on tea imports from China. Their replacement strategy proved highly successful: India became a major producer and at the time of Independence, it was exporting 70 per cent of its tea crop, primarily to the United

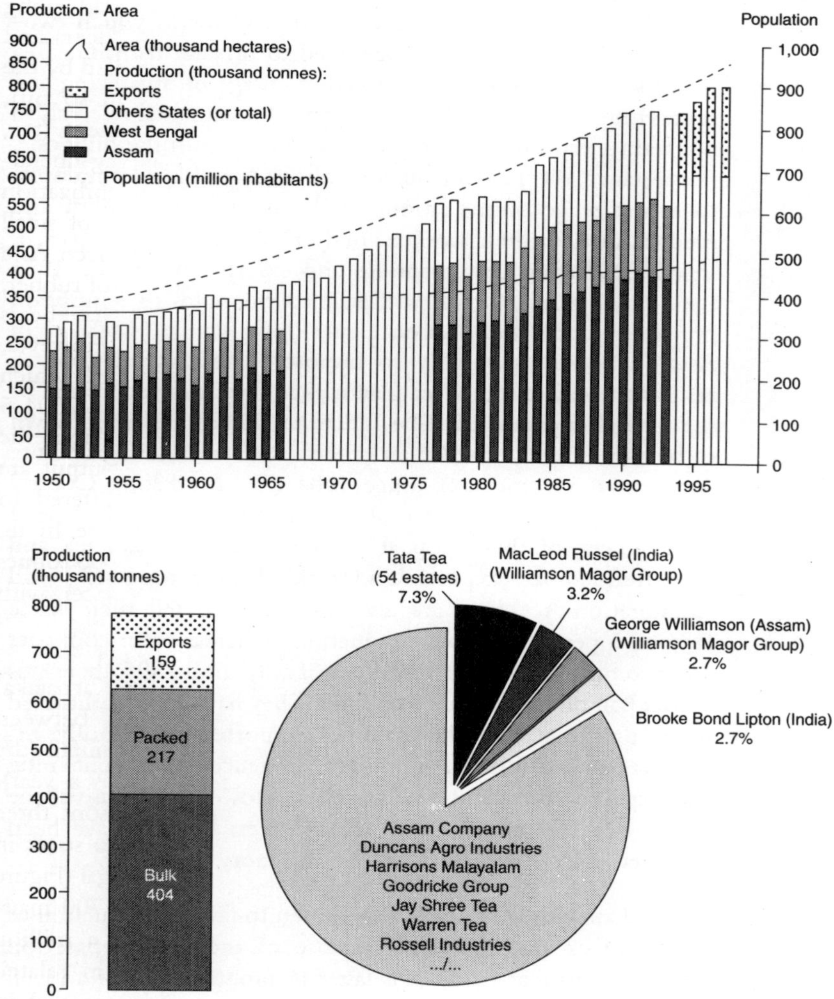

Sources: Based on Indian Tea Association, Centre for Monitoring Indian Economy, Economic Survey.

FIGURE 4: TEA PRODUCTION (1950–1 TO 1997–8)

Kingdom. It also became a major consumer, which subsequently prompted the establishment of numerous control and regulatory mechanisms aimed at supplying the Indian population first and foremost. For this young, constitutionally 'socialist' country, the aim was also very close supervision of a sector in which two-thirds of the cultivated area belonged to private firms. The Tea Board set up in Kolkata and placed in charge of organizing and supervising the commodity chain, from fundamental research to marketing, was one such instrument, but far from the only one. For instance, the 1951 Plantation Labour Act obliged employers to subsidize accommodation, food and energy supplies and medical care for their workers. In 1953, the Tea Act was passed, strictly regulating new plantings and external trade. The 1956 Land Ceiling Act, for its part, enabled the states to requisition previously unplanted land on estates (for instance 14,000 ha in Assam), and subsequently to impose various regulations to restrict the expansion of tea plantings in favour of food crops or the natural environment. The Indian tea industry is also known to be more highly taxed than others (state taxes on agriculture and central income tax). Since 1984 (Tea Marketing Control Order Act), producers have also been obliged to sell at least 75 per cent of their crop at auction, except packet tea and tea intended for export. Under the Prevention and Food Adulteration Act, they are also forbidden to sell their waste (around 5 per cent of total production), whereas other countries use it to make instant tea or caffeine. Lastly, until 1995, there was a strict ban on tea imports into India. They have been authorized since, provided that the volumes imported are wholly re-exported in one form or another (for instance blends containing cheaper Kenyan tea and local varieties). However, because of the WTO (see Chapter 8), such market access barriers have been outlawed since April 2001, at least in theory.

CTC Tea

The Indian authorities have also chosen to favour production of 'CTC' black tea, so-called because of the leaf preparation method (Cut-Tear-Curl). It is faster to produce and for a given quantity, makes around 500 cups compared to 350 for 'conventional' black tea, which is weaker and is sent for export (Darjeeling is the most famous variety). India also exports small amounts of green tea (the leaves of which are heated to prevent fermentation, and in which China has traditionally specialized). Between 1950-2 and 1995, CTC tea increased its domestic production share from 38 to 88 per cent (with 11 per cent conventional tea and 1 per cent green tea), and the Guwahati auction house in Assam is now the world's leading trading exchange for this variety. This policy of favouring quantity over quality for the domestic market has made India the world's largest producer (8,70,000 tonnes in 1998), and also the leading consumer (an average of 620 g per person, per year, with a figure of over 1.5 kg in states such as Jammu & Kashmir or Punjab). Production has shown a sharp decline in recent years (8,20,000 tonnes in 2004). It has been knocked off the top spot in the export tables, despite the fact that it exports three particularly reputed varieties (Darjeeling, Nilgiri and Assam): it was overtaken by Sri Lanka in the 1980s, and then by China and Kenya in the following decade. In 1998, less than a quarter of its output was exported (47 per cent to the former Soviet Union and 13 per cent to the United Kingdom), compared to 95 per cent for Sri Lanka, 89 per cent for Kenya and 35 per cent for China. In 2004 exports slumped to 145 million tonnes. Strategic errors (a ban on certain exports during the election campaign at the start of the 1980s), poor quality (up to 30 different teas may be blended in a given batch) or dubious standards (Germany denounced the pesticide levels in Indian tea in 1994), ethical problems (child labour), cost of production, issues surrounding effective certification of origins (three quarters of so-called 'Darjeeling' does not in fact come from the region), and the international situation (the disappearance of the USSR, its leading customer) are not the only factors behind the decline in exports.

Tata Tea, Brooke Bond Lipton and Co.

In fact, despite the recent rise in fizzy drink consumption in urban areas, domestic demand for tea is still huge and international competition is growing, but domestic production is failing to keep pace. The areas planted in the Himalayas could be extended, but it is important to consider the local tribal populations who still practise slash-and-burn, in zones that sometimes are also the scene of guerrilla warfare. In 1995 a total of 12,081 estates were recorded, including 10,988 of less than 100 ha in southern India (90 per cent of estates in northern India cover more than 400 ha): for all of them, extension is thus not really on the agenda, despite the fact that administrative controls on such operations have been relaxed in recent years. However, there is considerable room for progress in terms of productivity, which is currently low (the national average is around 1,800 kg/ha), particularly in the north, due to the cold that restricts harvesting to eight or nine months a year. Yields are higher in the south (2,400 kg/ha), albeit to the detriment of quality. Irrigation and drainage both leave much to be desired, but the priority is to replace large numbers of bushes, since their productivity drops after 50 years: by the end of the 1990s, 80 per cent of Indian bushes were already over 30 years old, and 45 per cent were over 50 (and even 80–100 in Darjeeling!). Lastly, in terms of quality and added value, there is substantial room for improvement by introducing packing and labelling plants (most packing and labelling is still done by foreign operators, or by Brooke Bond Lipton, Tata Tea and Duncans Agro Industries for the domestic market), improving marketing operations (certifying quality or origin), and exploiting emerging markets (tea bags in India, instant tea and organic tea in the export market). This should be facilitated by Tata Tea's purchase of the British firm Tetley in 2000, the largest ever overseas takeover by an Indian firm.

Coffee (Hindustan Lever, Nestlé and Co.)

Coffee originated in Yemen and Ethiopia, but owes its international success to the Arabs in the Middle Ages, and the Europeans (British, French and Dutch in India) from the seventeenth century onwards. With 2,75,000 tonnes in 2004–5 (1,72,000 tonnes of Robusta and 1,03,000 of Arabica), India is now the world's sixth largest coffee producer, thanks to its relatively high yields (more than 800 kg/ha for Arabica, which still accounted for 82 per cent of output in 1950–1), and depending on the year, is between tenth and fifteenth in the export rankings, with a total export value slightly below that of tea. As coffee growing calls for fertile, deep soils (because of the plant's tap root), and also not too extreme humid tropical climates or hot, medium-altitude zones, 70 per cent of the coffee produced in India comes from the mountains of Karnataka, with the rest concentrated in Kerala and Tamil Nadu (Figure 5). Of the 1,40,000 coffee growers, 85 per cent are small holders (less than 2 ha), who often grow more rice or other food crops than coffee. At the other extreme, 2 per cent of estates account for 40 per cent of the total output; these are generally large estates run by families (often set up by Europeans in the second half of the nineteenth century), and above all by commercial companies (Hindustan Lever, Nestlé India, Tata Tea's Consolidated Coffee,

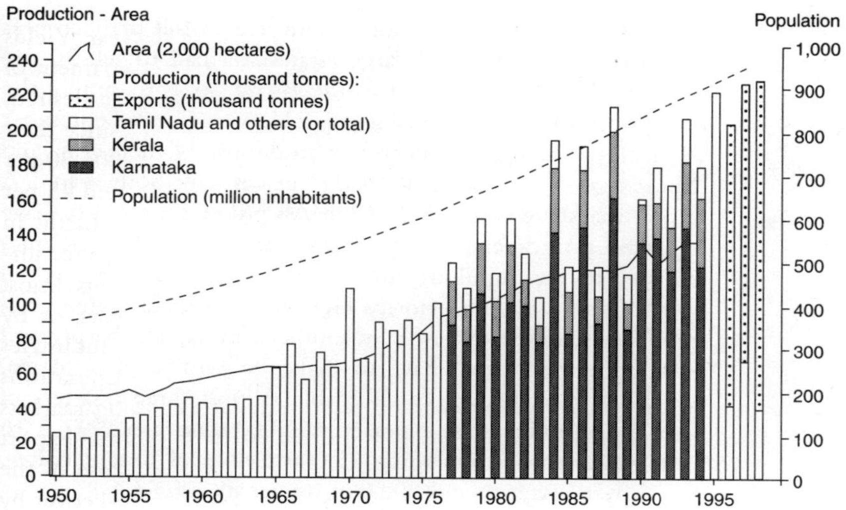

Sources: Based on Centre for Monitoring Indian Economy, Economic Survey.

FIGURE 5: COFFEE PRODUCTION (1950-1 TO 1998-9)

and so on). They are almost exclusively monoculture plantations, and have substantial resources, with modern 'cherry' processing factories often contrasting with the elephants used for forest logging operations. However, operations are still largely unmechanized, despite strong wage claims from full-time staff and a growing shortage of seasonal labour (due to emigration to the Persian Gulf, irrigation of some of the regions that used to supply the workforce, agricultural land distribution by the Karnataka state government). In terms of marketing, a period of global surplus production prompted the founding of the Coffee Board in Bangalore in 1942, in the hope of staving off the slump in exports. The Board awarded itself a monopoly on purchases from growers as well as on sales, in both the domestic and export markets. The latter sector was no longer seen as a priority, the main objective being to satisfy Indian producers and consumers. However, the Coffee Board was judged to be inefficient in the event of high world prices, and unable to provide adequate protection in the event of a price fall (as well as being accused of not sufficiently representing growers and fostering political divisions). The Board was forced to give up part of its monopoly in 1992. By 1995, small holders were free to sell their crop as they wished, although the large estates still had to sell 30 per cent of what they produced to the Board, so as to supply the domestic market at a reasonable price. However, since September 1996, all producers have been free to dispose of their crop, and export figures and domestic market prices have both soared. A futures market was set up in 1998. All producers seem to have benefited from liberalization, although small holders sometimes fall prey to unscrupulous buyers. Crop quality, which used to be poor, is a growing priority. However, domestic coffee consumption, almost exclusively in southern India, fell sharply, and poor consumers often have to make do with a glass of tea, which has remained more affordable. Almost three quarters of what India produces are exported: 160,000 tonnes in 1997-8 (to some 40 countries, including 15,000 tonnes of instant coffee, primarily to Russia) and 202,000 tonnes in 2005-6.

Cocoa (Cadbury and Co.)

Cocoa is the most widely consumed beverage base in the world, after tea and coffee. However, in India, cocoa does not grow as well as it does in the Amazonian rainforest, and plantations have not developed like they did in Africa after the Second World War. The crop was not introduced into the subcontinent until 1965 by Cadbury, and is still confined to Kerala and the coast of Karnataka, where it grows in the shade of coconut palms, areca palms or even rubber trees. It was relatively popular in the mid-1970s, when prices were attractive (Rs.14/kg of beans in 1978). However, the prices subsequently fell (Rs. 5/kg in 1981) due to the many obstacles to production development: Cadbury's purchasing monopoly, inadequate marketing structures, processing plants too far from the multitude of small holder producers, low domestic consumption, and so on. The area planted was halved between 1985-6 (20,948 ha, 7,715 tonnes) and 1995-6 (10,642 ha, 5,741 tonnes), and the commodity chain employed a little more than 28,000 people at that time. Since then there has been some revival (10,440 tonnes on 27,190 ha in 2004-5), with the advent of new buyers (Lotus Chocolate, Nestlé India, Amul, Britannia), the installation of large processing plants (the Campco cooperative in Mangalore has an annual capacity of 8,800 tonnes), and an improvement in cropping techniques (yields of 575 kg/ha in relation to a potential of 1,500 kg/ha), but in the meantime, the growing domestic demand for chocolate products will not be satisfied without importing cocoa beans, butter and other derivatives.

Tobacco (ITC and Co.)

Tobacco, which Christopher Columbus discovered in the Americas, has become a major crop, primarily non-irrigated (almost 60 per cent of the total area), in central India: in 1996-7, two-thirds of the 6,00,000 tonnes produced came from Gujarat and above all from Andhra Pradesh (Figure 6). Andhra Pradesh is the state in which Virginia tobacco production is concentrated (this FCV tobacco—around 20 per cent of the total produced in India—benefits from a minimum support price) and which houses the Central Tobacco Research Institute, in Rajahmundry. With an average yield of over 1,500 kg/ha, India is the world's third largest producer (4,90,000 tonnes in 2002-3) and eighth largest exporter (1,21,000 tonnes in 2003-4). The crop is officially closely supervised by the Tobacco Board (in Guntur, Andhra Pradesh), which authorizes a given area every year, but the actual figure is always at least 20 to 30 per cent higher, as a result of licensed farmers exceeding their quota, or of illicit growers (who make up around a third of the 36,000-odd growers in Karnataka, for instance). In fact, under pressure

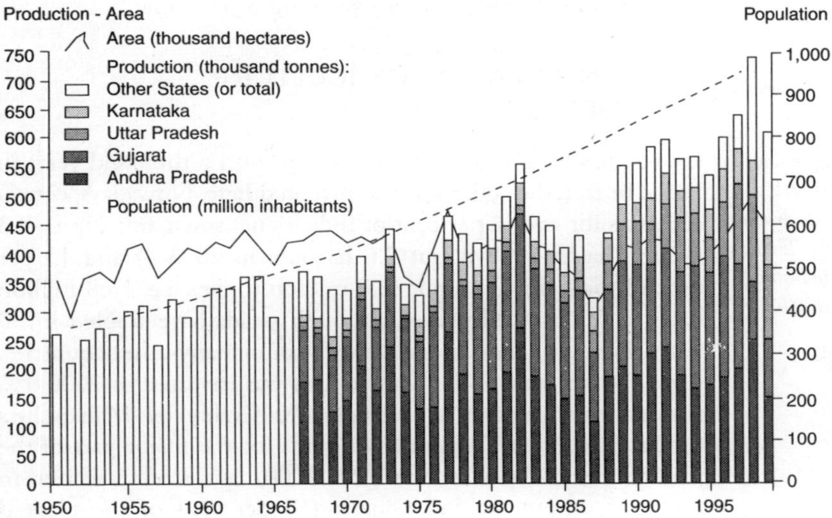

Source: Based on data from Ministry of Agriculture.

FIGURE 6: TOBACCO PRODUCTION (1950-1 TO 1999-2000)

from governments pandering to the farming electorate, year after year, the Tobacco Board has to resign itself to allowing this illegal tobacco to be sold through official auctions. This means that when the international market is sluggish, considerable stocks build up and prices fall; for instance, this forced the Tobacco Board to ban new plantings in Andhra Pradesh in 1999-2000. Nevertheless, like anywhere else, tobacco is a major source of revenue for the State: the 50 per cent tax on cigarette retail sales in India generated 40 billion Rs. in 1997-8. Cigarettes are still a relative luxury in the country, and are manufactured by major national groups, the largest of which is the Indian Tobacco Company (ITC). *Beedis*, for their part, are much more popular. These mini-cigars are made of tobacco rolled in *tendu* leaves picked by native communities in central India: they are eight times more popular than cigarettes and use 53 per cent of the tobacco crop (of which only 20 per cent—Virginia tobacco—is used to make cigarettes, with the rest used as chewing tobacco, snuff or in *hookah* pipes). In Karnataka alone, the main *beedi*-producing state, the industry employed some 8,00,000 people in the mid-1990s (and almost 10 million throughout India, including 4 million for *tendu* harvesting in season), often villagers (mostly women and children) working from home.

COTTON: BETWEEN AGRICULTURE AND INDUSTRY

Spinning Wheels, Khadi and the Textile Industry (KVIC...)

Cotton has been grown and woven for over a thousand years in India. In fact, the roller gin was invented here. Nowadays, cotton accounts for over 6 per cent of Indian's net sown area (up to 9.3 million ha in 1998-9, but 7.6 ha only in 2003-4) and 13 per cent of total global output (2.8 million tonnes, i.e. 13.8 million bales in 2003-4). However, although yields have trebled in 30 years (Figure 7), they are still lower than in many other countries. Only 34 per cent of the planted area was irrigated in 2000-1, a national average that is lowered considerably by Maharashtra (under 3 per cent). This state accounts for the major part of the planted area (37 per cent in 1999-2000), but is often second in terms of output, behind Gujarat (18 per cent of the planted area). The harvested lint is fixed to seeds (*kapas*, which have been used for just under a century to make oil, see Chapter 4),

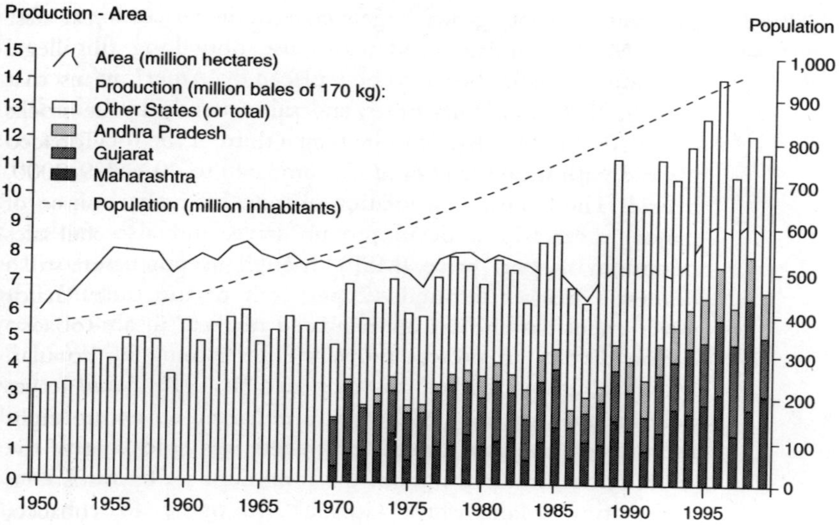

Source: Based on data from the Ministry of Agriculture.

FIGURE 7: COTTON PRODUCTION (1950-1 TO 1999-2000)

which have to be removed (ginning) before spinning. It was this type of fibre that enabled the textile industry in Manchester to flourish in the nineteenth century, before flooding the textile market in India, to the detriment of the many local small-scale producers. During the civil disobedience campaign headed by Mahatma Gandhi in the early 1920s, huge quantities of garments imported from Britain were burnt. The spinning wheel (*charkha*), which Gandhi often used for hours on end, rapidly became the symbol of the fight for independence. However, producing one's own cotton yarn and hand-weaving it into fabric (*khadi*) is not just a symbol of nationalism or asceticism; it is also a way of diversifying the rural economy and ensuring full employment. The Khadi and Village Industries Commission (KVIC) was set up for this purpose in 1952. Nevertheless, the *khadi* sector has continued to decline ever since, despite the steps taken to protect it. Cotton tends to be used in other production chains, still with handlooms, but also power looms and large textile mills: it represents two-thirds of all the raw material used by the Indian textile industry.

MSP and Procurement Price

The cotton variety grown largely governs the processing method used. Modern mechanized plants use only long fibres, and traditional varieties began to be replaced by 'American' varieties even in British colonial times, and subsequently by hybrids in the 1970s. In 2000, barely more than a third of the total area was planted with local varieties (*desi*), compared to 40 per cent with hybrids. The Cotton Corporation of India has embarked upon a major research and development drive, and also applies a minimum support price (MSP) through its purchases on the domestic market (around 12 per cent of the output). The government has also set up 'regulated markets' in almost every cotton district, to protect growers. After closing in 1962, the Mumbai futures market was reopened in 1998. Amidst these policies and structures, Maharashtra remained an exception: till recently all the raw cotton produced was sold to the state government, at a price above the minimum set by the Central authorities (Maharashtra Cotton Monopoly Procurement Scheme, launched in 1971). The aim was not only to support farmers' incomes, but also to encourage quality cotton production for the industry and thus consumers. However, this dual aim had not been reached, notably due to the prevalence of fraud among public and private players alike. Moreover, Maharashtra had cut itself off from the national market so as to cushion the variations in its output from year to year, and its borders remained closed to imports, to the delight of smugglers. Hence the Monopoly Procurement Scheme was eventually phased out.

Exports

Generally speaking, the Indian government has always hesitated between guaranteeing producers high prices for their cotton at the risk of holding back the textile industry, or encouraging a drop in fibre prices—even if it means importing—to help the industry satisfy domestic demand and banking on exports. In this last respect, it is worth recalling that the International Multi-Fibre Agreement expired at the end of 2004 with two consequences: the removal, long awaited by India, of certain commercial barriers set up by developed countries, and also the risk of cheaper imports from other Asian countries (China). As things stand, the textile industry accounts for 15 per cent of Indian exports ($19.3 billion in 2004–5). Cotton yarn and fabric exports alone account for more than 5 per cent of the country's total exports, amounting to almost half the total revenue generated by all agrifood exports combined. However, the cotton farming sector is still very fragile, particularly as the crop uses half the total amount of pesticides applied in India, which has obvious economic and ecological implications (see Chapter 7). This is why much talk, at least in research and ministerial circles, is now of organic cotton or of integrated pest management (IPM). However, GMO (Bt) cotton was cultivated on 3.6 million ha in 2006-7, and represented 39 per cent of the total cotton area. In any event, to achieve any real agricultural growth, it is clear that the commodity chain itself needs to be more integrated, perhaps following the example of the sugar commodity chain.

SUGAR CANE: A GREEN REVOLUTION FLAVOUR

Sugar cane

The Aryans may have been the first sugarcane planters in world history. Around 300 years BC, the Greeks observed a plant that they said produced honey without the need for bees, and by the sixteenth century, during the reign of Akbar, Bengal was the leading producer of sugar cane, a fact which was later exploited by European companies. After Independence, production gathered speed from 1960 onwards, almost trebling in volume terms in 40 years (Figure 8), making India the world's leading producer (300 million tonnes in 2000, with an average yield of 70 tonnes/ha, but only 236 million in 2003-4). Farmers generally grow just one or two ratoon crops, no doubt because the country's relatively low labour costs make it easy for them to replant. Uttar Pradesh accounted for 44 per cent of output in 2000, but Maharashtra and Tamil Nadu are also major players, and the crop employs some 35 million people (families farming just half a hectare of cane on average).

India is also the world's largest sugar cane consumer, as a result of its population size and diet: annual per capita consumption is 14 kg of refined cane sugar (in relatively well-off households, the catering and food industries), plus 10 kg of *gur* or *khandsari* (totally or largely unrefined brown sugars primarily eaten in rural areas). This is an average figure, and in urban Punjab, the figure for sugar consumption is over 70 kg per capita. On the whole, imports are commonplace (primarily from Brazil and the European Union), and peaked at 1.5 million tonnes in 1993-4.

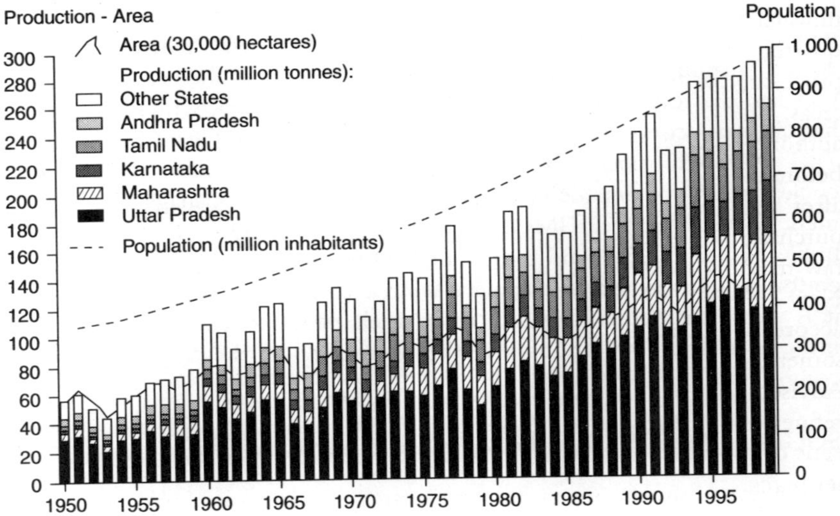

Source: Based on data from the Ministry of Agriculture.

FIGURE 8: SUGAR CANE PRODUCTION (1950-1 TO 1999-2000)

However, they are still discouraged by tariffs (at a rate of 61.2 per cent in 2005), and the fact that importers are obliged to sell part of what they buy to the state at a levy price. In some years, India is in a position to export sugar, mainly to Pakistan (the trade monopoly held by the ISGIEIC, a company managed by the private and cooperative sectors, was abolished in 1997). However, world prices still serve to discourage potential exporters, as they are well below those in the domestic market. In addition to import barriers, domestic production is also protected by an internal sugar cane price guarantee system, as production costs remain high.

SMPs and SAPs

Sugar cane production is demanding in terms of both inputs and water (89 per cent of plantings are irrigated), and thus also of credit, particularly since it does not provide any income whatsoever for a year after planting. It is the most common type of contract farming practised in India, which the State is keen to control. However, its links with the agro-processing sector, which provides most of the credit required, are somewhat unusual (Figure 9). A large share of the cane crop (between a quarter and half) is sent to the small-scale or semi-industrial processing sector to make *khandsari* and *gur*, generally in rural areas. The remainder goes to the major refineries, which the authorities began to encourage and protect as long ago as 1933, before introducing strict controls on their operations, particularly after the 1966 Sugar Control Order. Control begins with purchase and sale prices. Upstream, refineries have to buy the raw material from farmers at a price above the minimum set in New Delhi (SMP: Statutory Minimum Price), with bonuses paid according to sugar content. They also have to allow for the sometimes considerable bonus granted by the states (SAP: State Advised Price) to farmers who supply cooperatives or public refineries, the latter of which collect and control almost 60 per cent of the crop. Lastly, downstream, refineries have to supply a set percentage of their output (45 per cent in 1989, 40 per cent in 1993, 30 per cent in 2000, 15 per cent in 2001) at a levy price, to enable the authorities to build-up stocks for re-distribution via the Public Distribution System (PDS, see

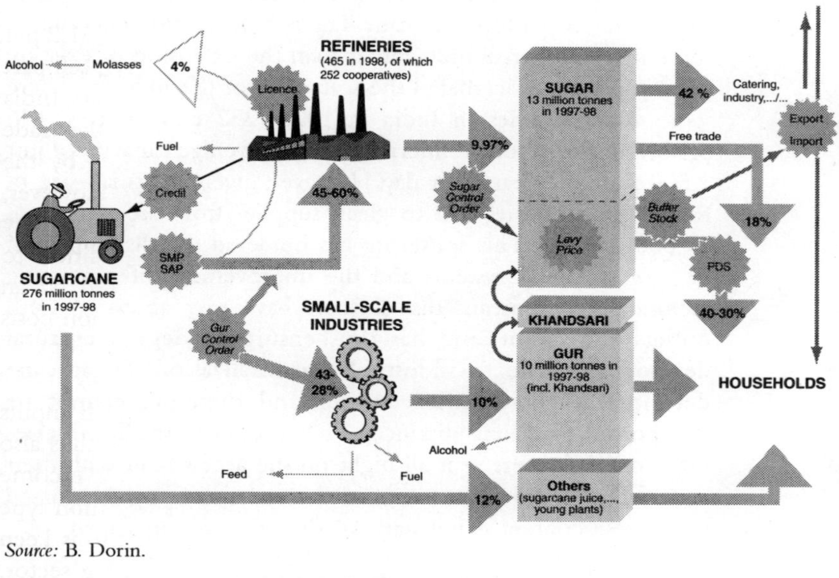

Source: B. Dorin.

FIGURE 9: SUGAR CANE COMMODITY CHAIN AND GOVERNMENT CONTROLS (*c.* 1998)

Chapter 3). This is the same sort of ambitious system as exists for rice and wheat: production and consumption subsidies guarantee farmers fair prices without penalizing consumers, with State funds covering most of the cost.

Refineries (Sugar mills)

State intervention is not restricted to fixing prices. The construction and extension of refineries is subject to official approval, and supply zones are determined by the authorities, which set production quotas for the various plants each month. Controls also apply to private trade (wholesalers have to hold a licence and their stocks are controlled). The refined sugar sector is thus very closely supervised by the government and it provides no incentive either to modernize or to increase efficiency: at the end of the 1990s, 36 per cent of mills were over 50 years old. However, a start has now been made on liberalizing the sector. For instance, since August 1998, new refineries have been exempted from supply quotas at the levy price for eight or ten years after their construction, which meant that in 1999, just 32 per cent of the total output was sold to the State, if not even less, due to fraud on the part of industrialists declaring a lower sugar content per tonne of cane. The new legislation encourages the building of small units rather than the extension of existing plants, and has exacerbated the scattering of the industry. There were 465 refineries in India in 1998 (252 cooperatives, 146 private and 67 public refineries), with an average capacity of just 2,500 tonnes of cane per day. However, given the small size of farms, the refineries had to glean supplies from an average of 17,000 growers. This scattering has hindered the dissemination of new cropping systems and the improvement of processing techniques, but means that farmers have easy access to both outlets and credit, and has thus ensured a degree of rural development due to industrial decentralization. Sugar cane deteriorates rapidly after cutting, and therefore cannot be transported over long distances. That said, even small refineries often make farmers wait all night on the access road with their carts full of freshly cut cane, and the system of payment based on sucrose content is not particularly efficiently managed.

Sugar, Gur and Khandsari

Things could not be more different in the *gur* (jaggery) and *khandsari* commodity chains: they are not subject to the constraints imposed on refiners, although the government can divert some of the cane supplied to them to the refineries under the Gur Control Order (1986), which since 1996 has limited the stocks held by any trader to 25 tonnes. Otherwise, they can sell their products at relatively high prices in the open market (the largest jaggery market is in Muzaffarnagar, in Uttar Pradesh), which compensates for the archaic processing methods used. The state tolerates these chains because prices nevertheless remain low and make the poor consumers satisfied, and they are a major source of seasonal rural employment. Farmers also often choose this unorganized sector rather than industrial refineries because the latter have an overly bureaucratic cutting permit, control and payment system. After making *gur*, farmers also sometimes recover the canes, which are shredded and fed to animals (otherwise, the refineries use them as fuel). All in all, it is the competition between these two sectors that is the main culprit behind the instability of the Indian market and its substantial price variations, which generally follow a 3- to 4-year cycle, since sugar production fluctuations are more abrupt than those in cane production.

Sugar Cooperatives

The north produces 70 per cent of *gur*, and in Uttar Pradesh, almost two-thirds of the cane produced is destined for this small-scale sector. This accounts for the fact that the State Advised Price (SAP) for sugar in the state is 40 per cent higher than those in the south. In southern India, there is less competition from *gur*, and the climatic conditions are also more favourable. In the west (Maharashtra), almost all the cane is processed industrially, by powerful cooperatives which also transport the raw material themselves, to minimize sucrose losses; the close links between the refinery and the 8,000 to 10,000 members of the cooperatives have also helped to improve cropping system productivity and profitability. The first cooperative in Maharashtra was set up in 1950, and over a hundred more have been founded since, most of them controlled by the Maratha caste. These cooperatives in fact operate like fiefdoms, under a small number of sugar barons, whom the state government has to pamper every time there is an election: politicians like Sharad Pawar (Nationalist Congress Party) have large numbers of clients there. The satisfactory income levels among members and the related momentum that boosts the surrounding rural economy cannot hide the corruption and dubious practices that reign supreme in a good number of cooperatives. Politicians all want to have a cooperative in their ward, and it's too bad if the available water resources—and public funds—run out as a result of extending the cultivated area in direct proportion to the number of voters they are hoping to win over.

Alcohol

Lastly, it is important to bear in mind that one of the main byproducts of the sugar industry is molasses, and that it (occasionally along with *gur*) is primarily used to make ethyl alcohol. However, since the central government lifted sales controls in 1993, molasses prices have fluctuated wildly (between Rs. 50 and 2,000 a tonne), which has resulted in the closure of almost half the ethyl production units. To protect this chemical industry (and thus preserve the revenue generated by the taxes on it), the states have set up their own regulatory systems, particularly by introducing varying rates of tax on molasses and alcohol movements into and out of their jurisdiction. As for the central government, which may one day set up the National Molasses and Alcohol Board that the profession is calling for, it decided in 1997 to allow companies (International Distillers, McDonald & Co., Mohan Meakin, Bacardi Rum, Pernod Ricard, Rémy Cointreau, and so on) to base production on molasses alcohol, which it had previously tended to discourage. The aim is in fact to avoid having to resort to imports (in 1999, customs duty varied from 118 per cent on alcohol to 243 per cent on spirits), as domestic alcohol consumption continues to rise: 2.5 billion litres in 2003, according to the FAO, or 1.7 litres/person/year, compared to 0.4 litre in 1961. This may be bad news for many Indian wives, but is a good vote bank for politicians, who often promise to ban production and consumption in their state (as in Gujarat, Manipur, Mizoram and part of Nagaland), with the blessing of religious authorities. However, prohibition is often short-lived due to the black market and to the colossal subsequent duty losses (total prohibition was in force in Tamil Nadu till 1971; in Andhra Pradesh, it lasted from 1996 to late 1997, and in Haryana, from 1996 to early 1998). Alcohol consumption centres on spirits (whisky, brandy, gin, rum, vodka), either locally produced (country liquor: 64 per cent of the market), or blended and bottled from imported bulk alcohols, concentrates or flavourings

(Indian-Made Foreign Liquor: 20 per cent of the market) by over 200 distilleries that concentrate 70 per cent of their operations in four states (Uttar Pradesh, Maharashtra, Karnataka and Tamil Nadu). However, in 1999, only 31 of those distilleries had a central government Carry On Business (COB) permit, 15 of which belonged to six groups: United Breweries, Shaw Wallace, Mohan Meakin, Balaji, Jagatjit and Narang Industries. The first three make most of the beer produced in India (16 per cent of the beers, wines and spirits market), consumption of which is growing strongly among wealthier consumers, as is that of wine, although this latter market is still in its infancy. The Indage group (which markets the only sparkling wine made in India, using the *méthode champenoise*), Golconda (part of Shaw Wallace), and Grover Vineyards (all in Karnataka or Maharashtra) are the market leaders in this sector, where there is strong demand for French expertise.

3. The Green (Cereals) Revolution

The term 'Green Revolution' was coined in the United States in 1968, to describe a process that concerned most of the countries in monsoon Asia at the time. Some years before, in densely populated India, it was well understood that cultivable areas were no longer extendable, calling for an unprecedented increase in productivity so as to make up the ground lost in agriculture both before and after Independence, put a stop to imports and to the threat of the 'food weapon' (when food exporting countries use this commodity as a blackmail tool). The country had to cover by its own steam the basic needs of an ever-growing population. The 1964-6 political and economic crisis acted as a catalyst for a set of measures that in turn led the authorities to (i) subsidize a production model based on new wheat and rice varieties requiring vast amounts of water and fertilizers; and to (ii) more or less guarantee profitable outlets for growers via State purchases that were subsequently redistributed to communities or areas suffering from shortages. This policy of low input and output prices, indirectly funded by the nationalization and extension of the banking system, enabled India not only to double its cereal output within 20 years, but also to build-up stocks of wheat and rice that could be exported from time to time.

THE MOTIVE: TO ASSERT THE INDEPENDENCE OF A YOUNG NATION

HUNGER IN BRITISH INDIA

The Indus Valley and the Mauryan Empire

The history of the Green Revolution in fact stretches back much further than the 1960s. The country's long tradition of agricultural development and intensification has in effect enabled it to support its growing population. In humid tropical regions, paddy (grown in flooded fields) is assumed to have first been grown—from India to southern China—over 6,000 years ago. In the arid north-west part of the country, the Indus Valley was the first place, after Mesopotamia and the Nile Valley, to have a water management systems, enabling flood retreat and irrigated crops (2500 BC). Further south, the Mauryan Empire (fourth to second century BC) was known for its public granaries, and the first irrigation systems on the Kaveri River date back to the second century. In Punjab, which now accounts for the major share of wheat production and supplies in India, development began in the fourteenth century when the sultans in Delhi opened up a pioneer frontier, starting from the Himalayan rivers (Yamuna). The British speeded up the spread of the front in the second half of the nineteenth century.

British Trade

The British colonial period nevertheless had an adverse overall impact in terms of food production. Expansion of the cultivated area, which was rapid after 1830, subsequently ran out of steam (+ 0.40 per cent a year between 1891 and 1947), while cereal and pulse production ('food grains' in Indian terminology) actually fell (- 0.18 per cent a year), and per capita output dropped by almost 1 per cent a year over the same period. On the other hand, so-called 'commercial' crop productivity, i.e. those crops that generate high added values in the export market (tea, cotton, sugar cane, groundnut), grew by 50 per cent in half a century. These factors, combined with oppressive tax policy, at least partly account for the series of famines following inadequate monsoon rains: two million deaths in northern India in 1860-1, four million in the Deccan Peninsula in 1876-8, and over five million in 1896-7, to quote only the most catastrophic.

The 1943 Famine

The early twentieth century was more favourable, thanks to the spread of permanent irrigation systems, the development of the rail and road networks, and also the introduction of a Famine Code in every province. Nevertheless, by the time of Independence in 1947, India was in a highly delicate position in terms of food supplies. It was forced to leave West Punjab, with its large-scale irrigation systems, to Pakistan, and it had been hard hit by the 1943 famine in Bengal, in which almost four million people died, including those killed by the subsequent epidemics. In this case, the famine was due less to the October 1942 cyclone than to the Japanese invasion of Burma, which upset rice import and distribution circuits, prompted the British to involve India in the war effort, caused chaos in the relevant administrative services, encouraged speculation and forced the authorities to requisition cereals in rural areas to feed Calcutta while refusing to give up their *laissez-faire* policy in the rest of the region. The trauma caused by the 1943 famine is largely the reason why India has never neglected the agricultural and food issue since Independence, even though it appeared to hesitate to implement any strict policies in this respect during the first two decades of its existence. Likewise, as he says himself, it was this famine that prompted Amartya Sen, who subsequently won the Nobel Prize for Economics, to embark upon a career as an economist, and to devote a large part of his research to poverty, having been traumatized by seeing starving rural refugees wandering around Calcutta in his childhood.

AGRICULTURE OR INDUSTRY?

'Grow More Food' Campaign

The famine in Bengal triggered a 'Grow More Food' campaign, which ran from 1943 to 1951 and was intended to steer farmers away from commercial crops such as cotton and towards food crops, increase yields through irrigation and fertilizer applications, and cultivate fallow or wasteland. In 1947, a target was set of achieving food self-sufficiency by 1952, with extra credit allocated for purchasing tractors and sinking tube wells. The First Five Year Plan (April 1951-March 1956), based on Keynesian economic theories, consolidated the restructuring effort while encouraging the concentration of seed and fertilizer development programmes in zones with guaranteed rainfall or irrigation systems: exactly what the green revolution was to achieve fifteen years later. In short, contrary to popular belief, considerable agricultural progress was made in the years prior to the Green Revolution. Between 1950-1 and 1964-5, agricultural production increased by 3.2 per cent per year, 0.8 percentage point above the population growth rate; the irrigated area spread by 26 per cent, and fertilizer use by 625 per cent. As a result, with the extension of the cultivated area, production of the main crops except wheat increased as much between 1950 and 1965 as between 1965 and 1990.

Planning Industrialization

However, a turning point was reached in 1956. While the First Five Year Plan allocated 37 per cent of its total budget to agriculture and irrigation, the Second (1956-61) and Third

(1962-6) Plans cut the figure to 21 per cent. Based on a Soviet-style model, priority was given to industrialization, and above all to heavy industry (machinery). Along with infrastructure, this was seen as the main factor in developing the national economy, which the Plans also protected from foreign competition and influence. There was a clear policy of import substitution, inherited from Mahatma Gandhi's *Swadeshi* movement, and of 'business socialism', whereby most of the main industrial families (such as the Tatas and Birlas) were closely linked to the Congress Party in power. According to the prime minister at the time, Jawaharlal Nehru, rural development depended on institutional-type changes, most of which had already been triggered: land reform, Primary Agricultural Credit Societies (launched in 1951, see infra), Community Development Programme (launched in 1952), and so on.

PL 480

It was also in 1956 that an agreement was signed with the United States. Within the framework of Public Law 480, it enabled India to import cheap agricultural goods and pay for them in rupees rather than dollars. The agreement was initially scheduled to cover three years and 3.5 million tonnes of wheat and 1,90,000 tonnes of rice, dairy products, cotton and tobacco (for a total of $362 million including shipping), but was rapidly extended. For the Americans, the aim was to sell off their agricultural surpluses, which were expensive to store, but also to thaw a political climate that had been decidedly frosty since the US had signed a military alliance with Pakistan. The Americans also wanted to make optimum use of their merchant fleet (50 per cent of the planned tonnage had to be shipped on American vessels) and build-up a reserve of local currency to enable them to conduct their various operations in the area. Until 31 March 1966, these funds were used as follows: 54 per cent loans (at an interest rate of 3.5-5.0 per cent until 1960 and 0.75-1.0 per cent thereafter), 26 per cent grants to the Indian government for development projects, 13 per cent for US government expenditure in India and 7 per cent for 'Cooley' loans (industrial collaboration between American and Indian private firms). For independent India, this was the only decade in which there was a clear urban bias favouring consumers, at the risk of reducing the incentives to produce more due to excessively low agricultural prices. Between 1956 and 1966, the area under wheat stagnated at around 13 million hectares, whereas it had grown by 43 per cent in the previous five years.

The Decisive Crisis

Subramaniam

As J.A. Bernard observed,

> Nehru died on 27 May 1964, with a broken heart [following India's defeat at the hands of China]. The Cabinet that the new Prime Minister [Lal Bahadur Shastri] submitted to the President on 9 June contained few changes in relation to Nehru's last, but the Prime Minister did ask the Minister for Steel and Mines, C. Subramaniam, to take responsibility for food and agriculture. Three new steel mills were launched in eight years, but the Indians were short of bread by the summer of 1964. The last two monsoons had been poor and governmental stocks had virtually run out. Famine reappeared in certain regions, such as Kerala. Traders speculated on price rises, while states with surpluses refused to supply those with shortages. In December 1964, the revolutionary faction of the Communist Party of India, which had split from the main party in July, was stirring up trouble among landless farmers in several regions.

War broke out with Pakistan in 1965, and in the end, everything hinged on the goodwill of the United States (PL 480), since the balance of payments could not sustain the triple burden of industrialization, defence and food. However, President Johnson deliberately delayed the departure of cereal transport ships, to force India to review its position on US policy in Vietnam. The situation was critical, yet the Planning Commission took an agonizingly long time to accept the proposals made by C. Subramaniam, inspired by American experts and the Japanese model. Indeed, it waited until cereal production had fallen by 17 million tonnes (-19 per cent) in 1965-6 and failed to recover the following year, and rice and above all wheat imports had topped 10 million tonnes (16 per cent of production) in 1966.

Swaminathan (IARI...)

The time was at last right for a policy based on a model recommended by a Ford Foundation team as long ago as 1959: increasing productivity by targeting supports (chemical fertilizers, credit, commercial infrastructures) in selected regions. In 1960, seven districts were chosen to benefit from the Integrated Agricultural District Programme. In 1965, 114 districts (of a total of 325 at the time) were covered by the Intensive Agricultural Area Programme. However, one crucial factor was still missing: cereal varieties capable of responding fully to fertilizer applications and irrigation. In 1962, the Indian Agricultural Research Institute (IARI) imported seeds of so-called 'HYVs' (high-yielding varieties) of wheat with short stems and large ears, from the future International Maize and Wheat Improvement Centre (CIMMYT, in Mexico). In 1963, the Director of CIMMYT, the future Nobel Peace Prize winner N. Borlaug, visited India at the invitation of an IARI researcher, M.S. Swaminathan, who was subsequently awarded the World Food Prize (1987). In 1964, C. Subramaniam embarked upon a reform of the research and agricultural administration sectors. M.S. Swaminathan was appointed Director of IARI, and suggested that 1,000 HYV demonstration plots of at least 2 ha be set up on volunteer farms, paying the farmers compensation in the event of failure. The operation was successful beyond his wildest dreams. As a result of the 1965-6 crisis, which swept aside the Minister for Finance's doubts about agricultural input imports, and also thanks to the funds advanced by the Rockefeller Foundation, India bought no fewer than 18,000 tonnes of HYVs from Mexico, the largest seed import deal in history. As for rice, seed was to be imported from the International Rice Research Institute in the Philippines, which M.S. Swaminathan was subsequently to head.

THE TECHNICAL SOLUTION: A 'PACKAGE' OF THREE INGREDIENTS

HIGH-YIELDING SEEDS (HYV)

State Seeds (NSC, SFCI, SSC, ICAR...)

The National Seeds Corporation (NSC) was founded in 1963, with technical support from the Rockefeller Foundation. The initial aim was merely to promote local production and distribution of hybrid maize, sorghum and millet varieties. However, it rapidly found itself at the head of a well-established national seed industry, with the State Farms Corporation of India (SFCI), created in 1969, and 13 State Seed Corporations (SSC), which were set up with support from the World Bank under National Seed Projects I (1975) and II (1981). As it was not feasible to ensure the independence and development of the sector without mobilizing and developing the research sector, considerable efforts were also made in that respect. The sector now includes 18 regional agricultural universities and 6 Indian Council of Agriculture Research (ICAR) institutes, including IARI; 20 State Seed Certification Agencies (SSCA); and 96 State Seed Testing Laboratories (SSTL). The Indian researchers' first task was to adapt the imported varieties to local ecological and consumer demand while preserving their acknowledged advantages: expected high yields, short ripening times (between 140 and 110 days, if not less), and the absence of photoperiodism, to ensure that the varieties could be distributed as widely as possible throughout India. For rice, following on from IRRI and its popular IR 8 variety, efforts remained centred on improving seed intended for irrigated fertile soils. It was not until the late 1970s that thought was given to upland, i.e. non-irrigated, rice. Similarly, whereas the aim had always previously been to shorten the cropping cycle so as to enable two or even three crops per year, the emphasis subsequently shifted to increasingly late varieties capable of withstanding the hazards of rainfed inundated paddy growing. Lastly, India began producing hybrid varieties in 1990, at the instigation of ICAR, supported by the UNDP. However, yields were not much better than with normal varieties, and barely compensated for the high purchase cost of such varieties. As a result, the operation has not been a great success (1,00,000 ha of hybrid rice in 1999, compared to 15 million in China); but research is continuing, notably on transgenic plants, and increasingly in the private sector, which has really taken off since the late 1980s.

Private Seed (Mahyco, ProAgro & Co.)

A start to dismantle the State monopoly was made in 1988, with a new policy aimed at relaxing the very strict constraints on imports, encouraging foreign investment and recognizing the merits of quality non-certified seeds (a category that was not covered by the 1966 Seeds Act). Then phase III of the National Seeds Project (NSP) was launched in March 1990, still with World Bank support, but this time $30 million were set aside for preferential loans to private companies wanting to invest in seed production and distribution. Demand in India was still high in terms of both quantity and quality, and the public sector was far from able to cope with demand throughout the country. Lastly, since February 1992, foreign companies have been authorized to hold a 51 per cent share of the capital invested in joint ventures, without any specific licence, which has considerably boosted the establishment of cooperative projects with international private groups of varying sizes. Within a few years, the sector has had over a hundred private operators belonging to an influential organization (ISCA) centring on five cities (Delhi, Mumbai, Aurangabad, Bangalore and Hyderabad). Many are still very small-scale, but ten groups had a turnover of over $4.2 million in 1997: Mahyco or Maharashtra Hybrid Seeds, the world's leading cotton hybrid producer ($30 million), ProAgro Group of Companies ($15 million), Indo-American Hybrid Seeds ($11.5 million), Nath Seeds ($10.3 million), Rallis India ($9.4 million), Cargill Seeds India ($9.4 million), Mahendra Hybrid Seeds Co. ($9.2 million), Novartis India ($7 million), ITC ($4.6 million) and J.K. Agri-Genetics ($4.6 million). Using foreign technologies has enabled these firms to set up research and development services and biotechnology laboratories. Mahyco (73,000 farmers under contract) and Monsanto have launched a joint venture to produce rice and cotton hybrids. However, other Indian companies have actually been taken over: ProAgro was bought by the German firm Agrevo in 1999.

GMO (Monsanto, Pioneer, Rallis & Co.)

The new seed policy in 1988 radically changed the sector: ten years later, private and public operators had almost equal shares in the market ($545 million in 1997) and output (7,55,000 tonnes), with the former having slightly over 50 per cent in terms of turnover and the latter the same share in terms of volume. Around 90 per cent of the areas under wheat and 70 per cent of those under rice in India are now sown with HYVs. There are still excellent development prospects, since public and private seed production in India accounts for just 20 per cent of the 3.8 million tonnes of seeds consumed by Indian farmers each year. Many farmers often still use seed from their crops (open pollination). Private operators are therefore still free to continue their efforts, in fields overlooked by the Green Revolution (vegetables, oilseeds, pulses, etc.), or in conjunction with the public sector. This is not likely to pose a threat to the public sector, since it has a guaranteed future by dint of the major functions it fulfils: producing and distributing HYVs that farmers can then reproduce from one year to the next (India did not sign the 1991 version of the UPOV, which granted breeders exclusive rights to exploit their registered varieties: see Chapter 7), producing and selling hybrid seeds for crops such as millet, which are not popular with private operators (who are interested in more secure markets, such as sunflower, maize, castor, sorghum, rice, wheat, etc.), selling seed (particularly to small companies) or buying seed (up to 25 per cent of the total volume for the Andhra Pradesh SSC) from the private sector so as to ensure more efficient technology transfer to rural areas. Lastly, with respect to transgenesis techniques, India is still very cautious (three organizations are watching the research being conducted in the country officially), and has even expressed shock at the suggestion of genetically modified organisms (GMOs) using the so-called 'Terminator gene'. It is nevertheless very active in this field. For instance, in the late 1990s, both private (Mahyco-Monsanto, ProAgro-Pioneer, Rallis India) and public players (ten universities and institutes) were conducting research and trials, with financial support from the Rockefeller Foundation and the World Bank, but also from Monsanto. In 2000 the Ministry of Science and Technology's Department of Biotechnology authorized Monsanto to grow and market its Bt transgenic cotton variety in India, to the dismay of anti-GMO campaigners. In 2008 cotton is still the only GMO crop allowed for commercial cultivation in India. Officially it was grown on about 4 million ha in 2006-7, but the actual area may be more if we include stealth seeds (Navbharat) and informal crossings made by the farmers with non-BT hybrids. One hope is that research will eventually make it possible to reduce the demands of HYVs, which are so pesticide-, water- and fertilizer-intensive.

Chemical Fertilizers

Fertilizers To fulfil their potential, the green revolution's HYVs require substantial amounts of inputs, particularly water and fertilizers, although those amounts theoretically vary depending on the crop, soil type and annual organic matter applications and removals. In particular, they need three to four times more nitrogen (N) than traditional varieties, in addition to essential phosphorus (P) and potassium (K) supplements. Average chemical fertilizer consumption, in either single form (such as urea for N, phosphate or single super phosphate for P, and potash or muriate of potash for K) or combined formulas (such as MAP or DAP, fertilizers combining N and P), increased from 5 kg per cultivated hectare in 1965 to almost 75 kg 30 years later (more than the figure for the United States). This means a market worth $3 billion, largely based on urea (57 per cent). Consumption reached 90 kg/ha in 2001-2. It centres on a small number of crops (wheat, rice, cotton, sugar cane) and irrigated areas (69 per cent, with 112 kg/ha compared to an average of 34 kg/ha in non-irrigated zones in 1995-6). It tops 173 kg/ha in Punjab (2001-2), the granary of India, which is almost as high as the average figure in France. India is now the third largest fertilizer consumer in the world, after China and the United States (14 million tonnes in 1999-2000, that is 10 per cent of global consumption), and year in, year out, is also the third largest importer (2 to 4 million tonnes or roughly 3 per cent of global imports). Until 1991, two state-owned companies had a monopoly on imports: India Potash for potash and Minerals and Metals Trading Corporation (MMTC), which still controls or oversees a large number of transactions concerning the three nutrients of which India has limited (phosphates), if any (potash) natural reserves. However, as regards nitrogen and phosphates, the country has managed to establish a substantial production capacity, either within its borders or, more recently, under joint ventures abroad (Senegal, Jordan, Iran, Oman).

IFFCO, KRIBHCO & Co.

In 40 years, India has multiplied its fertilizer production by 100 (Figure 10), placing the country third in the world (14.5 million tonnes of fertilizer in 2002-3, or 10 per cent of global output). Like China and other large developing countries in general, the Indian Union has founded its agricultural development on industry. The first chemical fertilizer factory opened in 1906, but it was not until the country's Independence in 1947 that the industry really developed (half its nitrogen fertilizer plants are now over 20 years old), supported by large-scale extension campaigns and a well-organized distribution network, which

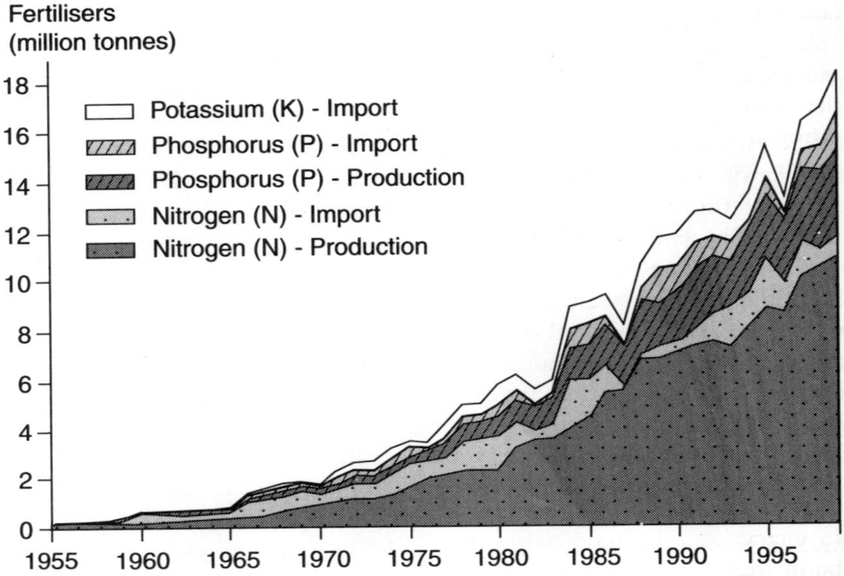

Sources: Based on Fertilizer Association of India and Ministry of Agriculture.

FIGURE 10: FERTILIZER PRODUCTION AND IMPORT (1955-6 TO 1999-2000)

now has 2,75,000 points of sale. Producing single and complex nitrogen fertilizers (such as DAP, which accounts for over 60 per cent of Indian phosphate consumption) calls for significant investment, in both installations and operations. It also has to allow for advances to farmers. The main ingredient, ammoniac, is made from costly raw materials: naphtha, petroleum, coal, and above all natural gas (6.5 billion m^3 consumed in 1995, 40 per cent of total gas production in India). These financial barriers partly explain why five producers: two cooperatives, Indian Farmers Fertiliser Cooperative Limited (IFFCO), and Krishak Bharati Cooperative, Limited (KRIBHCO), two State-owned firms (National Fertilisers Limited and Rashtriya Chemicals and Fertilisers) and one private company (Gujarat State Fertilisers Limited) account for 45 per cent of nitrogen production capacity (around 10 million tonnes a year produced by 40 urea and 10 DAP plants). The phosphate fertilizer (primarily SSP) sector is more splintered, with over 800 mainly private factories, although the total capacity is even more under-used than it is in the nitrogen sector: in 2003-4, the average capacity utilization at Indian fertilizer plants was 89 per cent for N and 67 per cent for P.

Retention Price Scheme (RPS)

The boom in production capacity is primarily a result of direct support from the central government, whose power to intervene in the highly strategic fertilizer sector was confirmed by the 1955 Essential Commodities Act. From 1943 to 1966, all nitrogen fertilizers, imported or not, were under the control of a central pool, which allocated them to the various states at set prices, and took charge of transport operations. After the first oil crisis (1977 to 1979), the Retention Price Scheme (RPS) was introduced. The scheme set out on the one hand to guarantee Indian industrialists sufficiently high revenue to boost their activities and development, and on the other hand to guarantee farmers sufficiently low purchase prices to encourage them to apply products that were considered crucial in ensuring the country's food self-sufficiency. To this end, each year, the State pays industrialists a subsidy corresponding to the difference between two prices: the sale price to farmers, which is set and imposed by the authorities, and a so-called 'retention price', which is generally considerably higher. The latter, which is calculated for each factory and product, is in fact a theoretical sales price at which the industrialist, regardless of his production costs, would obtain a 12 per cent return on his capital investment, operating at a utilization rate of 85 to 90 per cent. In addition, twice a year, representatives of the Ministries of Transport and Chemicals and Fertilizer meet with industrialists to decide, based on regional demand, where each factory can or must sell its products, and in what quantities, given that the government will cover transport costs. For instance, the country's largest fertilizer producing state, Gujarat, supplies a major part of the Ganges Valley to the west, and sometimes areas as far away as Tamil Nadu in the south of the peninsula.

Fertilizer Subsidies

The RPS has boosted domestic fertilizer production, but failed to prevent imports, which are another expense for the State: so-called 'import' subsidies are based on the same philosophy and mean covering the difference between a 'market' price (in this case the purchase price overseas) and a 'fair' price for sales to farmers. In addition, there are considerable indirect subsidies linked to domestic energy price control, i.e. the cost of naphtha, petroleum and coal consumed by nitrogen fertilizer manufacturers. Under the RPS, until 1991, prices for fertilizer consumers were kept low and highly stable: agricultural applications and yields increased in intensively farmed areas, as did the cost to the public purse. This last point was severely criticized by the IMF during the 1991 financial crisis (see Chapter 8). A series of measures and counter-measures was introduced that year and in subsequent years, with every announcement followed by often violent farmers' demonstrations, reflecting the considerable difficulty of reforming the sector. Since then, urea sales prices have generally increased overall (+40 per cent in July 1991, cut to +30 per cent in August, –10 per cent in August 1992, +20 per cent in June 1994, +10 per cent in February 1997, +10 per cent in January 1999, etc.). In the meantime, in August 1992, the RPS was abolished entirely for phosphate and potassium fertilizers. This sent prices sky high, with a corresponding drop in demand for P and K fertilizers and an imbalance in terms of NPK applications that jeopardized soil fertility (over-use of N fertilizer). A so-called 'ad hoc' or 'concessionary' subsidy was introduced in October of the same year. These subsidies are paid to P and K fertilizer producers and importers based on the number of units sold, and in fact enable the government to set a maximum sales price each season for the various products concerned. As a result, the bill for fertilizer subsidies is continuing to grow (see Chapter 8), and the phasing out of the RPS for urea is always postponed: fertilizers will continue to account for a major share of government agricultural support, along with two less visible but perhaps equally important aspects: irrigation and water.

Irrigation

Water

With rainfall levels above the global average (1,194 mm/year compared to 991), India receives over 4,000 billion m^3 of water a year. However, that rainfall is very unevenly distributed in terms of both geography (1,600 m^3 in West Bengal but less than 100 in Rajasthan, for instance) and time, since 3,000 of those 4,000 billion m^3 fall during the main monsoon season, from June to September. After evaporation (around 700 billion m^3) and infiltration (around 1,700 billion m^3), 1,800 billion m^3 go into the country's rivers (20 basins) and 1,500 billion m^3 flow directly into the sea, carrying some 6 billion tonnes of alluvia and at least 8.5 million tonnes of fertilizer (as of the late 1990s). The main challenge for Indian farming is to control water flow more efficiently, so as to capture and distribute the available water over time and space, stabilize and increase yields and cultivate new areas. Some deltas of the east coast (Kaveri) have been equipped since ancient times. Even before the Great Mughals, a start was made on building canals in the Ganges Valley. This was the beginning of a vast network that was considerably developed by the British from the nineteenth century onwards, and subsequently by independent India. The whole upstream section of the Indo-Gangetic plain is now irrigated, and various parts of Punjab have been converted into a veritable pioneer front: diversion canals leading from the powerful rivers of the Himalayas serve to irrigate this semi-arid area, and the resulting influx of farmers has resulted in larger than average farms, with a geometric plot layout. In Deccan, somewhat later, large reservoir dams were built on the major rivers to enable crop farming during the dry season; one example is the dam built on the Kaveri River by the Maharaja of Mysore in 1932 (72,000 ha of irrigated land). However, these dams have sometimes jeopardized the large irrigation schemes in downstream delta areas, which are at risk of water shortages. This is one of the reasons behind the current more or less open conflicts between upstream and downstream states fighting over the waters of various rivers (see Chapter 7).

Canal Irrigation (CWC, CAD, Wara-bandi...)

The building of large reservoir dams, the 'temples of modern India' as Nehru dubbed them, continued apace after Independence. However, once completed, these 'medium' (2,000 to 10,000 ha) or 'major' irrigation projects (over 10,000 ha) still failed to supply all the areas that were supposed to benefit, since water was wasted in some places and remained scarce in others. The overly technocratic nature of the projects, which were launched and managed by highly skilled engineers who nevertheless mostly failed to grasp the economic, ecological and human aspects of what they were doing, led to the launch, in 1974, of the Command Area Development (CAD) programme. The aim was no longer merely to build and maintain canals, but also to make optimum use of their potential for agricultural production and for guaranteeing a return on public investment. (The Accelerated Irrigation Benefits Programme (AIBP), launched in 1996, fitted in with this objective.) The approach was intended to be 'coordinated, integrated and multi-disciplinary'. In addition to the concerns expressed about water supplies by the Department of Irrigation (at the ministry of the same name) and the Central Water Commission (CWC), there were also issues concerning cropping systems, agricultural credit, how to provide water to crops and for how long, and how water should be shared between individuals and communities upstream and downstream of projects. As a result, an attempt was made to impose the *warabandi* system, which enables relatively sophisticated water supply rotations, particularly in the north of the country. However, on the whole, despite regular confirmation over the years of the relevance of the CAD approach, the results show that there is still considerable room for improvement. It has also failed to ensure that users at least cover the cost of operating and maintaining the networks installed, for want of sufficiently high tariffs (the minimum and maximum figures levied per state in 1992 were around Rs. 35 and 350, respectively). There was huge public investment in developing irrigation systems during the first seven five-year plans (1950-90), amounting to some Rs. 600 billion (at 1988-9 prices), or $41.8 billion (at the exchange rate at the time). Of that investment, only 40 per cent was in 'medium' or 'major' projects, since the Green Revolution primarily invested in stepping up the use of a hitherto neglected resource: ground-water.

Wells (MWS...)

In 1965, the regional disparities in agricultural India primarily hinged on the existence (or lack) of a canal system. In southern India in particular, there is a tradition, dating back to mediaeval and even earlier times, of village ponds and tanks, which serve to extend the cropping season a little (the tanks, which also help to top up the water table, are now managed by the state, with villagers only responsible for the smallest ones). There are also open wells, generally 8 m in diameter, which are used to collect water along with ancient water skins, norias or beams. However, these techniques were largely insufficient for the production model the Green Revolution set out to popularize, and a 'well revolution' was therefore also required. By dint of subsidized loans in particular, there was an initial drive to encourage new digging operations, including at existing wells, to increase their depth from 10 to 40 m (dug-cum-bore wells), and by installing centrifugal diesel pumps. So as not to exclude Dalits and tribes from the process, the Ministry of Rural Areas and Employment launched the Million Wells Scheme (MWS) in 1988, which involved digging open wells free of charge for the benefit of such communities. Ten years later, in 1998, after digging over 1.15 million such wells (at an average unit cost of Rs. 30,000-35,000), the MWS was extended, notably to include tube wells. There has been unprecedented development of tube wells since the 1970s (Figure 11), also thanks to financial support from the

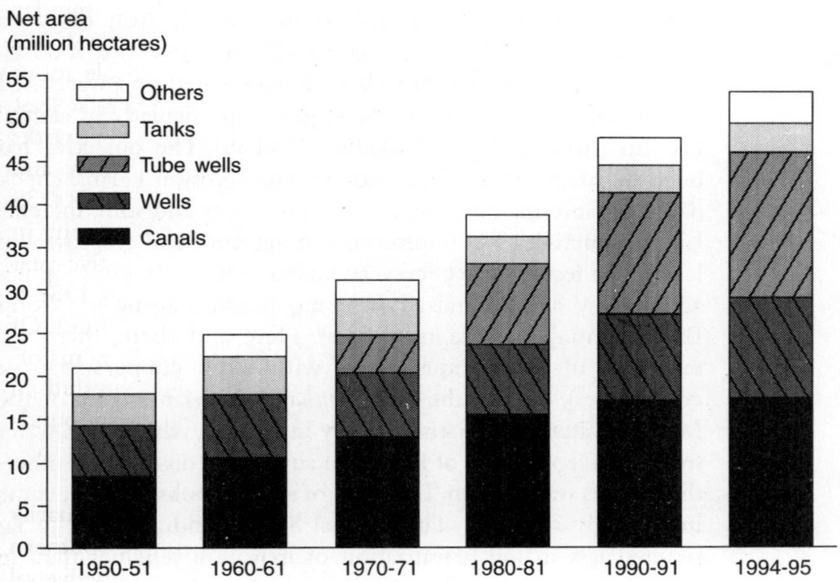

Source: Based on data from the Ministry of Agriculture.

FIGURE 11: NET IRRIGATED AREA SOURCE-WISE (1950-1 TO 1994-5)

government. Tube wells are extremely deep (up to 150 m and more), and call for submersible electric pumps. Provided electricity is available (power cuts or supply sharing with local industry are common), such wells ensure a greater flow rate at a lower cost than diesel pumps, since electricity for agricultural purposes is heavily subsidized, and even free in some states (Punjab and Tamil Nadu). They also bear witness to the efforts made to ensure constant access to the water table, which is falling fast now that there are so many wells.

Watersheds and Water Cooperatives (PIM...)

In four decades, the gross irrigated area was multiplied by 2.7, from 28 million ha in 1960 to 75 million in 2000-1, largely thanks to well development (59 per cent of the net irrigated area in 1999-2000 as against 30 per cent in 1960). India now accounts for 20 per cent of the total irrigated area worldwide, albeit with significant variations within the country (in 1999-2000 the national average for the proportion of land with irrigation was 41 per cent, with 94 per cent in Punjab but only 17 per cent in Maharashtra and Kerala). The price to pay is growing in both financial (see Chapter 8) and ecological terms (see Chapter 7). This has led to the introduction of more economical, equitable and eco-friendly resource use models. Since 1982, programmes have been implemented on a watershed scale in zones with little, if any, irrigation, particularly in central Deccan (Andhra Pradesh, Madhya Pradesh). The objective has been to safeguard the local ecology (anti-erosion berms, check dams, organic manure use, to conserve water and soil), increase land productivity and improve living standards and employment levels. The results have been very mixed, as have the philosophies adopted by agricultural advisers and funding agencies (World Bank, central or state ministries). Here and there, there are examples of micro-experiments with water cooperatives (or committees), such as the *Pani Panchayats* in Maharashtra or the Mohini Water Cooperative Society in Gujarat, which buys water from the Department of Irrigation and sells it on to its members through its own system. This type of system looks set to become increasingly common. The gradual State withdrawal has so far resulted less in full privatization of irrigation schemes than in cooperation between the authorities and users, with water rates being set under an independent financial system. As a result of an Act passed in 1997, it is Andhra Pradesh that has gone the furthest down the 'Participatory Irrigation Management' (PIM) road, thanks to World Bank funding. The state has more than 10,000 associations officially created for managing 4.7 million ha. Provided care is taken to draw up measures that protect smallholders, full devolution of small-scale irrigation scheme management to the irrigators themselves could enable truly 'sustainable' irrigation, which is unfortunately far from being the case at present.

THE ECONOMIC SOLUTION: PROCUREMENT AND REDISTRIBUTION

PROCURING GOODS WITH ATTRACTIVE FARM PRICES

Regulated Markets

Guaranteeing agricultural producers attractive prices and protecting them from price slumps became a real priority for India during the Green Revolution. As regards the first point, based on a recommendation made in 1928 by the Royal Commission on Agriculture, the states of the Union first passed trade laws setting up Regulated Markets, primarily in the 1960s. The primary aim was to improve trading conditions for farmers in primary markets (*mandis*). The texts differed, but the aim was to ensure that agricultural product buyers and sellers could meet in a place where they were truly in competition, with reliable weight and quality controls, authorized brokers taking a set rate of commission (generally 2–2.5 per cent), storage facilities and accommodation for producers who lived some distance away. Two decades later, in 1988, the Ministry of Agriculture listed 6,052 Regulated Markets in India, almost two-thirds of which were in six states: Bihar (798), Maharashtra (736), Punjab (670), Uttar Pradesh (630), Andhra Pradesh (568) and Madhya Pradesh (498). Of those figures—which should be viewed with caution (some so-called Regulated Markets are in fact merely deserted patches of concrete in the middle of the countryside), 36 per cent are major centres that supervise the others, through a 'Market Committee' with between 8 and 20 members (generally civil servants) and a chairman, vice-chairman and secretary, the last of whom may either be elected or appointed, depending on the state, and who has authority over the market's employees.

He also oversees the smooth running of daily sales, which generally operate along three main lines: auctions, sealed bids or mutual agreements. It is also at these markets that the wholesale prices of goods included in the main Indian price index, the Wholesale Price Index (WPI), are recorded. Above all, these markets are where MSPs are both displayed and, if need be, applied.

Minimum Support Prices (MSP, MIS, NAFED)

The MSP programme, implemented at the same time as the efforts made to develop and structure agricultural markets, was intended to protect producers from sharp price falls by guaranteeing sales at a price that would cover their production costs and generate at least a small profit in the most advanced zones. The body in charge of the scheme is the National Agricultural Cooperative Marketing Federation (NAFED), which was founded in 1958 to help organize and promote agricultural product marketing. In 1990, the federation's members included the Union Government and the National Cooperative Development Corporation (NCDC), 24 state-level Marketing Federations (MARKFEDs) and 3 territory MARKFEDs, 13 state-level Tribal and Commodity Federations and 251 cooperative or processing companies at district or regional level, representing around 6,000 Primary Cooperative Marketing Societies (PCMS).

Nowadays, MSP are set by the Commission for Agricultural Costs and Prices (CACP) for 24 crops that account for over 80 per cent of the gross cultivated area: the main cereals, main oilseeds and pulses, copra, cotton, jute, Virginia tobacco and sugar cane. Other goods such as onions, potatoes, ginger, chillies, black pepper, castor and certain fruits, are covered by a less centralized system, the Market Intervention Scheme (MIS) under which the Union and individual states work together to set price thresholds, so as to share the cost of any intervention. In practice, they very rarely have to intervene under either the MIS or the MSP scheme, and these minimum prices are more useful as a reference in determining procurement prices for cereals.

Procurement Prices (PP, SMP)

Since 1970-1, the Indian Union has announced Procurement Prices (PP), somewhere between the MSP and the market price, for cereals alone (wheat and rice in practice, plus maize, sorghum and millet in theory). These PPs are also set by the CACP (the government may increase them if need be), and have to be sufficiently attractive to enable building up large public stocks that can redistributed at low prices to communities or areas suffering from shortages, or used to counter the adverse effects of poor monsoons. In the case of rice, which has to be hulled before storage, the system is combined with compulsory procurement from rice mills (sometimes up to 75 per cent of their output, particularly in Punjab and Haryana). In 1991, the PPs for cereals officially became MSPs, in part with good reason, since PPs in any event acted as MSPs (with the government buying all the stocks offered at the set price), but in part wrongly, since they also continued to act as PPs, leading to actual market intervention. As with sugar cane and its Statutory Minimum Price (SMP), which is intended to build-up public stocks while ensuring that some refinery profits are redistributed to farmers, there is an incentive to produce the goods concerned. In effect, in optimum areas, farmers are guaranteed a healthy profit. This government guarantee, and the fact that the government is in turn sure of obtaining sufficient supplies, obviously comes at a price, which needs to be kept to a minimum. One solution is a systematic ban on grain trading between zones with surpluses and others with shortages, to 'encourage' the sale of any surpluses to the authorities. However, these barriers to free trade and circulation of goods are currently being dismantled, in particular with the 2002 order softening the controls by the Essential Commodities Act. (In 1973, the central government had gone so far as to award itself a monopoly on wheat wholesale trading). They are occasionally reintroduced to facilitate purchases by the Food Corporation of India (FCI), see infra, or by the states themselves, which sometimes close their borders so as to build-up their own stocks or control inflation. However, it is clear that during the 1990s, the cost of procurement by the FCI increased in line with the closure of the gap (often orchestrated for political ends) between the prices offered by the government and those on the domestic market, which themselves grew steadily.

Redistributing Stocks to Consumers at Low Prices

Food Corporations (FCI, CWC)

The FCI, which is under the aegis of the Ministry of Food and Civil Supplies, was founded at the end of 1964 to manage the procurement, transport, storage and redistribution of food products that the government wished to make available to the population in sufficient quantities, throughout the country and at all times. State procurement was not a new concept in India: it had existed on a small scale since colonial times, and even earlier in some areas. In 1951, it amounted to almost 4 million tonnes (primarily cereals and some pulses), i.e. 7 per cent of output. However, it subsequently declined and was non-existent by 1956, albeit rising to 1.4 million tonnes in 1964 (under 2 per cent of output): the country was counting more on imports to fill its grain godowns (warehouses). After 1965, this was no longer the case. There was strong and regular growth (around 10 per cent of annual cereal production) in public purchases on the domestic market (Figure 12 and Map 8), with occasional peaks, for instance in 1993 (28 million tonnes, 16 per cent of output).

In terms of transport, the FCI benefits from preferential rates from the Indian railways for its 600 to 800 25-tonne wagons that crisscross the country each day. For storage, it has its own installations, but also rents from state governments, private warehouse owners and above all warehouse corporations. These corporations (Central Warehousing Corporation and 17 of State

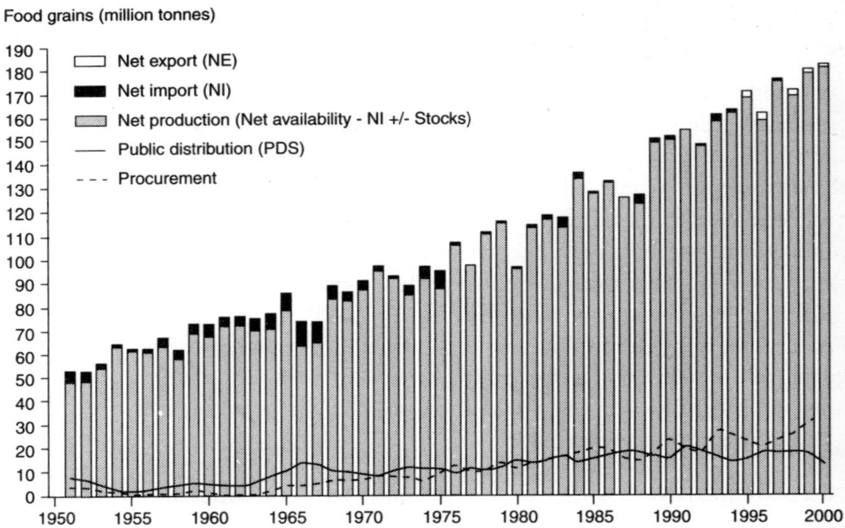

Source: Based on Economic Survey.

FIGURE 12: FOOD GRAINS PRODUCTION, IMPORT, PROCUREMENT AND DISTRIBUTION (1951 TO 2000)

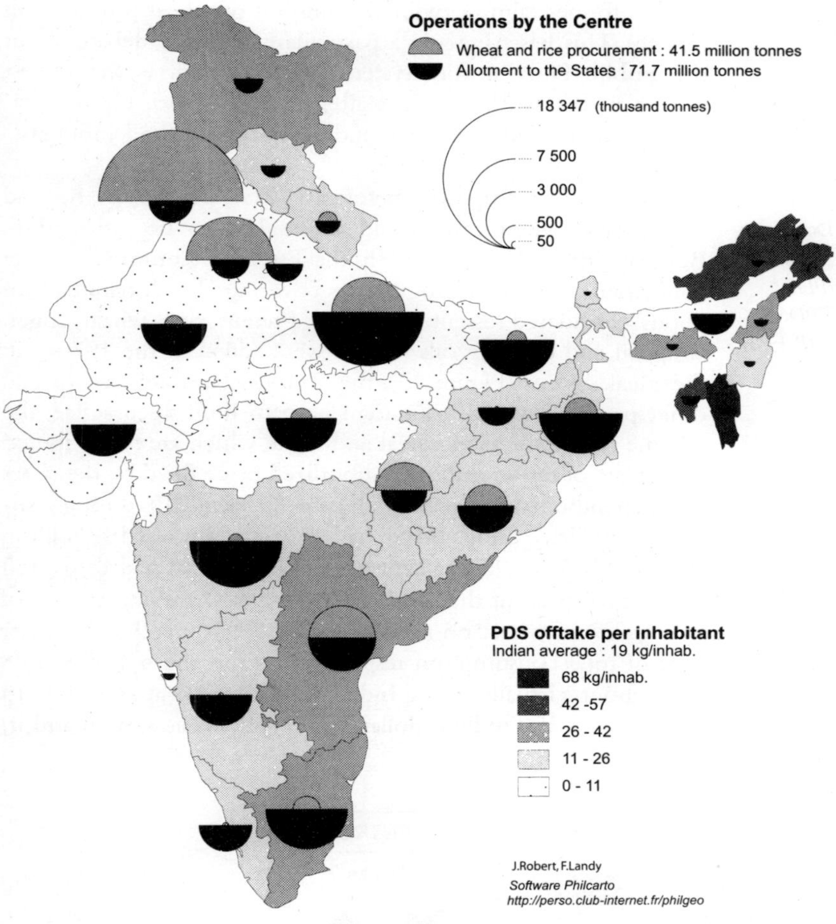

Source: Based on data from the Department of Food.

MAP 8: WHEAT AND RICE PROCUREMENT AND CENTRAL ALLOCATION (2004-5)

Warehousing Corporations), which represented 33 per cent of the 25.8 million tonnes of covered storage capacity available to the FCI in 2005, are also in charge of managing public fertilizer stocks on behalf of the Union. This type of stock management is often criticized, as for instance in mid-1996, when the FCI found itself with 30 million tonnes of cereals, with some rotting in the warehouses, and in 2001-2, when stocks were over 60 million tonnes (almost twice the amount of wheat produced in France). This has triggered a particularly virulent debate about the Public Distribution System (PDS), which is the largest system in the world, perhaps after that in China, for redistributing domestically procured and/or imported food products.

Public Distribution System (PDS, TPDS, CIP, FPS)

The PDS was set up well before the FCI, during the Second World War, when cereals and pulses had to be rationed in Bombay and Calcutta. In 1955, the Essential Commodities Act confirmed a national programme covering the distribution of goods considered 'essential', viz., at present rice, wheat, sugar, lamp oil and cooking oils (which were added in the 1970s). In the ideal system (Figure 13), the various states are free to add other products, which they then have to fund. In practice, the scheme centres on rice, wheat and sugar, which are redistributed to holders of ration cards at a subsidized price fixed by the states but depending on the Central Issue Price (CIP) through so-called Fair Price Shops (FPS). In 2002, an estimated 199 million households (over 90 per cent of the population) had cards, and the annual value of the food issued (almost 9 million tonnes of rice and 7 of wheat on average in the 1990s, i.e. 9 and 13 per cent of total consumption respectively) from the 4,40,000 FPS throughout virtually all of India was estimated at over Rs. 15 billion (over 356 million dollars). The cost of the system and its

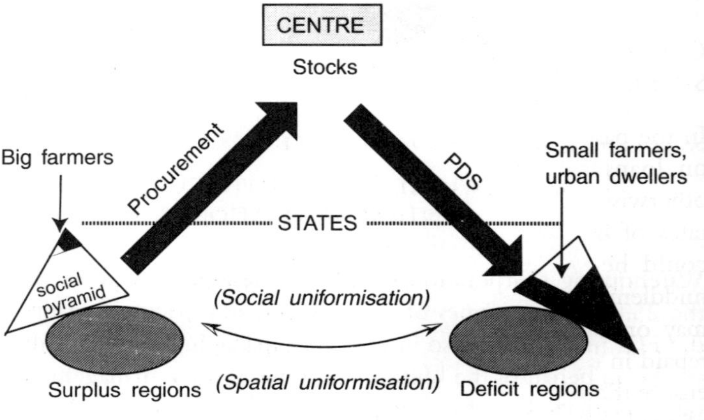

FIGURE 13: AN IDEAL VIEW OF THE PUBLIC FOOD SYSTEM

obvious malfunctions (poor families were far from the only beneficiaries, see Chapter 6) led to restructuring in the 1990s, with formulas intended to target those zones or populations that were really in need. On 1 January 1992, the Revamped PDS (RPDS) was launched, with the aim of offering 20 kg of grain per month for half a rupee less than the CIP to poor families living in the administrative blocks chosen for the operation (2,446 in 1995, i.e. 267 million people). However, fraud proved to be rife (some 11.5 million bogus cards were withdrawn in 1994–5), and the 'revamped' system was replaced by a 'targeted' PDS (TPDS) on 1 June 1997. This encompassed a dual price system: a heavily subsidized CIP for Below the Poverty Line (BPL) households, with an annual family income of less than Rs. 15,000, and a CIP similar to the market rate for those judged Above the Poverty Line (APL). In the former case, the grain allocation was limited to 10 kg per month (35 kg from 2002 onwards), given that the central government had set an annual quota of 7.2 million tonnes for the 60 million target households (BPL) and 10.3 million tonnes for the others (APL). Additional allocations (theoretically at the APL price, in an attempt to cover FCI operating costs) may be negotiated with the various states, which have the unenviable task of identifying BPL and APL households before distributing the volumes allocated to them. The states are also free to increase the quotas distributed to the households and reduce the issue prices, but at their own budgetary cost.

Collecting and Distributing Savings More Efficiently

Rural Credit and Usury

In the past and even now, many Indian farmers have depended on loans from family members or friends, if possible, and otherwise from unofficial lenders who generally charge interest rates of between 2 and 5 per cent per month. These lenders could be successful farmers, travelling traders, marketplace middlemen (*arhtias*), small-scale dealers, etc. These loans, which may or may not be secured (generally on gold jewellery), are repaid in cash or in kind, and are a good short-term solution to ensure the family's survival and future income (to fund purchases of seed and other inputs) and its honour on certain occasions (particularly to pay for weddings and dowries). However, although they are quick and easy to obtain, they can also work out very expensive and mean that the whole family is burdened, sometimes over several generations, with a loan that the lender postpones and increases if the family cannot pay and which they try to repay by taking other loans. The consequences are sometimes fatal: almost 300 cotton growers in Andhra Pradesh committed suicide in 1998 after their crop failed. The creation of 'rice banks' or of small-scale savings and credit associations (money clubs, *bishis*, *chit funds*, *chitties*, urban credit societies, and so on) that generally involve people from the same caste or socio-economic group may help to avoid the need for these usurers, but the latter are still a major source of loans in rural areas where informal funding in parallel with the official system still accounts for over 50 per cent of agricultural loans (at least 60 per cent of rural households did not have a bank account in 1994). Despite appearances, the authorities' efforts to remedy the situation have been relatively effective; the results obtained are highly respectable in relation to many other developing countries, and also compared to the situation in India in the middle of the last century.

Primary Agricultural Credit Societies (PACS)

A major national survey in 1954 revealed that official institutions granted just 7 per cent of loans in rural areas. The government therefore decided to give strong support to the development of Primary Agricultural Credit Societies (PACS) in villages, and a wide-ranging network rapidly grew, supervised by the districts, states and the central government. These PACS primarily supply short-term crop loans, often half in kind (primarily fertilizers), at an interest rate of around 1 per cent per month. In some cases, they also sell various consumer goods or fertilizers, and serve as 'FPS' under the PDS. However, despite all the technical, administrative and financial support the government was forced at the end of the 1960s to recognize that most cooperatives were corrupt and led by local elites fulfilling their own political ambitions, who discouraged repayment so to increase their stronghold over debtors. As a result of this observation and of the subsequent shift in strategy, there were only half as many PACS in 1981 as in 1961. This marked the end of the first development phase and of the monopoly held by cooperative structures (1954–69).

RBI, NABARD and Commercial Banks

The second phase (1969-91) aimed both to improve access to institutional credit and release savings in rural areas, to fund the Green Revolution. It began by nationalizing the 14 largest deposit banks. Six others followed by 1980. The commercial banking sector was transformed into a veritable government monopoly, under the aegis of the National Bank for Agriculture and Rural Development (NABARD). In ten years (1968-77), the number of branches in rural areas was multiplied by six, and the number of deposits by five. These newly nationalized institutions fulfilled a range of functions in this new environment. Firstly, they contributed to the capital of Regional Rural Banks (RRB), created in 1975 to provide the most underprivileged rural classes with access to credit. Since 1982, they have also allocated loans and subsidies via the Integrated Rural Development Programme (IRDP), which has much the same objectives as the RRBs (in favour of agricultural workers, Dalits, tribal communities, craftsmen and small-scale traders, young unemployed people, women, etc.). Since the mid-1970s in particular, the Lead Bank Scheme has given the leading bank in each district the task of working with other credit organizations in its geographical area to draw up an Annual Action Plan and a longer-term District Credit Plan. These plans are supposed to integrate directives from the cooperative sector, the state government and the central government (loan conditions, interest rates, credit allocation for jobs specified in the plan, etc.). The NABARD attempted in 1987-8 to loosen these constraints by proposing a programme of Potential-Linked District Credit Plan (PLP), giving districts a little more autonomy. Since April 1989, the Reserve Bank of India (RBI), for its part, has been promoting a local service approach or Service Area Approach (SAA), aimed at simplifying and accelerating requests for loans (centralized processing at village level by the nearest bank). However, these initiatives have failed to overcome the increasing concerns and malfunctions in the profession.

Reforms of 1991 and Structural Adjustment Plan

The situation is in fact critical. Ever since nationalization, the strict control the government and the RBI exercised over credit volumes and the amount of currency in circulation in India had spared India from long periods with high inflation. However, a series of poor harvests, exacerbated by the severe drought in 1987, and a succession of electoral campaigns prompted a large-scale move to encourage rural inhabitants not to repay their loans, which obviously proved very popular. In the end, a programme was introduced on 15 May 1990 to write off Rs. 10,000 of each farmer's loan from the various credit organizations, which were verging on bankruptcy at the time. The RBI estimated the cost of the operation at Rs. 15 billion, but a year later, in May 1991, over Rs. 50 billion (Rs. 77 billion by 30 November 1993) had already been allocated to more than 22 million beneficiaries. This situation, compounded by other difficulties, meant that the whole country was facing bankruptcy by July that year (see Chapter 8). The RBI had just three weeks of reserves left.

The IMF's Structural Adjustment Plan and the firm undertaking to liberalize the economy led the government to embark upon a third complex reform: making credit institutions more functional, efficient and above all financially viable. The recapitalization of the banks and deregulation of their operations (greater flexibility in setting rates, guarantees, investment, etc.) also meant certain constraints, particularly in terms of the Cash Reserve Ratio (CRR) and Statutory Liquidity Ratio (SLR). The entry barriers surrounding rural credit were also lifted. Since August 1996, the RBI has authorized the creation, albeit under certain conditions, of small Local Area Banks (LAB), operating over an area covering not more than three neighbouring districts.

Mini-banks and Microfinance (SEWA, SHG...)

In February 1997, the international Micro-Credit Summit in Washington demonstrated the merits and profitability of setting up savings and credit structures in developing countries, such as the Grameen Bank in Bangladesh, Bank Rakyat Indonesia, Bolivia's Banco Solidario and SEWA Bank in India, which has lent money to almost 50,000 women in the Ahmedabad region. On a subcontinental level, it also increased the Indian government's recognition and encouragement of experiments other than cooperative mini-banks (PACS). The NGOs involved (SHARE or RDT in Andhra Pradesh, RDO in Manipur, WWF in Chennai, MYRADA) can now form recognized Self-Help Groups (SHG) and join networks involving other similar groups or banks (a formula introduced by the NABARD in 1992-3).

They may also use the LAB formula, or that of the Small Industries Development Bank of India (SIDBI), which was launched in 1994 to support the establishment of micro-enterprises and had granted Rs. 80 million worth of loans within four years to 72 NGOs (including 55 women's organizations) with 48,000 members on very low incomes. By 31 March 2004, there were 1.1 million SHGs (compared to 225 in 1992–3 and 30,477 in 1999), on which commercial banks, RRBs and cooperative banks had spent Rs. 39 billion since 1992. This is a considerable sum, but it has to be considered in relation to total agricultural credit volumes in the country (Figure 14).

THE REWARD: CEREAL SELF-SUFFICIENCY

Productivity

The substantial release of household savings just after the start of the Green Revolution helped to fund irrigation operations, domestic fertilizer and high-yielding seed production, and support measures aimed at ensuring that producers and

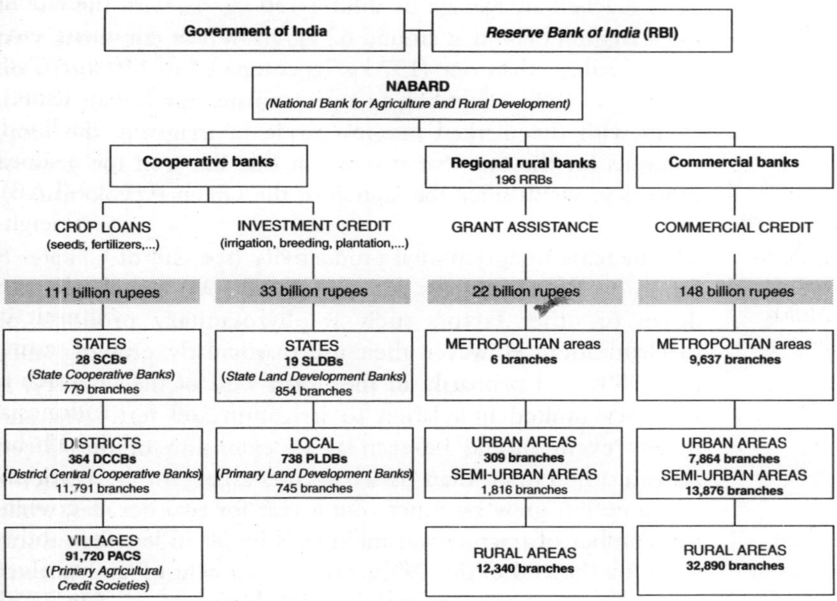

Source: Based on data from NABARD and Economic Survey.

FIGURE 14: RURAL CREDIT OFFICIAL ORGANIZATION (1997–8)

consumers did not have to bear the cost of increased intermediate consumption (policy of low-cost inputs and outputs). For rice, and above all wheat, the results were obvious: between the early 1960s and the end of the century, yields per ha doubled and trebled respectively on average throughout India, with an even greater increase in the most active regions. In fact, these two crops, and the regions best suited to growing them, largely benefited from the new mechanisms. In addition to the development of HYVs, 65 per cent of the 43 million ha newly irrigated between 1960 and 1995 were used for wheat and rice (an extra 19 million ha for the former and nine for the latter, which already occupied areas with a good natural water supply).

As regards fertilizers, at the end of the 1990s, it was seen—for want of crop-by-crop application statistics—that the six leading rice- and wheat-growing states in India (accounting for 63 and 67 per cent respectively of the total tonnage produced by the country in 1997-8) consumed almost 55 per cent of the fertilizers applied in India, whereas they accounted for barely 35 per cent of the gross cropped area. Fertilizer applications in those six states reached an average of around 130 kg/ha, with the rest of India lagging behind at around 62 kg/ha. Wheat consumes even more fertilizer than rice (137 kg/ha compared to 110 kg/ha on average in 1995, according to our estimates for India), which, along with the marked progress made in irrigating the crop, accounts for the fact that it is wheat that has seen the greatest growth in yields since the launch of the Green Revolution.

Pesticides and Mechanization

The increase in agricultural productivity (see end of Chapter 8 for an overall analysis for the period 1980-95) can also be put down to other factors such as phytosanitary products or mechanization. However, their use (particularly growing since the 1980s, and primarily in the north-west of the country) is still very limited in relation to irrigation and fertilizers, and in any event should be seen as an extension of the Green Revolution rather than as a specific aspect of it. Pesticide consumption grew by 6 per cent a year for two decades, while the number of tractors was multiplied by 30 in less than thirty years (by the end of the 1990s, only 55 per cent of land was still being ploughed using animal draught). However, in addition to the specific constraints in India (small plot size), public policy in this respect remained cautious, with few incentives and indeed many obstacles, since mechanizing agricultural operations and using herbicides instead of hand-hoeing plots are a threat to agricultural employment: it is land that is scarce in India, not labour. As a result, as recently as the mid-1980s, an 18 per cent tax was still imposed on tractors, although it has since been abolished for those under 25 HP. Although they are now a relatively common sight in the Indian countryside, much more so than rototillers, this is because they are more often used to transport stone or people than to plough fields. Punjab—where there is one tractor for every 10 ha—is the only state in which combine harvesters are common. However, for some time now, the rate of mechanization has gradually been increasing, for instance in certain rice-growing regions with a diversified economy, where labour tends to be relatively scarce and costly. Moreover, the cut in the tax on powerful tractors has made them more attractive, and the multinationals, which have now been authorized to sell their goods throughout the country, may well be about to put a stop to the quasi-monopoly previously held by small 35-HP tractors.

Wheat, Rice and Other Cereals

In the meantime, since the launch of the Green Revolution, the technical and economic advantages of growing rice and wheat have led to an increase in the area sown, and in some cases to monoculture systems. With the simultaneous increase in yields, Indian rice production was multiplied by 2.4 and wheat production by 6 in less than 40 years (Figure 15 and Table 1). By the end of the 1990s, India was running a close third to China and the United States, and accounted for over 20 per cent and 10 per cent of total world output for the two crops respectively. India eventually overcame the USA in wheat production. It is even able to export now (between 2 and 5 million tonnes of rice a year and less consistent volumes of wheat since 1995). In the case of rice, over 80 per cent of domestic production comes from eight states (West Bengal, Uttar Pradesh, Andhra Pradesh, Punjab, Bihar, Tamil Nadu, Madhya Pradesh and Orissa), the first three of which accounted for over 50 per cent of the total in 1999-2000. The degree of concentration is even greater for (soft) wheat production, since just five states in the north of the country account for 88 per cent of supplies: Uttar Pradesh

TABLE 1: FOOD GRAIN AREA, YIELD AND AVAILABILITY (1950-1 TO 2000-1)

		1950-1	1960-1	1970-1	1980-1	1990-1	2000-1
Gross cropped area (GCA)) (million ha)	Rice	30.8	34.1	37.6	40.1	42.7	44.7
	Wheat	9.8	12.9	18.2	22.3	24.2	25.7
	Total cereals	78.2	92.0	101.8	104.2	103.2	100.7
	Pulses	19.1	23.6	22.6	22.5	24.7	10.7
	India	131.9	152.8	165.8	172.6	185.7	187.9
Irrigation (irrigated GCA/GCA)	Rice	32%	37%	38%	41%	46%	54%
	Wheat	35%	33%	54%	70%	81%	88%
	Total cereals	21%	22%	28%	34%	41%	51%
	Pulses	10%	8%	9%	9%	11%	13%
	India	17%	18%	23%	29%	34%	40%
							(1997-8)
High Yielding Varieties (GCA with HYV/ GCA)	Rice	-	3%	15%	45%	64%	74%
	Wheat	-	4%	36%	72%	87%	86%
	Total cereals	-	2%	15%	41%	63%	75%
	Pulses	-	-	-	-	-	-
Fertilizers (kg of nutrients per ha of GCA)	Punjab	-	-	37	112	171	162
	Tamil Nadu	-	-	34	63	115	145
	Haryana	-	-	14	43	128	147
	Andhra Pradesh	-	-	22	46	133	160
	Uttar Pradesh	-	-	18	49	90	115
	West Bengal	-	-	10	36	90	117
	India	-	2	14	32	68	87
Yield (quintal per ha)	Rice	6.7	10.1	11.2	13.4	17.4	19.0
	Wheat	6.6	8.5	13.1	16.3	22.8	27.1
	Total cereals	5.4	7.5	9.5	11.4	15.7	18.4
	Pulses	4.4	5.4	5.2	4.7	5.8	5.4
Production (million tonnes)	Rice	20.6	34.6	42.2	53.6	74.3	85.0
	Wheat	6.5	11.0	23.8	36.3	55.1	69.7
	Total cereals	42.4	69.3	96.6	119.0	162.1	185.7
	Pulses	8.4	12.7	11.8	10.6	14.3	11.1
Population (million inhab.)		363.2	442.4	551.3	688.5	851.7	1033.2
Production per capita (kg per year)	Cereals	116.7	156.6	175.2	172.8	190.3	179.7
	Pulses	23.1	28.7	21.4	15.4	16.8	10.7
Per capita availability (kg per year)	Cereals	122.0	146.0	152.4	152.3	171.0	141.0
	Pulses	22.2	25.2	18.7	13.7	15.2	11.0

Source: Based on Ministry of Agriculture, Fertiliser Association of India, Economic Survey.

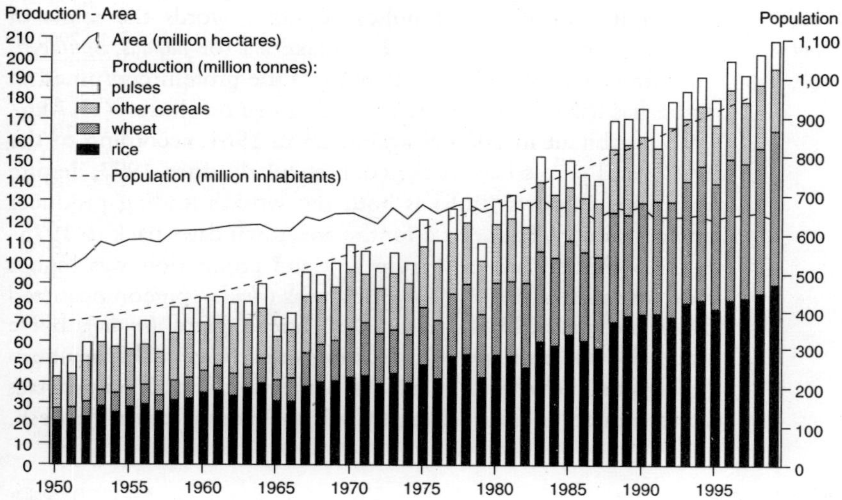

Source: Based on data from Ministry of Agriculture.

FIGURE 15: FOOD GRAIN AREA AND PRODUCTION (1950-1 TO 1999-2000)

(34 per cent), Punjab (21 per cent), Haryana (13 per cent), northern Madhya Pradesh (11 per cent) and eastern Rajasthan (9 per cent). Including the occasional cereal imports since the end of the 1970s (to top up government reserves after poor monsoons), and allowing for exports, stock movements, losses and the volumes used as seed and as animal feed, according to the FAO, per capita annual cereal availability has increased from 144 kg in 1961 (395 g/day) to 159 kg in 2003 (436 g/day). This is cause for both satisfaction and concern: satisfaction because the population grew by over 613 million over the same period, and concern because the increase centred on wheat and rice, which have now reached their limits in terms of the area sown and perhaps of yields. Production of other cereals (classed as 'coarse cereals' in India), primarily maize, barley and millets (sorghum/*jowar*, pearl millet/*bajra*, finger millet/*ragi*, little millet, Italian millet, common millet, kodo millet, etc.) stagnated at around 28 million tonnes during those four decades of strong population growth (and the gross area sown even decreased, from 45 million hectares in 1960 to under 30 since 1998-9).

Pulses, Legumes

Per capita availability of pulses, in other words the fruits of legume crops that are cooked to make *dal* (or *papads*, *namkeens* and other snacks) and provide most of the protein consumed in India, has halved since the start of the green revolution (11.7 kg/year/inhabitant in 2003 as against 23 in 1961, according to the FAO), and prices have rocketed, particularly since 1993, despite increasing imports (India is both the world's leading producer and consumer). The record for the area sown dates back to 1975-6 (24.5 million ha, see Figure 16), and production was higher that year than in 1997-8 for chick peas (*chana*), pigeon peas (red gram/*tur*, *arhar*), black gram (*urad*), green gram (*mung*), horse gram (*khulti*), lentil (*masur*), chickling vetch (*khesari*), kidney bean (*rajma*) and cow pea. In all, 70 per cent of total output was concentrated in four states (Madhya Pradesh, Uttar Pradesh,

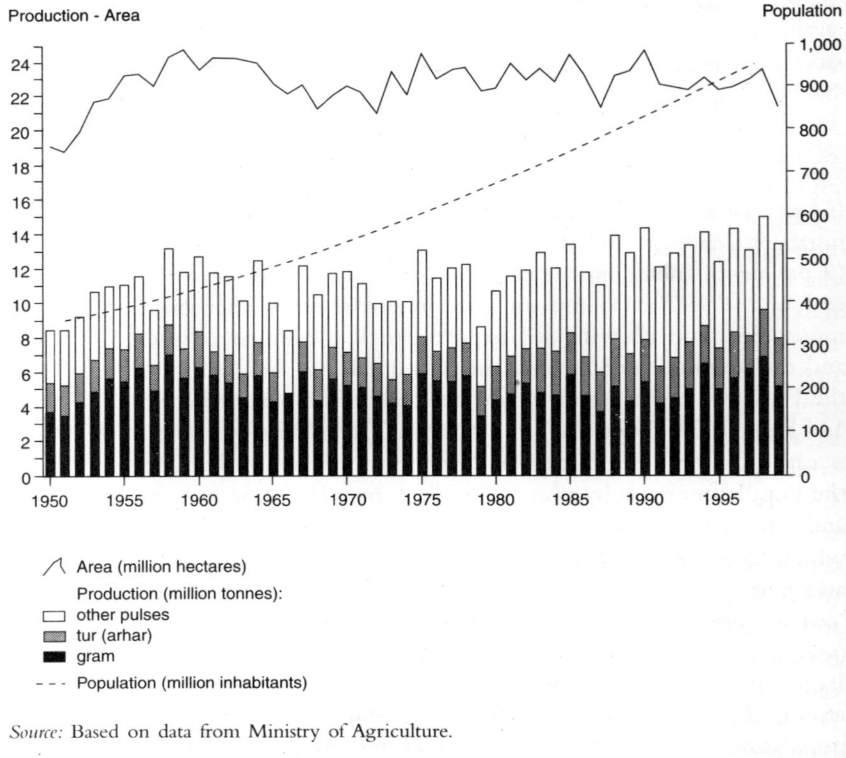

Source: Based on data from Ministry of Agriculture.

FIGURE 16: PULSE AREA AND PRODUCTION (1950-1 TO 1999-2000)

Maharashtra and Rajasthan) in 1999-2000, and most of cultivation was restricted to non-irrigated areas and/or the dry season. Unlike other legumes used to make oil and cake (groundnut, soyabean, and so on), pulses did not even contribute to the yellow (oilseed) revolution in the early 1990s (see Chapter 4), despite its ambition at one stage to pull these 'poor relations' of the green revolution out of the rut they were in.

Mills, Bakeries and Biscuit Factories

The Indian Green Revolution therefore has not been a revolution in terms of all 'food grains', despite what this constantly growing hotchpotch of statistics that too often is quoted might suggest (Figure 15). Neither has it been one in terms of grain processing, if indeed this needs pointing out to temper results which have nevertheless exploded the Malthusian theory. Rice processing is restricted to hulling paddy, with the bran used as animal feed and increasingly, thanks to the subsidies available, to produce energy or oil. Rice may also be precooked and packed (by Satnam Overseas, Thapar Agro, United Riceland, Sachdeva and many others), but Indian consumers prefer to buy it in bulk. Wheat flour mills are obviously more common: around 850 in the organized sector at the end of the 1990s (NEPC Agro Food, Kovilpatti Lakshmi Roller Flour Mills, Ambuja Flour Mills), along with some 3,20,000 small mills (*atta chakkis*) in the non-organized sector. However, the very inconsistent quality of the end-product is a considerable obstacle to its use in bread-making. Indian flour has a shelf life of just 15-20 days, compared to six months in Europe or the United States, since the germ is not removed for lack of suitable equipment. As a result, 80 per cent of flour is consumed directly by households, mainly to make bread and flat bread (like *chapatis* and *naans*). The remainder, which may be produced from imported wheat (from Australia, Canada, Argentina, etc.) is primarily used by some 50,000 small-scale, largely unmechanized firms to make biscuits (1.2 million tonnes in 1997-8), sandwich bread (1.1 million tonnes) and cakes (6,00,000 tonnes). With very few exceptions, bread-making is still a protected sector, restricted to small-scale industries, as was biscuit-making for considerable time. At the end of the 1990s, only fifteen large firms had modern plants (Britannia, Modern Food, Parle Biscuits, Kwality Biscuits, Bakemans, SmithKline Beecham, among others). Nevertheless, as the largest cereal producers have benefited from the Green Revolution and the associated increase in incomes, they, like urbanites, have aspired since the end of the 1980s to consume products other than chapattis or rice, for instance bakery products (Saf Yeast, a subsidiary of the French Lesaffre group, holds a 50 per cent share of the Indian yeast market), but also milk, fats, poultry and many other foods that planners in the 1960s had never really thought of.

4. The Anand White and Yellow Floods

In one sense, the White (dairy) Revolution and the Yellow (oils and oilseeds) Revolution were merely an extension of the drive for national food self-sufficiency that fuelled the Green Revolution. However, the means involved were quite different. The White Revolution made ingenious use of food aid: rather than competing with local produce, the foreign milk powder was sold on to fund a policy that made India the world's leading dairy producer. Above all, thanks to the National Dairy Development Board (NDDB) based in Anand (Gujarat), it was supported by a cooperative network broadly representative of social diversity among Indian farmers, and regions that were not necessarily those that benefited most from the Green Revolution, and from a whole century of agricultural growth. The yellow revolution, in which the NDDB also played a part in the late 1980s, set out to revolutionize Indian bureaucracy by fostering decentralized decision-making, consultation between public services and cooperation with the private sector. For a while, it was a great success in economic terms (trade surplus) for oilseed crops that had previously been relegated to dry zones or dry seasons. However, that success was short-lived: lobbies and fears of jeopardizing the cereal production led India to become once again the world's leading importer of vegetable oils by the end of the 1990s.

THE WHITE REVOLUTION OF MILK: RECYCLING FOOD AID

Getting up Steam

Anand, Amul and Kurien

India is one of the few countries worldwide that do not support dairy prices or producer incomes. That does not mean to say that the State does not intervene, quite the opposite. It began by supporting the development of what was to become one of the largest cooperative management structures in the world: the NDDB. It all started in Bombay Province, prior to

Independence. The colonial government had given Polson's dairies a monopoly on milk collection from villages, so as to be able to redistribute it more easily in urban areas (this 'City Milk Scheme' was extended to other cities in the 1950s). However, in 1946, farmers in Kaira District, 400 km north of Bombay, refused to deliver their product to middlemen who were underpaying them, and eventually won their fight to be allowed to sell their product direct to the state. They also took the opportunity of setting up, and in 1955 registering, a cooperative union, the Kaira District Cooperative Milk Producers' Union, which is now widely known under the brand name Amul. A few years later, in 1964, Prime Minister Lal Bahadur Shastri visited the organization's head office in Anand, Gujarat. At a time when India was importing some 60,000 tonnes of powdered milk per year, he observed that its operating performance bore no relation to that of the dairies run by the states or the Union. Was it because the producers owned the installations and elected their managers? Or because their leaders, the nationalist Tribhuvandas Patel and the young Christian engineer Verghese Kurien, were exceptionally good at drumming up enthusiasm for their technical, economic and social objectives? In any event, Lal Bahadur Shastri was convinced that the spirit of the Anand operation and its organizational structure had to be reproduced throughout India. To this end, the NDDB was set up in 1965, headed by V. Kurien, who held the post for over 30 years, before handing over the reins to Amrita Patel in 1998, having achieved both national and international recognition (for instance the FAO World Food Prize in 1989). His strategy, which required considerable strength of character, was not to rely on over-political, inconsistent state or Union budgets and thus to remain independent of government agencies, while taking care to avoid offending them so as to obtain favours if necessary, on behalf of the cooperative movement and to the detriment of private industry.

Operation Flood

Three years after it was set up, in 1968, the NDDB presented Phase I (1970-81) of a strategy aimed at extending the Anand model, dubbed 'Operation Flood', and in 1970, it persuaded the Indian government to agree to an FAO World Food Programme project, viz., a donation of 1,26,000 tonnes of powdered milk and 42,000 tonnes of clarified butter (*ghee*) over a five-year period. At the same time, four 'Mother Dairies' were set up in the four corners of India (Bombay, Delhi, Calcutta and Madras) to reconstitute these imported goods and make milk for sale in the domestic market, so as to generate the million rupees required for the first phase of 'Operation Flood'. International food aid was not allowed to compete with domestic products by simply being sold in the domestic market, and thus served to help the country achieve self-sufficiency.

The operation was a great success: ten years later, in 1980-1, there were 13,270 Village Milk Producers' Cooperatives (VMPC), belonging to unions at district level and federations at state level, with almost 1.8 million members in all. Domestic milk production rose from 22 million tonnes in 1970 to 34 million (+ 55 per cent) over the same period. This was the cue for Phase II of the operation (1981-5), supported by the World Bank and the European Community. It served to guarantee supplies to 148 Indian cities via a 'national grid' linking those urban centres with 136 dairy production basins in rural areas. The number of dairy cooperatives also continued to grow significantly, as indeed it did during Phase III (1985-95), which was still supported by the same funding agencies and by self-funding generated by the NDDB, and which set out to assert the independence and viability of those organizations. By 1995, there were over 70,000 of them, with more than 9 million members in 170 production basins, supplying 610 urban complexes with milk, butter, *ghee*, cheese, chocolate, ice cream, yoghurt and flavoured milk drinks (some of which were also exported). The annual volume collected by the cooperatives reached 3.8 million tonnes in 1994-5, which amounted to less than 6 per cent of domestic milk production (or 8-9 per cent including the milk consumed by members, see Figure 17 and Map 9), but 60 per cent of the 10 per cent collected, processed and marketed in India by firms in the formal sector (Figure 18). Later, in 2003-4, rural milk procurement reached 6.4 million tonnes, produced by 12 million farmers belonging to 1,08,570 societies (including conventional societies and taluka unions). However, since 1991, private dairy firms have also been jumping into a market from which they were previously barred.

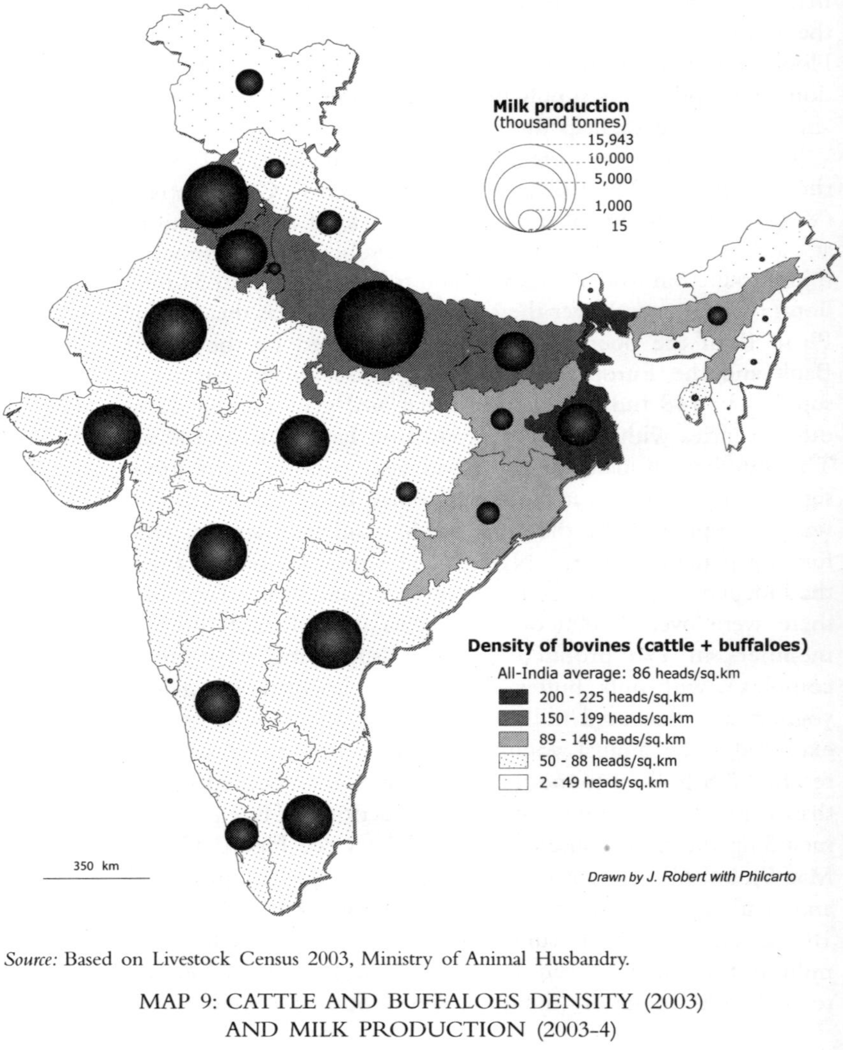

Source: Based on Livestock Census 2003, Ministry of Animal Husbandry.

MAP 9: CATTLE AND BUFFALOES DENSITY (2003)
AND MILK PRODUCTION (2003-4)

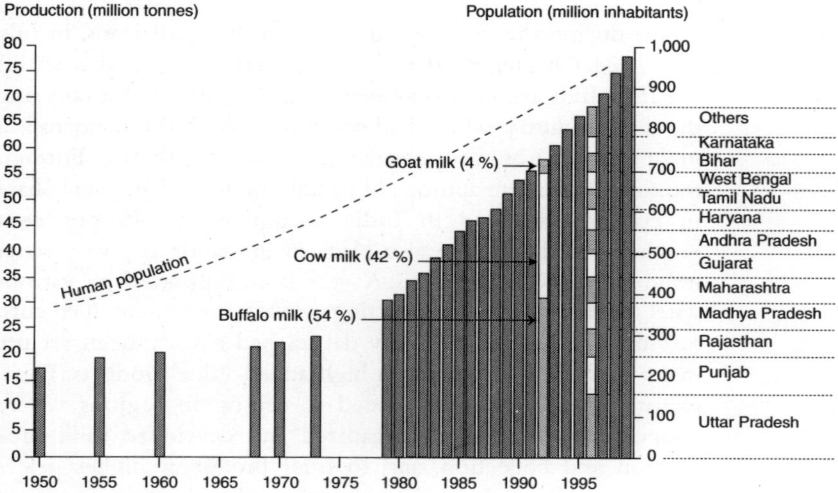

Source: Based on Mininistry of Agriculture.

FIGURE 17: MILK PRODUCTION (1950-1 TO 1999-2000)

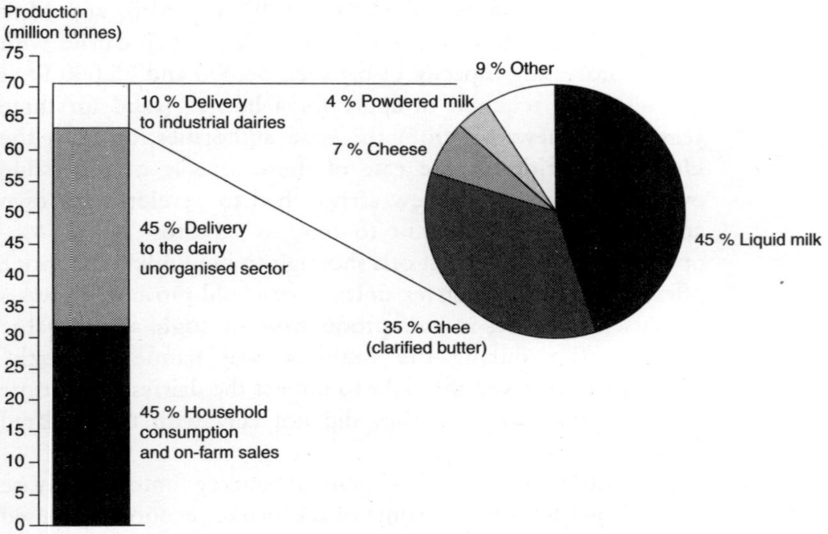

Sources: Based on Rabobank International and India Dairy Year Book.

FIGURE 18 : MILK PROCUREMENT AND PROCESSING (1997-8)

The Liberalization Circuit Breakers

MPPO It was during the country's most severe financial crisis, in July 1991 (see Chapter 8), that central government decided to lift the 1951 Industries (Development and Regulation) Act covering the dairy industry, which had previously blocked the expansion prospects of non-cooperative firms in the sector. Foreign multinationals were authorized to hold up to a 51 per cent share in companies based in India (compared to 40 per cent previously). There were also plans to dismantle the very strict import and export barriers. A year later, supported by various state policies aimed at attracting private investment (tax cuts, subsidies, etc.), over 100 new dairies had already been set up, many of them specializing in high added-value products. These private firms obviously tended to set up in regions where cooperatives had already organized and developed milk production and collection, and to offer producers higher prices than the cooperatives. The accompanying increase in fraud (adulterated or contaminated milk sales) was another reason why V. Kurien contacted Prime Minister P.V. Narasimha Rao directly to explain the threat faced by the whole of the cooperative system. Shortly afterwards, in June 1992, the Milk and Milk Products Order (MMPO) was issued, under which dairies with a daily processing capacity of between 10,000 and 75,000 litres of milk were required to apply for a licence (valid for three years and renewable) from the state authorities, or from the Union authorities in the case of those capable of processing over 75,000 litres. Any new arrivals had to develop their own collection basin, so as not to trespass on those of the cooperatives, or in the event of a shortage, to buy milk at the price offered by the cooperatives, unless they could prove there was a surplus. Lastly, off-season production of high added-value products (i.e. during the summer) was banned, and the government reserved the right to inspect the dairies at any time and seize their stocks if they did not tally with the declared figure.

The order prompted a general outcry among private industrialists who, in the name of the market economy, accused the government of giving cooperatives an unfair advantage in addition to the considerable public aid from which they had already benefited in the past. The MMPO was slightly amended in May 1993 (licences were extended to five years, renewable, and were no longer required for capacities of less than 75,000 litres). For its part, in 1995, the NDDB launched Phase IV of its operations, the main aim of which was to bail out the many dairy unions that were operating at a loss. This time, Kurien accused the government of being too free-market oriented.

NDDB and Rural Development

True, it is important not to deny the aid received in the past. Between 1971 and 1992, the food aid received by the NDDB (butter and powdered milk) represented a monetary equivalent of a good billion dollars in real terms (1990 basis). In addition, there were World Bank loans ($586 million at 1990 rates), government expenditure on developing the dairy sector from the Fifth to the Seventh Five Year Plans (over a billion dollars between 1974 and 1990), and various other privileges granted during that period (preferential rates for bank loans and customs duty; systematic import controls until 1994; funds from the Technology Mission for dairy development, an interministerial programme launched in 1989). Kurien had not forgotten the first part of the equation (Rs. 20 billion of investment in Phases I, II and III of Operation Flood), but in the meantime, domestic production had trebled, which, with a litre of milk costing Rs. 6, meant an extra Rs. 240 billion of revenue. The World Bank itself saw this as an exceptional input/output ratio, particularly as in this case, the revenue generated directly benefited the small-scale farmers belonging to the Anand structure (20 per cent of whom were landless and 70 per cent of whom had a maximum of two milch cows or buffaloes).

Operation Flood may well have been the largest successful employment programme in history. It has also provided smallholders with a service: training in democratic and cooperative life skills, technical support, veterinary services, cattle feed supplies, artificial insemination or embryo transfer, etc., and has meant ongoing training and research and development operations, the first result of which was to adapt the equipment used in dairy industries in the Western world to the specificities of buffalo milk. Lastly, it is a unique management model, and is proof that Indian production structures are not necessarily condemned to remain on the fringes of the modern economy. Thousands of rural families, each with two or three milch cows or buffaloes producing just a few litres per day (3–4 litres per cow and 6-7 per buffalo on average in India), now have a guaranteed additional source of income from milk, which is collected daily at a price based on its quality (fat and protein content) and immediately refrigerated, before being processed, packed and transported to cities so as to optimize the added value generated. According to Kurien, all this has considerably boosted the development of the sector as a whole, and the particular interest that foreign multinationals are now showing.

Nestlé, Glaxo and Co.

Since 1999, India is the world's leading dairy producer (13 to 14 per cent of global output, with a production of 88 million tonnes of milk in 2003-4), ahead of the United States. Its dairy herd in 2003 was estimated to be 65 million adult cows (87 per cent of female cattle is indigenous, 13 per cent is exotic or crossbred) and 51 million adult female buffaloes: 283 million bovines in all, alongside some 124 million goats and 62 million sheep (see Chapter 5). Some 70 million families at least partly live on the income from dairy production, which now accounts for nearly 10 per cent of agricultural GDP. Low productive local races are still in the majority despite various genetic improvement programmes (particularly crossing with Holsteins), but their advantage is to be more robust and to need less care.

Annual per capita milk availability was 68 kg in 2003 according to the FAO, i.e. twice the 1973 availability, whereas the population had almost doubled (+80 per cent) during this 30-year period. Moreover, there is still considerable room for development, since a large proportion of people still consume less than what the WHO recommends (204 g/day), and the remainder have increasingly sophisticated tastes. This means many potential openings for large private firms (Nestlé, Glaxo, Bongrain, Britannia, Horlicks, Cadbury's, and so on), which, as Kurien says, will probably take just ten years to achieve what it took forty to fifty years to do in Anand: increasing daily collection and processing volumes from 200 to 1 million litres.

In 2002, the revision of the Milk and Milk Products Order, 1992, has allowed private companies to set up dairy plants processing more than 10,000 litres a day without any assigned 'milkshed area'. The concept of milkshed area, which provided collection monopoly to one dairy in the area, was withdrawn, to the advantage of newcoming multinational or Indian firms. Such companies are indeed frighteningly efficient, and imports of dairy products are growing (like from New Zealand) due to the decrease in tariffs and the end of non-tariff barriers. The cooperatives are not necessarily doomed to failure. Nevertheless, if the government decides to liberalize the sector, it will also have to free the cooperatives from the civil servants and politicians on their boards, who still govern all the decisions made on investment and restructuring. Their involvement in the cooperatives has proved disastrous, and is leading straight to bankruptcy. Kurien has therefore raised the question of how, under these conditions, the cooperatives can be expected to compete with multinationals such as Nestlé. It is vital that this issue be resolved, particularly since Anand has invested its social capital in other fields (fruits and vegetables, vaccine manufacture, salt production, among other things), and since many of the cooperatives set up under its 'Operation Golden Flood' (of oils and oilseeds), launched in 1979, has proved to be also invaded by the same bureaucrats.

THE YELLOW REVOLUTION OF OILSEEDS: AN IMPOSSIBLE MISSION?

The Workings of the Scandal

In India, there is a wide range of vegetal materials from which edible or industrial oils can be extracted. Some play a major role in the current national vegetable oil production. Others have been developed more recently. Lastly, several materials have been identified as having potential, some of which having already been used in the past. These materials can be split into five categories: *Oilseeds*

- Annual crops: Nine species are cultivated in India, suitable for food use (groundnut, rapeseed/mustard, safflower, niger, sesame, soyabean and sunflower) or industrial use (linseed and castor);
- Tree crops (coconut and oil palm), which are concentrated in the south of the peninsula and the neighbouring islands;
- Byproducts of commercial crop (cottonseed, rice bran, tobacco seed, maize germ, tea seed, jute, hemp, etc.);
- Fruit and vegetable kernels, seeds or pips (mango, tung, apricot, *sitaphal*, sapota plum, grape, etc.). Some of these, like in the above category, have been used more intensively

since the mid-twentieth century, thanks to the development of the solvent extraction technique;
- Seeds of wild or forest species (*sal*, *mahua*, *neem*, *karanja*, *khakan-pilu*, *kusum*, *dhupa*, pistachio, cashew nut, etc.), which are primarily collected by tribals and their commercial associations more or less controlled by the government.

After single or double pressing and/or solvent extraction, these oilseeds yield oil and a residue, the oilcake, which has become the prime source of protein feed for animals in the Western world since the Second World War, with the spread of the American 'maize + soyabean cake' formula.

Vegetable Oils

Until the First World War, colonial India, along with Senegal (groundnut) and China (soya) unquestionably dominated the international oilseeds market: up to 50 per cent of the groundnut and 60 per cent of the rapeseed/mustard produced in the country were exported outside the subcontinent. However, within a few decades, the situation had changed drastically, with the globalization of the 'soyabean complex' that had taken hold in the United States and Brazil between the two world wars. Despite the competition from America, India managed to remain a net oil exporter until the mid-1960s, thanks to global demand after the war and to restructuring efforts on the part of Indian industrialists. But this was a turning point, and domestic oil prices subsequently rose steadily, particularly during the 1971, 1972 and 1973 droughts. American food aid (between 30,000 and 1,00,000 tonnes of soyabean oil per year until the mid-1970s) was largely insufficient to stabilize prices, and the production of oilseeds, for which the green revolution did not pay attention, increased by barely 1 per cent a year, well short of the population growth rate.

This surge in prices was quickly denounced by consumer associations (such as the one launched by Mrinal Gore in Bombay) and political movements (such as Navnirman in Gujarat), and forced the central government to take another look at its protectionist policies and to import 4,00,000 tonnes of vegetable oil in 1976-7. In subsequent years, the figure topped a million tonnes, making India the world's leading vegetable oil importer (Figure 20). A record was reached in 1987-8, a drought year, with 1.9 million tonnes, plus an additional 1,00,000 tonnes in aid. From 1981-2 to 1988-9, this meant an average annual outlay of Rs. 7.2 billion (the second import item after oil), which was particularly disastrous in that it placed an extra burden on the country's dwindling foreign currency reserves in the late 1980s.

Bureaucracy and Corruption

Since the borders were opened, oil imports have also provided large-scale and attractive opportunities, given the difference between domestic and international prices. International prices were particularly low during the 1980s, with some countries trying to sell their surpluses (European and Canadian rapeseed oils, Brazilian soyabean oils, and so on), and others to strengthen their hold on specialist export markets, for instance Malaysia and its palm oil (a country and a product favoured by India due to the geographical proximity and the wish to strengthen cooperation with ASEAN members). Between 1982 and 1988, the average price of the oils purchased by India on overseas markets was Rs. 6.56 kg (CIF), while the most common domestic oils (groundnut and rapeseed/mustard) cost Rs. 18.50. These low prices could have been a boon to India's poorest inhabitants, who did not eat enough fat: the annual difference between import values at the border and their minimum value on the domestic market was Rs. 17.1 million on average between 1982 and 1988. But the reality was somewhat different. After paying (i) the State Trading Corporation (STC) which handled all imports (2 per cent *ad valorem*, i.e. 60 per cent of its 1988 turnover), (ii) the various types of tax and commission levied on imports into the Union and then into the various states (Rs. 8.7 billion of revenue per year on average between 1982 and 1988, including 1.8 for the states), (iii) attributing a share of those imports at a preferential price to the *vanaspati* industry which was the only one authorized to mix them with local oils (a discount equivalent to Rs. 3 billion per year in relation to domestic prices), there was only a small slice of the cake left for the PDS (an annual Rs. 5.4 billion out of the total Rs. 17.1 billion). Furthermore, at least 50 per cent of the volumes officially allocated to the PDS (0.9 million of the 1.4 million tonnes imported each year on average between 1982 and 1988) were in fact misappropriated by corrupt civil servants and dishonest oil manufacturers, and sold for the full price under another name. Indian consumers largely failed to benefit from these mass low-cost oil imports, as did oilseed producers. Processors and traders were sufficiently well organized to buy at a low price at harvest time, store their purchases and resell them at a higher price. Moreover, it often—somewhat curiously—just so happened that oil imports were released in production zones just after the harvest, hence pushing agricultural prices down even further.

SAM'S OILCAN

Rajiv Gandhi, Sam Pitroda and Technology Missions

It was the Rajiv Gandhi government that decided to take the bull by the horns. When it took office in 1984, there was feverish activity among the administrative elite in Delhi. While *Garibi Hatao* (down with poverty) had been his mother Indira's slogan, the young new prime minister opted for 'India in the twenty-first century'. Rajiv impressed public opinion and his party with his hitherto unsuspected sense of authority, but also his style, that of a manager keen for fast results, less bureaucracy and more efficiency, integrity and modernity. Interministerial committees began meeting more regularly and tackling a wider and thornier range of issues. Five issues were made the object of five 'Technology Missions' (although technology was not the only matter covered), one of which (Technology Mission on Oilseeds, TMO) concerning oilseeds. However, the missions remained discreet, and it was not until the arrival of Sam Pitroda at the end of 1987 that they first came to the attention of the media—and indeed of certain ministers—and proudly proclaimed the specific aim that 'Sam' now wanted them to fulfil: 'to change the work ethos of the government and the bureaucracy for radically changing a system that remained colonial and feudal even forty years after Independence'.

Pitroda, who had been very close to the prime minister since his return from the United States, where he had made his fortune in the telecommunications sector, worked to make his teams and the general public more aware of what, according to him, will govern the success of public policies in India: 'management', 'community participation', 'information and communications', and 'centre-state coordination'. It was within this framework that a revised version of the TMO was launched at the start of 1988: it did not change anything in terms of the (limited) budget and (ambitious) targets set in the first version for the years 1990, 1995 and 2000, but it did upset the routine at Indian government services, encouraging them to be more coordinated and work closely together, not only horizontally (research, agriculture, industry, trade, and so on) and vertically (central government, states and districts), but also with various other agents (cooperatives, private firms, associations, retired civil servants).

TMO, MIO and NDDB

The services and agents involved in each of the four 'Mini-Missions' making up the TMO (crop production technology; post-harvest technology; input and service support to the farmers; price support, storage, processing and marketing) responded with varying degrees of enthusiasm to the recommendations made by Pitroda and P.V. Shenoi, the TMO's new director. However, to shake things up somewhat, the Prime Minister's Office decided to grant the world's largest agricultural cooperation structure—the NDDB—the power to implement a special Market Intervention Operation (MIO) in 1988-9, aimed at guaranteeing more stable farm prices that would guarantee better incomes among oilseed producers. Why the NDDB? As long ago as 1977, after the dairy sector, NDDB decided to move into the oil sector, with which it was competing (butter/vegetable oil) and on which it was also dependent (oilcake to feed dairy herds). Its strategy was similar to the one implemented ten years previously for the dairy sector: to recycle aid in kind (in this case American, Canadian and European vegetable oils) so as to develop oilseed producers' cooperatives able to better control the whole oils and oilseeds commodity chain. The NDDB thus followed Operation Flood with Operation Golden Flow. Its presence on the political stage was relatively discreet until the mid-1980s, as it was busy intercepting aid, a favour that the central government had eventually granted. However, it subsequently became more vociferous, and was quick to denounce the many malfunctions in the sector following the disastrous 1987-8 season, including the degree of tax evasion among its 'counterparts' (processors in the private sector). The virulence of the attack (and the corresponding backlash) paid off. With the MIO under its control, the NDDB set out to destabilize the powerful processors' and traders' organizations, but also several government services, including the Ministry of Civil Supplies. The plan was relatively simple:

- to divert a share of the volumes imported so as to sell them at the right time and place;
- to buy oilseeds and oils in regions and at times when yields were high;
- to cover the country with a storage, transport and packing network so as to reduce the differences in supply and demand between regions and seasons, from which speculators had previously made considerable profits;
- to popularize pre-packed oil sales, partly to create a parallel market capable of buffering the impact of speculative operations in the wholesale sector, and partly to discourage adulteration.

The Yellow Revolution

This programme proved as eventful as it was controversial. However, thanks to the progress made by other players involved in the TMO, production of the nine oilseeds reached 16.8 million tonnes in 1989-90. It had even topped 18 million tonnes the previous year, with an excellent monsoon. With other oil bearing materials (rice bran, cottonseed, copra, *sal*, *neem*, *mahua*, mango, etc.), domestic vegetable oil production amounted to 5.5 million tonnes in 1989-90—5 million of them for food use, which was exactly the target set a few years earlier. The vegetable oil import bill, for its part, was not halved (the TMO's second target for 1990), but virtually divided by five in two years. From Rs. 9.7 billion in 1987-8, when a disastrous world record was set following the century's worst drought, it fell to just Rs. 2.3 billion (2,93,000 tonnes of oil). Although India was on the verge of bankruptcy and would have had difficulty importing any more, it had reason to celebrate. Not only was the bill by far the lowest of the decade, it was accompanied by a significant increase in exports of oilcake (notably soyabean) and, to a lesser extent, oilseeds (particularly sesame and peanuts). In all, in 1989-90, for the first time in many years, there was a trade surplus, of Rs. 5.6 billion. This increase in value obviously corresponded to an increase in export volumes, and also resulted from a determined trade offensive outside the Rupee Payment Area (between India and the then USSR), a particularly wise move since India was very short of dollars at the time. After the green (cereals) revolution and the white (dairy) revolution, this was classed as the yellow revolution. The speed with which it was implemented proved that it was even more efficient than the first two, as it had much less in the way of financial resources. With a budget of Rs. 3–4 billion spread over the five years of the Seventh Plan, the TMO could claim to have largely paid back the public funds invested.

Business as Usual

Marico, ITC, Hindustan Lever, Godrej & Co.

The Indian oils and oilseeds market also offered a host of opportunities in the early 1990s: various strategies were in competition, which had not been the case a few years previously. New players came onto the scene, headed by the NDDB and its 'Dhara' brand, which the TMO helped to establish. Above all, the NDDB demonstrated that the oils and oilseeds market was a forum for strategic expansion, requiring modern human resource management and techniques. This prompted restructuring and investment on the part of semi-public bodies such as the Hindustan Vegetable Oil Corporation (HVOC) or National Cooperative Development Corporation (NCDC), processors' organizations such as the Central Organisation for Oil Industry and Trade (COOIT), Groundnut Extractions Export Development Association (GEEDA), Solvent Extractors' Association (SEA), Soyabean Processors' Association (SOPA) or Vanaspati Manufacturers' Association (VMA), along with agri-foods giants such as Marico Industries (with the 'Safola' and 'Sweekar' brands), Indian Tobacco Company (with 'Sundrop'), Hindustan Lever (with 'Flora') and Godrej Foods (with 'Sunflower' and 'Cooklite'). Some moved into the new pre-packed oils market, while others opted for vertical integration strategies, gaining a foothold in areas previously monopolized by the authorities (seeds, agricultural input distribution, research and development, crop technologies, risk management, farmer payments, etc.) or by private processors and traders further up the chain (storage, transport, processing techniques, oilcake use, oil marketing, foreign relations, etc.).

Agricultural producers were not left out: the area sown with oilseed crops expanded as a result of higher and more stable prices, particularly after 1989, when the MIO truly came into operation for groundnut and rapeseed/mustard. However, at the start of the 1990s, oil prices also began to rise, at a much greater rate than the overall price index (see Chapter 8), which hit Indian consumers particularly hard. To ensure that consumers had a daily average of 25 grams of fat by the year 2000 (the target set by the TMO), India either had to step up its efforts, or resume imports. It indeed did so in the mid-1990s, by which time the powers of both TMO and NDDB had been reduced for political reasons and also for fear of a drop in cereal production. By the end of the 1990s, imports were running at 3 or even 4 million tonnes (over $1.8 billion a year, whereas the PDS only really distributed 1,51,000 tonnes in 1998-9), while public wheat and rice stocks were huge. In 2003-4, palm oil imports still reached 3.6 million tonnes.

Groundnut, Rapeseed/mustard, Soyabean and Sunflower

This late and brief 'yellow revolution' nevertheless placed India in the world's top five oil and fat producers, behind the United States, the European Union, China and Malaysia. Most of its vegetable oil (more than 8 million tonnes in 1998-9, including around 90 per cent for food use) came from the nine oilseed crops (26.2 million ha and 24.8 million tonnes of seed in 1998-9—see Figure 19—but only 21.2 million hectares and 15.1

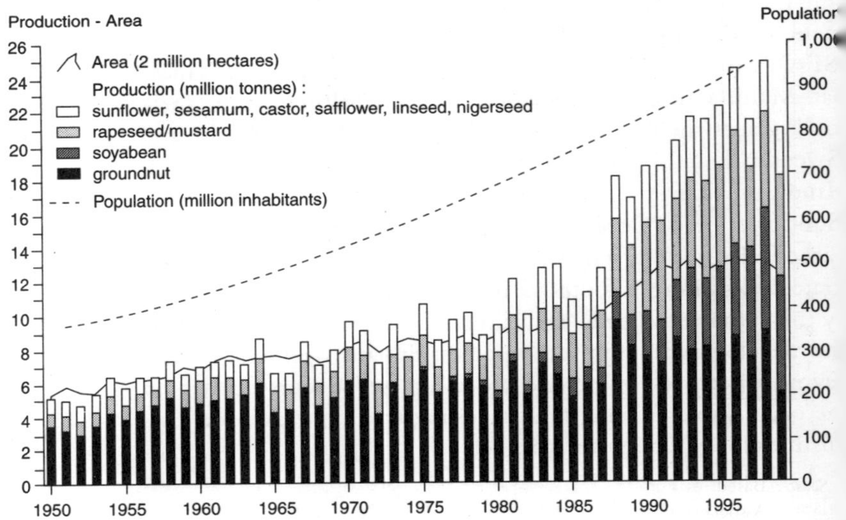

Source: Based on Ministry of Agriculture.

FIGURE 19 : OILSEED AREA AND PRODUCTION (1950-1 TO 1999-2000)

million tonnes in 2002-3), which agricultural development in India has always restricted to dry zones or dry seasons (a quarter of the area sown is irrigated). Groundnut (which is grown in the south of the peninsula, and has stagnated since the early 1980s) and rapeseed/mustard (grown in the north, increasingly intensively, in the *rabi* season, after the wheat harvest) are the leading crops, with 1.2 and 1.8 million tonnes of oil respectively in 2003-4. Sunflower and above all soyabean, two crops that were almost non-existent in India at the start of the 1980s, compete strongly with other oilseed crops (castor, sesame, safflower, linseed and niger, in order of importance). Soya oil production reached one million tonnes in 2003-04. These two crops are concentrated in the states of southwestern and central India: Karnataka and Maharashtra for sunflower, and Madhya Pradesh for soyabean (4.7 million tonnes of soyabean harvested in that state in 2003-4, about 60 per cent of the national production) whose oilcake boosted Indian exports (see Chapter 8; aflatoxin is still a major handicap for other types of oilcake).

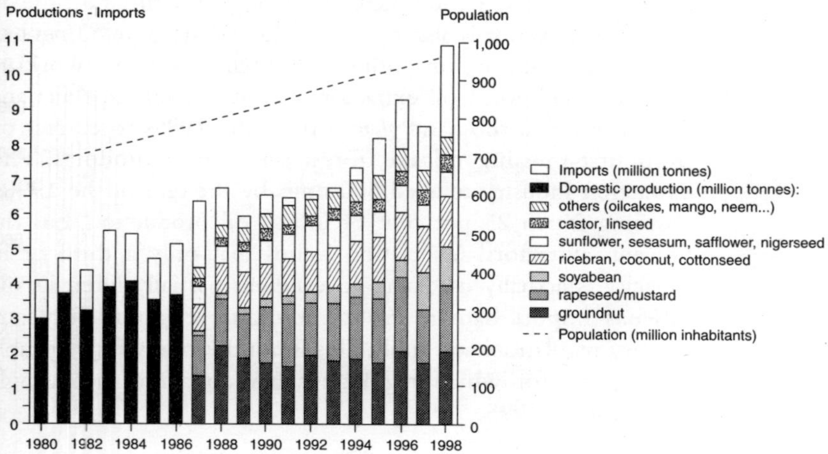

Source: Based on Dorin (1994), Vanaspati Manufacturers' Association, Solvent Extractors' Association, Economic Survey.

FIGURE 20: VEGETABLE OIL PRODUCTION AND IMPORT (1980-1 TO 1998-9)

Coconut, Cotton seed and Rice bran

However, there are other sources of oil that should not be overlooked, including the coconut plantations that supply the copra oil popular in the south: they are estimated to provide a living for more than five million people in four states though yields are decreasing due to pests (Kerala, Karnataka, Tamil Nadu and Andhra Pradesh in order of the areas planted; 1.91 million ha throughout India in 2002-3 for 3,50,000 tonnes of oil). Oil palm plays a much smaller role, if any, in Indian production statistics: large areas are being planted and harvested in the south of the peninsula (Andhra Pradesh), but there is no hope of matching the yields obtained in countries such as Malaysia.

It is even more important nowadays for India to think about extracting oil from byproducts. Cottonseed (primarily grown in the west and south of the country, see Chapter 2) is already used (5,20,000 tonnes of oil in 2003-4), as is rice bran, from which India currently extracts one of the largest volumes of oil worldwide (6,00,000 tonnes in 2003-4, including around a third for non-food use, particularly soap manufacture). The rise of this last product is linked to new bran stabilization techniques that have overcome the main obstacle to its use (Monsanto and RiceX Co. offered India new technology for this purpose in 1999). However, it is also obviously due to the development of the solvent extraction industry, which has been working alongside traditional oil extractors (about 50,000 expellers and several hundred thousand *ghanis*) since the 1980s to extract oil from first-pressing oilcake, forest seeds or byproducts. This extraction industry totalled 600 units by the end of the 1990s, ensuring 20 to 25 per cent of Indian oil production, but the Solvent Extractors' Association claims that only a third of its capacity is actually used: the government partially lifted its old oilseeds import ban in 1998, but drastic customs duty and sanitary regulations still apply. This is not the case with vegetable oil imports for which regulations have become increasingly relaxed since 1995.

Vanaspati, Butter and Ghee

Most of the vegetable oil produced is still sold as is (Figure 21), despite an obligation since September 1998—following another fatal poisoning scandal—to pack oils and control their quality. Double filtration and refining (400 units for less than 8,00,000 tonnes per year), along with packing, were not really developed

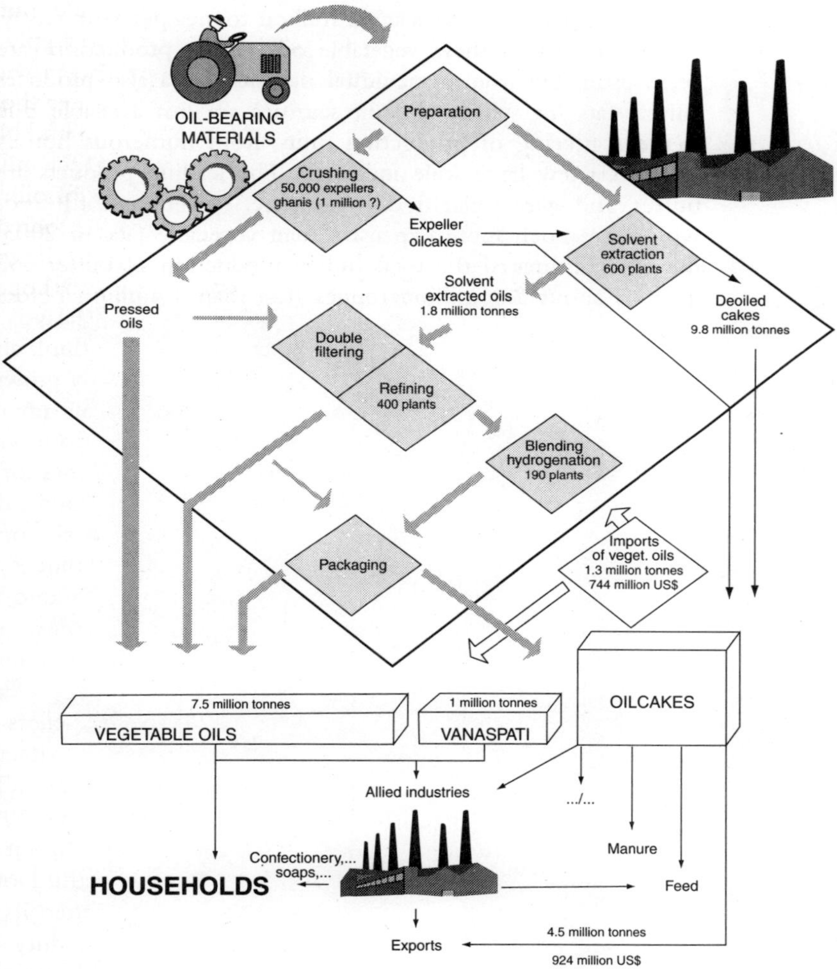

FIGURE 21: VEGETABLE OIL COMMODITY CHAIN

until the 1980s. However, for some considerable time, a large share of the oil produced has been used to make *vanaspati*, with a network of 190 factories in 1997-8 subject to stringent government control. *Vanaspati* is solid at room temperature since it is a hydrogenated blend of vegetable oils only (unlike margarine, which is not popular in India). Production has been struggling since the early 1980s to reach a million tonnes per year. Lastly, in addition to all these vegetable oils whose productions are often estimated from agricultural outputs, India also produces animal fats for which relevant statistics are not available due to the scattering of production units, from numerous households to a few large-scale industries. The leading products are butter and *ghee* ('clarified' butter, i.e. boiled and filtered) which are much more expensive than vegetable fats. In 2003, the FAO estimated the total Indian production of butter and ghee at about 2.6 million tonnes (less than 1 million before 1990).

5. The Resurgence of Vitamins and Proteins

Might this be the future for Indian agriculture? Horticulture, aviculture and fish farming, which have hitherto suffered from public policies in favour of cereals that discouraged the agrifoods industry and restricted exports, are now growing rapidly. Times have changed, particularly since the liberalizing reforms of 1991. The flourishing agribusiness sector has given rise to dynamic firms, primarily private and increasingly involved in international agreements, which have brought in foreign currency as well as new techniques and management methods. On a domestic level, urbanization and the increasing importance of the middle classes have firmly steered demand not towards cereals which India now knows how to produce in big quantity, but towards eggs, fruit and vegetables, meat, processed foods, and so on. However, there are always limitations. Domestic consumers' low purchasing power means that these emerging sectors must still deal with the ups and downs of international markets, besides factors intrinsic to India: the multiplicity of middlemen, poor or inconsistent product quality, lack of refrigeration facilities, saturated transport infrastructure, limited industrial packing and processing capacities, competition between man and animals for food—not counting various other obstacles to growth, be they cultural (taboos concerning beef and pork), political (obstacles to economic concentration) or ecological (adverse environmental effects of fishing and aquaculture).

HORTICULTURE: A GROWING NURSERY

A Garden for Middlemen

Fruit and Vegetables

Despite the vast range of fruit and vegetables on the subcontinent and the wealth of vitamins and minerals they contain, Indian horticulture suffered for a long time as a result of the country's food policies, centring solely on cereals. However, the sector is now booming: India is the world's second largest vegetable producer (89 million tonnes in 2001-2, compared to 72 in 1992-3) and fruit grower (43 million tonnes compared to 33 million in 1992-3), behind China. It is the largest or second-largest producer of mangoes (almost 1,000 varieties, including the famous Alphonso: 60 per cent of the world crop in 1998), cauliflowers (44 per cent of global production), papayas (24 per cent), bananas (15 per cent – the current average yield of 30 t/ha has grown by 4.5 times in 25 years), litchis and onions (Figure 22). Growth has been both vertical (increased yields) and horizontal: in 1998-9, an extra 1 million ha were planted with fruit and vegetable crops, compared

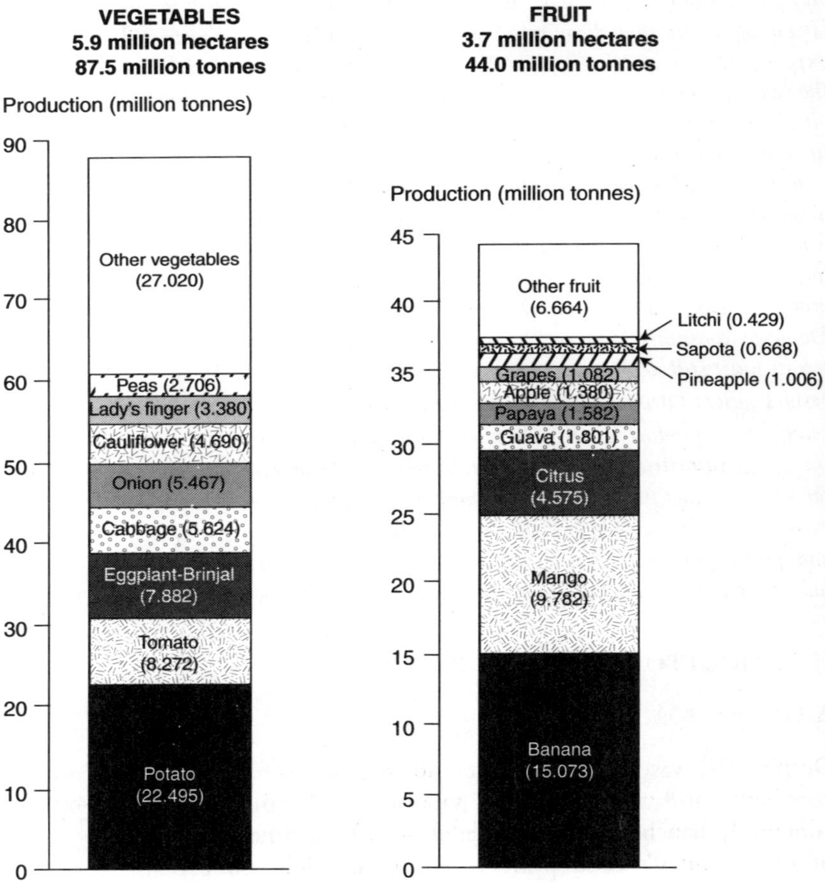

Source: Based on National Horticulture Board.

FIGURE 22: FRUIT AND VEGETABLE PRODUCTION (1998-9)

to 1991 (9.6 million hectares in all), particularly in semi-arid and mountainous areas that generally do not benefit from public subsidies for irrigated agriculture. This is a real boom, centring on the main cities and on eight states, which accounted for 75 per cent of fruit and vegetable production in 1997-8: West Bengal and Uttar Pradesh (the leading vegetable growers), Bihar, Orissa, Karnataka and Andhra Pradesh (the leading fruit producers), Tamil Nadu and Maharashtra. With its 32 ha, Azadpur, near New Delhi, is said to be the largest fresh fruit and vegetable market in Asia.

Losses and Wastage

However, there are many bottlenecks in the sector, which will take some time to clear. First and foremost, the production systems are generally still largely unproductive in global terms. With one exception (Kerala), India does not have a tradition of well-tended 'vegetable patches' or 'kitchen gardens'. Moreover, horticulture falls under the laws restricting land ownership, since it is not officially seen as a 'plantation' crop. It is therefore generally practised by small land holders with limited investment capacities, which is a particular hindrance to fruit tree development. This problem is compounded by the lack of interaction with players higher up the agrifoods production chain: fewer than 1 per cent of horticultural farmers are under contract with industrialists, which does not do anything to facilitate the dissemination of techniques, advice, seed and other appropriate inputs. Lastly, and above all, the segmentation of marketing circuits, combined with the poor storage and transport infrastructures, means huge losses: at least 20 per cent of Indian fruit and vegetable production is in fact lost either on farms, or during transport and at traders' premises, at the cost of some Rs. 15 billion, according to a 1997 McKinsey study.

That is not all. There are also depreciation costs on the remaining products due to inefficient processing (Rs. 105 billion) and the cuts taken by the excessively large number of middlemen (Rs. 125 billion), which bring the total loss of profits to Rs. 230 billion, almost 50 per cent of the figure generated by fruit and vegetable production in India, or 100 per cent of that generated by car production at that time!

For fresh products, the usual marketing chain includes village markets, then district markets (*mandis*), and then wholesale markets (Azadpur in Delhi, Navi Mumbai market, etc.), i.e. an average transport distance of 1,500 km, generally without refrigeration, despite the climate. At present, there are between five and seven middlemen between producers and retailers, who all take a significant cut, in view of the losses and risks they incur. In short, Indian horticultural farmers apparently receive barely 25 per cent of the end price, which includes a 30 to 50 per cent cut for the middlemen. This last figure is less than 7 per cent in the United States, with their integrated cooperative sector in which 50 per cent of the consumer price goes to farmers.

Safal from NDDB

Boosted by its success in the dairy sector, the NDDB accepted a government proposal in 1987 to transpose the experiment to the fruit and vegetable sector, in order to link producers and consumers more efficiently and supply the Indian capital and its suburbs. A decade on, the network is centred on the 2-ha Mangolpuri sorting and storage facility 15 km north-west of Connaught Place, New Delhi's central square. The facility has an annual capacity of 1,20,000 tonnes and equipment that is not available elsewhere: grading and quality sorting equipment, large temperature- and humidity-controlled cold rooms, controlled-atmosphere rooms for long-term storage and ripening (particularly of bananas and tomatoes), a tunnel freezer, loading and unloading bays, a staff canteen and bank, etc. Further up in the chain, the village communities targeted by the NDDB are encouraging farmers to join the network. In return, they benefit from various types of advice (choice of varieties, production calendar, cropping techniques, etc.) and are paid based on product quality. On average, 250 tonnes of fresh products (including 110 potato varieties) are delivered to Mangolpuri each day, via primary collection centres, with green vegetables coming from within a 200 to 300 km radius of the capital, tomatoes and onions from Maharashtra, and fruits from all over the country. Further down the chain, the distinctive green plastic crates supplied to farmers can be seen at retail outlets: 200 self-service shops in 1996 in the Delhi territory and the large sub-urban city to the south-east (Noida, in Uttar Pradesh), 75 per cent of which are close to the NDDB milk booths, at sites provided by the local authorities at a low rent. These 'Safal' shops (Safal being a company and brand name derived from the Hindi words for 'fruit' and 'vegetable') have an average floor space of

120 m^2, are supplied twice daily, include a small cold storage room, are often run by retired military personnel who are free to employ an assistant if they wish (at their expense), and sell fruit and vegetables at clearly marked, set prices that are generally lower than elsewhere. Purchases are weighed electronically and customers are given a receipt.

Fresh Products

The Safal experiment, whose viability and reproducibility are partly dependent on the cooperation of the local authorities, is therefore also original in terms of the sales methods used. Otherwise, goods are usually sold door-to-door (on carts) or, as with other fresh products (milk, meat, fish, etc.), through very specialized small shops (separate fruit and vegetable shops, in addition to those specializing in bananas, which are sold all year round), grouped in certain streets of the bazaars or in the covered markets built by the British (such as Crawford Market in Mumbai), and which have different opening times from grocers' shops. The shopkeepers also take particular care over how they display their wares. According to the FAO, in 2003, after deduction of (low percentage of) wastes and of (fast growing) net-export (1,57,000 tonnes of fruits and 1.186 million tonnes of vegetables, including 8,60,000 tonnes of onions), the per capita annual availability was close to 69 kg of vegetables and 38 kg of fruits (compared to about 143 and 96 kg respectively in France), i.e. almost half the global average (118 and 62 kg respectively, including India). Moreover, this is only an average figure, with consumption varying considerably in line with income levels. This income elasticity is even greater for processed products, since India is still primarily a fresh product market (a good half of what it produces is consumed by farmers and their families), and processes barely 1 per cent of its fruit and vegetables, compared to 15 per cent in China, over 80 per cent in Malaysia and 30 per cent on average worldwide (end of 1990s).

A Slow Process

Fruit Juices, Preserves, Pickles and Chutneys

The processing industry doubled its capacity between 1991 and 1996, reaching 2 million tonnes in 1998, but only 50 per cent of that capacity is actually used. Half of the industry's output is fruit juices and drinks, which have only recently become popular, with the rest comprising preserves (17 per cent), pickles and chutneys (9 per cent), frozen foods (less than 8 per cent), jams and jellies (less than 7 per cent), tomato sauce and ketchup (6 per cent), etc. The main part of the sector, around 3,300 decentralized small-scale units producing less than 50 tonnes per year, is ignorant of the techniques commonly used elsewhere. Their goods are therefore of poor quality, and rarely original. However, some 40 firms (less than 1 per cent of the total number of units at the end of the 1990s), often on the edges of large towns, have a capacity of over 250 tonnes/year and account for almost 35 per cent of the volumes processed. They are using increasingly complex techniques and are venturing into new areas such as frozen fruit pulp, flavourings, pre-packed vegetable curry, bottled mushrooms, resins, etc.

However, there are still severe constraints on the sector: the multiplicity of scattered production zones, the excessive seasonality of the raw materials used (Table 2), insufficiently consistent raw materials, excessive losses, an inadequate packaging industry (the sector is legally reserved for small-scale industries), high taxes on processed goods, consumers reluctant to pay higher prices for fruit and vegetables, particularly as they prefer them fresh, etc. The low domestic demand, which is limited to the upper classes and the armed forces, means that this burgeoning industry has so far had to look to the export market for a quarter of its outlets. In 1997-8, domestic demand was dominated by dried or preserved fruit and vegetables (63 per cent), mango pulp (16 per cent), and pickles and chutneys (11 per cent).

Agrifood Policy (APEDA...)

Fruit and vegetable processing and export operations were still almost negligible at the end of the 1990s, due to the size of the domestic market for fresh products, and also to a lack of attention to the food processing sector on the part of the authorities. But things had begun to change in the mid-1980s: the National Horticulture Board was set up in 1984 and placed in charge of improving production systems, transport and product processing (the cold chain). The Agricultural and Processed Food Products Export Development Authority (APEDA) was created in 1986, and the Ministry of Food Processing Industries in 1988. In the same year, seed imports were authorized, and over 30 per cent of the area under tomatoes and cabbages (but only 4 per cent of

TABLE 2: MAIN SEASONS AND REGIONS FOR FRUIT AND VEGETABLE PRODUCTION (1995-6)

	Main producing States (States accounting for at least 50% of the 1995-6 Indian production)	Seasons (market availability)											
		Sept.	Oct.	Nov.	Dec.	Jan.	Feb.	Mar.	Apr.	May.	Jun.	Jul.	Aug.
Banana	Tamil Nadu, Maharashtra, Karnataka												
Pineapple	West Bengal, Assam, Andhra Pradesh												
Mushroom	Tamil Nadu, Maharashtra, Punjab, Haryana, UP												
Sapota (Chiku)	Karnataka												
Cauliflower	Bhiar, Orissa												
Apple	Jammu & Kashmir												
Onion	Maharashtra, Gujarat, Karnataka												
Papaya	Karnataka, Orissa												
Cabbage	Uttar, Orissa, Bihar												
Tomato	Bihar, Karnataka, Orissa												
Guava	Bihar, Karnataka, U.P., Gujarat, M.P., Maharashtra												
Potato	Uttar Pradesh, West Bengal												
Grapes	Maharashtra, Karnataka												
Mango	Andhra Pradesh, Uttar Pradesh, Bihar												
Lady's finger (Okra)	Bihar, Orissa, West Bengal												
Peas	Uttar Pradesh												
Litchi	Bihar												
Citrus	Andhra Pradesh, Maharashtra, Karnataka	—	—	—	—	—	—	—	—	—	—	—	—

Source: Based on Vikas Singhal and Rabobank

that under cauliflowers) were planted with hybrids produced by both public and private firms. Above all, since 1991, the processing sector has no longer been reserved for small-scale industries (SSI). Subsidies are also increasingly being granted, at least on paper, to enable the use of greenhouses, plastic growing equipment and drip irrigation systems. 'Food parks' grouping agrifoods industries around shared infrastructures are also under construction, and since 1999, the agrifoods industry has been classed as part of the 'priority sector' to which banks are legally obliged to grant a major share of loans. Export revenue is tax-free, and so are the export-oriented units. Lastly, health and quality standards have been introduced: industrialists now have to conform to the Fruit Products Order.

Kissan, Vadilal, Godrej, Pepsi, Nestlé & Co.

Large Indian or overseas companies are increasingly moving into the sector (Hindustan Lever's Kissan Products, Godrej Foods, Kejriwal group's Tropical Fruits International, Tarai Foods, Thapar group's Global Green Company, Wimco, Nestlé India, Pepsi Foods, Enkay Texofood, Dabur, Parle Foods, Agro Dutch, Coleman, etc.). It is a result of a major shift in agricultural policy as a whole, which had previously been wary of big businesses and vertical integration, of seeing small holders become slaves to processing firms, of Indian land being taken over by foreign multinationals. As recently as 1996, the Hindu nationalist party RSS' slogan was still 'Computer chips, yes. Potato chips, no'. Eight years earlier, in 1988, Pepsico had only been allowed into Punjab under a range of conditions (which in the end were not strictly respected) concerning employment, diversification of the local agricultural sector and protection for Indian fizzy drink producers. The authorities now encourage such private investment, even if it is foreign. In 1998, the government company Gujarat Agro Industries Corporation intervened with the local authorities to support a request by the American Del Monte group, which was keen to set up two pineapple processing plants, provided the law restricting major land purchases (in this case 200 ha) to farmers from the state was suspended. The argument was that if Del Monte were allowed to build its factories, it would bring in currency through exports to the Middle East: the authorities' social ambitions were satisfied by the hope that the sector, which is highly capital- and labour-intensive, would help to reduce rural under-employment while boosting small holders by allowing them to farm under contract.

A Political Ground

Onions

However, for many people, such operations are still a gamble, particularly since given the increasing price tension on the domestic market, consumers are ruthless in the event of sharp or excessive price rises. It is not unreasonable to suggest that the BJP, which was previously in power in New Delhi, lost the 1998 legislative elections as a result of a rise in the price of onions (+ 900 per cent). Production had fallen by just 15 per cent, but unwise exports, imports that failed to meet demand and speculation on the part of some operators had contrived to make onions a leading political issue (they are a staple ingredient in Indian cooking, except for orthodox Brahmans and Jains, who do not eat either onions or garlic). A temporary export ban was introduced, onions were placed under the country's Essential Commodities Act (under the direct control of New Delhi), and the NAFED was given greater power. Nevertheless, this was proof of the difficulties faced by a government that was reluctant to give up its precious foreign currency revenue (India is the world's third largest exporter of onions, which represent 90 per cent of its vegetable exports in value terms, albeit barely 1 per cent of its total agricultural exports), but that needed to satisfy its domestic market. It had little room for manoeuvre. Until then, India, which has the largest area under onions in the world (30 per cent of it in the Nasik region of Maharashtra) but which is only the second largest producer due to its poor yields (10 t/ha), had previously chosen to control the commodity chain closely: imports were banned until 1988, separate export permits were granted for each variety and subject to a minimum price, and the NAFED was placed at the centre of overseas trade and domestic price support operations. Does the system now need to be completely reformed? How can a compromise be found between the interests of producers and consumers and the balance of trade?

Potataos

There are probably as many possible solutions as there are fruits and vegetables in India. For instance, the case is different with potatoes, since although they account for a fifth of the area planted with vegetables (India is the world's third largest producer after China and Russia), they are much less important in terms of exports. Average yields are far from low (18 t/ha), as a result of irrigation and the use of selected varieties. In Uttar Pradesh, the leading producer ahead of West Bengal, 94 per cent of the area planted with potatoes was set up with HYVs. It is estimated that in terms of production and productivity, the progress made with potatoes is comparable to that made with wheat, and greater than that with rice. The labour-intensive and fast-ripening nature of Indian potatoes is a major asset on a national level. However, potato growing is still a risky undertaking, both agronomically and economically. Small holders, who make up three quarters of growers, are badly organized and have difficulty coping with high seed costs and unstable sales prices (there is no legal minimum price). The country's cold storage capacity (particularly in the public sector) amounts to 8 million tonnes (40 per cent of the total crop), but is not used efficiently, and in any event, refrigeration damages potatoes. Moreover, crisp and chip manufacturers complain about the lack of standardization, inadequate supply circuits and very low domestic demand for their products.

Mushrooms Cultivated mushrooms are an even more specific case. They were first grown in 1670-80 in King Louis XIV's vegetable garden (France), but it was not until the second half of the twentieth century that mushroom growing really took off worldwide, and it did not catch on in India until the 1990s. However, now that India has moved into the sector, things are going well. Production (primarily *Agaricus* and *Pleurotus*) increased from 7,000 tonnes in 1990 to almost 40,000 in 1997-8 (including 10,000 tonnes in Tamil Nadu and 7,000 in Maharashtra), a figure that remained the same in 2004 (fourteenth largest producer). For some years the commodity chain was booming, having recovered from the crisis triggered by the arrival on the global market of huge quantities of Chinese mushrooms in early 1993, as a result of which 30 of the 44 operators involved in the sector in India (Tata Tea, Ponds, Alpine Industries, Tactron, Premium Mushroom, Mandeep Mushrooms, Transchem, RLF, Saptarishi Agro Industries, Agro Dutch Foods, etc.) found themselves in deep financial trouble. Judicious financial investment since then has resulted in greater productivity at both farms and processing units, and India is once again competitive on export markets: most of what it produces is now exported processed, to the United States and Europe. By the end of the 1990s, it accounted for 5 per cent of world trade in mushrooms, partly thanks to the success of Agro Dutch Foods, a group set up by Punjab Agro Corporation and a Dutch trading company (which supplied most of the cold-drying, drying and freezing equipment). Exports of wild mushrooms (*Guchhi*: boletus, chanterelle, etc.), which are picked in the Himalayas after the snow melts, are also worth watching, as they are set to increase, since the added value that can be achieved on export markets is even higher.

Flowers

A more decorative and much more traditional crop than mushrooms, flowers are an integral part of life in India, from the orange Marigolds used in religious ceremonies to the jasmine that women weave into their hair every morning and the garlands placed around the necks of honoured guests or statues of the gods. Almost half of the 80,000 ha planted with flowers in 1997 was given over to these traditional flowers, primarily grown by small holders. There is a huge contrast with the other flower production chain, which was still almost non-existent in the 1980s: cut flowers grown on large farms or by firms. It is this chain that is responsible for the recent growth in flowered areas (+ 56 per cent between 1988 and 1994), making Karnataka the leading producer. It also triggered the appearance of a host of street florists in India's large cities, selling roses and gladioli. Lastly, India is also counting on the cut flower chain to boost exports (for instance, the APEDA is trying to set up cold storage facilities at the country's airports). However, in view of the competition in the global market, the phytosanitary problems with Indian flowers that have been criticized by importing countries (which India has in turn accused of thinly disguised protectionism), the unauthorized use of varieties created abroad, the poor marketing infrastructure and the dubious profitability of export-oriented units, given that it takes Rs. 30 million borrowed at 18 per cent interest to set up 3 ha, it is debatable whether the best prospects for development do not in fact lie in the domestic market. Is it just a coincidence that the cut flower auction market that opened in Bangalore in 1998 is solely geared towards the domestic market? If proof were needed, it lies in the huge increase in the popularity of Valentine's Day among the upper classes in India, to the disgust of Hindu groups that have denounced this form of Westernization, along with beauty contests, although India as a whole is hugely proud of its beauty queens.

ANIMAL PROTEIN: HATCHERIES AND HINDRANCES

CATTLE MEAT: A WORLD APART

Animal Husbandry, Breeding

The Green Revolution and India's achievement of cereal self-sufficiency since 1977 were followed by a surprising resurgence in the livestock sector (Figure 23). Between 1980-1 and 1995-6, its share (in value terms) of Indian agricultural production increased from 19 to 27 per cent (at current prices), and its share of agricultural GDP trebled or quadrupled, according to estimates (from 6 to 19 per cent or 22 per cent of GDP at

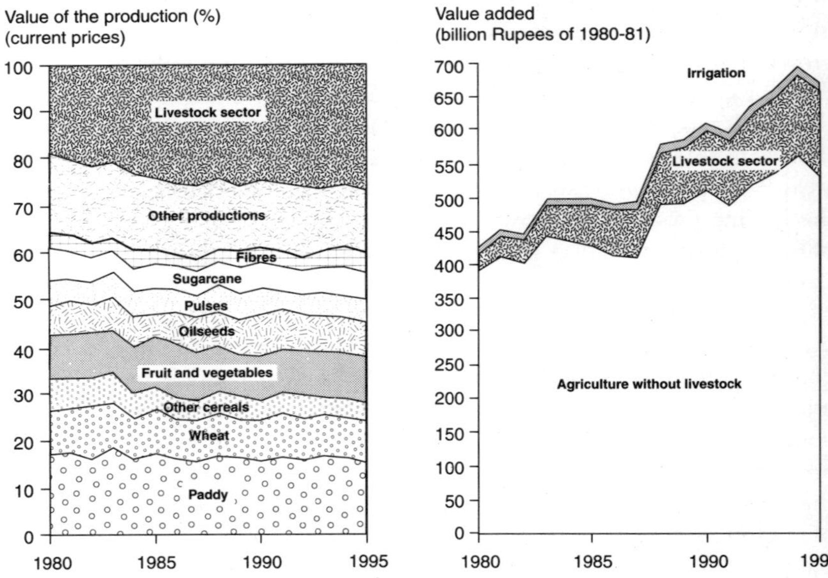

Source: Based on Central Statistical Organisation.

FIGURE 23: THE GROWING IMPORTANCE OF LIVESTOCK (1980-1 TO 1995-6)

current or constant prices). The dairy sector plays a dominant role, since it accounts for almost two-thirds of the total livestock production value in 1995-6, compared to 20 per cent for meat and eggs (with 3 per cent for eggs and 7 per cent for chicken), over 9 per cent for manure and fuel (dung), and 6.5 per cent for other products (leather, wool, silk, etc., and 3 per cent increase in stocks). The resource itself is impressive (Figure 24): the subcontinent has just 3 per cent of the world's land, but 57 per cent of the total number of buffaloes (98 million head, according to the 2003 survey, including 80 million females), 14 per cent of cattle (185 million head, including 65 million adult cows), and 16 per cent of goats (124 million head). Lastly, and most importantly, while the number of animals (bovines, sheep, goats, pigs and others) per inhabitant has almost halved in 40 years (0.8 head/inhabitant in 1952 and 0.5 in 1992 as well as in 2003), they still play a crucial role, particularly among the poorest people, for whom they are a means of survival. Three quarters of rural dwellers own animals, and smallholders (farmers with less than 2 ha) rear 56 per cent of the large animals and 62 per cent of the sheep in India.

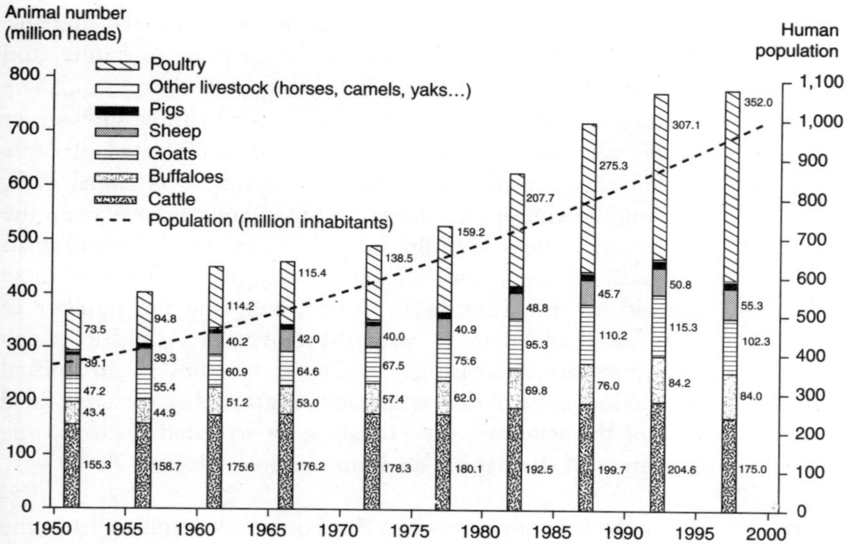

Source: Based on Ministry of Agriculture.

FIGURE 24: LIVESTOCK POPULATIONS (1951 TO 1997 CENSUSES)

In a subsistence economy, animals play fundamental roles that are not fully reflected in GDP figures: draught (a quarter of the buffaloes and half the bovines are used for ploughing: the equivalent of 30,000 megawatts), savings (a means of setting money aside, along with gold), milk production (88 million tonnes in 2003-4), wool (48,500 tonnes that year, including 40 per cent from Rajasthan), fuels and/or fertilizers (dung) and lastly, leather and meat. However, meat is still a world apart, and the corresponding statistics are extremely vague, unlike those for the number of artificial inseminations (28 million in 2003-4) or veterinary facilities: 8,720 veterinary clinics, 17,820 dispensaries and 25,433 more or less mobile units in 2003.

Pastoral Nomadism

In fact, according to the official statistics, there are no meat races in India, or programmes to develop meat production: with both bovines and smaller animals, the sector is dominated by largely non-intensive 'domestic' rearing, where feeding solely in stalls is rare and reserved for the dairy cows introduced during the white revolution (see Chapter 4). That land is in short supply for crops and particularly for grazing in India is a significant obstacle to any moves to satisfy the very real increase in demand for dairy and meat products. Crops are primarily grown to feed humans, crop waste and household rubbish are a poor substitute, and the concentrates industry has not yet got off the ground. The shortfall in terms of green and dry fodder in India grows ever greater each year: with every monsoon, 15,000 head of cattle are left to graze illegally in the Ranthambore National Park, pending the end of the harvest, and thousands of cows roam the streets and avenues of Delhi. It is easier to move sheep and goats in search of food, which explains why 30 per cent of these animals are still nomadically reared, and why the number of goats has doubled in 30 years. Moreover, in Rajasthan, sheep and goats are increasingly replacing bovines in an animal production system that seasonally migrates between the arid west of the state and the Himalayas or irrigated plains, to the detriment of the natural environment (see Chapter 7).

Cattle Meat

The only way of overcoming the bottleneck resulting from the lack of land is to intensify. However, this means including improving meat productivity in India's development targets, which is still a difficult and tricky issue for the authorities. The taboos Hindus place on beef and Muslims (and most Hindus) place on pork have a lot to answer for. However, in 1998, according to FAO estimates (Figure 25), beef and veal production (1.4 million tonnes) was much the same as that of buffalo meat, seven times that of lamb, and around three times that of goat meat (also known as 'mutton' in India), pork and poultry. If these figures are accurate, they suggest that since the early 1960s, beef (along with pork) has increased its share of total meat production, whereas increased agricultural mechanization, the use of more productive races and feed availability problems in over-grazed areas have led to a decrease in the number of cattle (185 million head in 2003, excluding 98,000 buffaloes whose number is increasing). The price of beef, which is at least twice cheaper than that of mutton, undoubtedly has something to do with this (for the same reason, most male buffaloes are slaughtered at birth). It may be that some of this output supplies the growing meat export sector (Rs. 7.6 billion in 1998-9), although beef exports are theoretically banned (unlike buffalo meat exports). Although meat consumption in India is generally much lower than elsewhere (5.2 kg per capita in 2003 including 2.4 kg of bovine meat, whereas the world

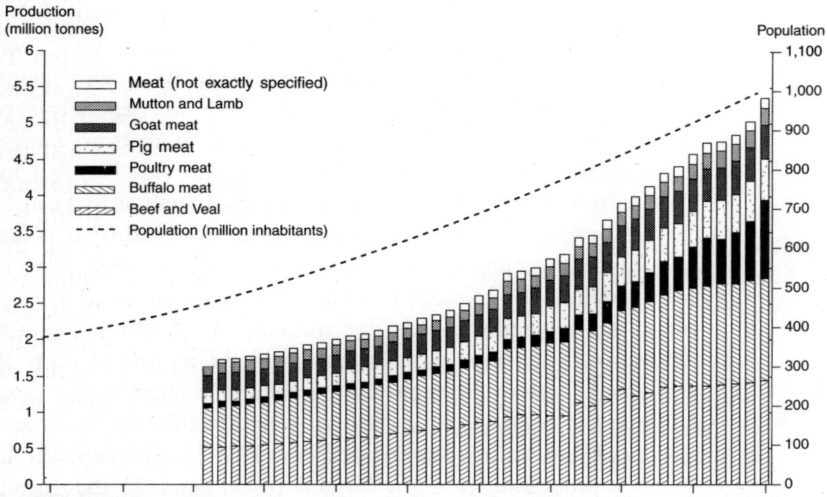

Source: Based on FAO.

FIGURE 25: MEAT PRODUCTION (1961 TO 1999)

average is 40 kg according to the FAO), only some Indians are vegetarian for religious or dietary reasons (24 per cent of urbanites are vegetarian, according to a 1992 survey). Demand for animal protein is thus bound to increase significantly with the growth of the middle classes, urbanization and, more generally, a legitimate wish to diversify a diet that was previously largely dominated by cereals, and a limited range of pulses (lentils and peas) whose price has rocketed since 1993.

Abattoirs (Allana, Hind Industries, Al-Kabeer & Co.)

Pending a 'red revolution', the cattle slaughtering rate reported at the end of the 1990s was just 1.5 per cent for 'traditional' bovines, compared to 3.5 per cent for buffaloes, 35.6 per cent for goats, 32.5 per cent for sheep and 26.3 per cent for pigs. Slaughtering cows is forbidden in most states, and Gujarat even has a ban on beef trading. Article 48 of the Constitution also stipulates that 'the State . . . shall take steps for . . . prohibiting the slaughter of cows and calves and other milch and draught cattle'. Those states that do not obey these 'recommendations', such as Kerala, with its Christian and Communist influences, receive a million head of large animals from neighbouring states each year. There are also huge numbers of clandestine operators: of the country's 34,700 abattoirs in 1996, over 90 per cent were small, unlicensed units, accounting for some 40 per cent of the country's total meat output. Of the other operators, which are subject to minimum quality and hygiene regulations laid down in the 1973 Meat Product Order, and which are generally run by the State or municipalities, only six modern abattoirs satisfy international standards (Aurangabad, Goregaon and Nanded in Maharashtra, Rudraram in Andhra Pradesh, Derabasi in Punjab and Usgaon in Goa). Animal slaughtering conditions in India thus leave something to be desired: for goats and sheep, as well as for poultry, the butcher (a Muslim or someone from a very low caste) generally bleeds the animals, in appalling hygiene conditions. Meat processing at the 150-odd registered units is hardly any better, although 25 are relatively large (some also slaughter the animals), since they are geared to the export market (Allana, Hind Industries, Al-Kabeer, PLM Industries, etc.). Primary processing is often limited to tenderizing the meat, cutting up the carcasses and sometimes freezing the cuts. Secondary processing to make high added value products represents just 1 per cent of meat production, primarily pork:

sausages, salami, ham and bacon are made at units in the north (Tibetan enclaves) and north-east (under Chinese and Burmese influence).

Exports

Officially for religious reasons, India has a ban on meat and meat byproduct imports, except horsemeat (with the exception of quotas for luxury hotels and the diplomatic community), but willingly encourages exports (except of cow meat), notably through the APEDA. In 1997-8, of 1,84,000 tonnes of exports with a value of Rs. 8 billion (including barely Rs. 20 million worth of processed products), 1,76,000 were buffalo meat, for which processing operations are booming. Fifteen export-oriented units were set up between 1996 and 1998. The Middle East and South-East Asia are the main clients, thus the fact that animals are slaughtered using the *halal* method in India is a major asset, along with India's geostrategic position between these two Muslim regions. Furthermore, given the domestic market potential, foreign investment began to flood in the 1990s (Seanet PTY from Australia, Asian Investment Corporation from the Philippines, McDonald Corporation from the United States to name a few), and has helped to modernize the commodity chain as a whole (animal feed, refrigeration, processing). This modernization could have a beneficial effect on the leather production chain, which exports large volumes but which has to import some of the skins used because of the often inappropriate slaughtering techniques practised in India. This is paradoxical, given the number of animals in the country. In any event, there is still a long way to go, particularly if the aim is to ensure that sectorial growth does not only benefit the booming industrial-scale animal production chain, but also farmers from almost all the social classes, as has been the case for dairy, albeit much less so for aviculture.

Aviculture: Soaring over Cities

Aviculture (CARI, NECC...)

Is this a just reward? The Harappa and Mohenjo-Daro civilizations domesticated poultry around 2,500 BC, and it is now the descendants of the red jungle fowl (*Gallus gallus murghi* or *Gallus bankiva*) that are being reintroduced in the subcontinent (457.4 million heads in 2003, compared to 307.1 in 1992, and 73.5 in 1951). This was after a long voyage and major changes in the West, particularly in the United States, where a veritable industry grew up in the mid-twentieth century that has since spread throughout the world, albeit with some variations. The first avicultural research department in India was set up in 1936, under the Indian Veterinary Research Institute (IVRI) in Izatnagar, Uttar Pradesh. However, it was not until 1979 that it become an institute in its own right (Central Avian Research Institute [CARI]). Likewise, the 1940s saw a wave of state model farms producing eggs (the first hybrid layers were introduced in 1955), followed by a multitude of programmes (DPAP, IPDB, IRDP, LPP) aimed at organizing small holders, primarily in cooperatives. However, broilers were not introduced until the early 1970s, and the first professional organization—the National Egg Coordination Committee (NECC)—was founded as recently as 1982. Likewise, it was not until 1981 that imports of foreign strains were limited so as to concentrate on crossing races suited to the climate in India, particularly to the heat, and on encouraging the independent development of the national production sector.

Despite a lack of any substantial international aid or government investment, Indian aviculture embarked upon a period of sustained growth (in double figures), becoming the most dynamic agricultural sector in the last two decades of the twentieth century. However, its development centred on the industrial sector, which benefited from tax exemption on a third of its income. The size and intensiveness of the new units played a major role in growth, resulting in substantial economies of scale: between 1985 and 1993, the real price of eggs and meat fell by 8 per cent. By 1994, the average annual number of eggs per chicken had topped 300, and broilers were reaching a weight of 1.5 kg in under 40 days. In addition to small-scale producers (farmers or cooperatives, as in Maharashtra), there are now large firms, often working with foreign partners, which now produce a major share of total output. Development has not only been intense in time, but also in spatial terms: roughly speaking, at the end of the 1990s, 75 per cent of chicken and egg production in India was concentrated in urban areas, which was home to 25 per cent of the country's population.

Eggs

With 30 billion eggs in 1998 (Figure 26; including 5 per cent duck eggs) and 40 billion in 2003-4, India is now the world's

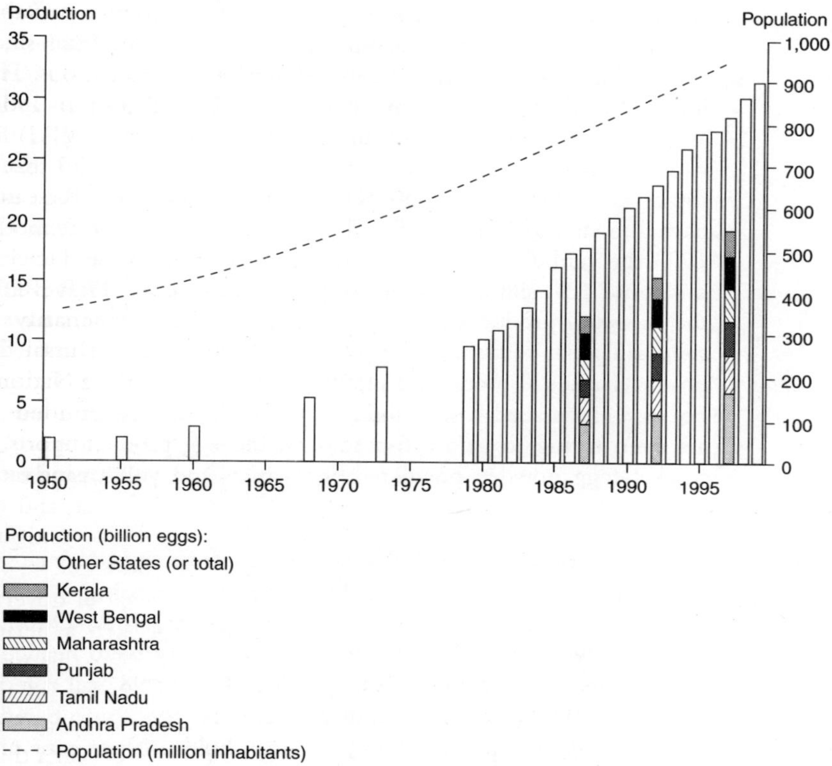

Source: Based on Ministry of Agriculture.

FIGURE 26: EGG PRODUCTION (1950-1 TO 1999-2000)

fifth largest producer, but is still a very small consumer since according to the FAO, in 2003, the annual per capita availability was just 1.8 kg compared to a global average of 8.6. The situation in rural areas is of great concern, as people consume fewer than 15 eggs per year on average, compared to almost 100 in urban areas (the WHO recommends 180). The high price (as a result of high animal feed costs in India) or the excessive seasonal production fluctuations (+ 40 per cent between April and November), despite attempts by the NAFED to buy and resell eggs, are not the only reasons for these low consumption figures. The concentration of hatcheries (331 in 1997, 61 per cent of them private) near urban areas with higher purchasing power is compounded by the recurrent problem of distribution infrastructures: regions with surpluses, such as Andhra Pradesh, the egg basket of the subcontinent (20 per cent of Indian output in 1997–8, followed by Tamil Nadu, Punjab, Maharashtra and West Bengal, which each account for around 10 per cent), find it difficult to supply rural areas where the local races used (*desi* fowls) now produce just 30 per cent of India's eggs. Diseases have also driven some small holders out of business: in March 1993, the viral disease Gumboro (infectious bursal disease) wiped out some 4.5 million birds in Andhra Pradesh alone. However, the state still produces a surplus, as some poultry farmers have solid financial resources. Despite their insufficiently standard products and still precarious supply circuits, some, such as Balaji Foods, a Hyderabad-based subsidiary of the Venkateshwara group, are even trying to gain a foothold on the egg product export market (egg powder, powdered egg whites and yolks, eggshell lysozyme).

Venkateshwara & Co.

At the end of the 1990s, India had just 20 or so egg processing units and barely more than 15 chicken processing plants (MAFCO, Deejay, Capon Foods Specialities, Indo-Dutch Protein, Ovobels, Godrej Agrovet, etc.), but they were headed by a group that, as *Business India* put it in June 1998, still ruled the roost. B.V. Rao's Venkateshwara empire, the Pune-based 'largest integrated poultry group in Asia', holds 70 per cent of the Indian market for one-day chicks intended for laying or for the table. When B.V. Rao died in January 1996, nine months before the International Congress of the WPSA (World Poultry Science Association, 108 member countries), he had dreamed of holding in India, his eldest daughter Anuradha Desai took over and organized things so efficiently that she was unanimously voted president of the Association for the next five years. This was the first time that such a meeting had been held in a developing country, and that a woman had been appointed president. Moreover, Ms Desai was elected at a record age (just 33 years), but it cannot be denied that she had an impressive record. With seven companies, including three that are now very large (Venkateshwara Hatcheries, Bromark and Balaji Food) and four in partnership with foreign companies (three American and one French), the Venkateshwara group is not content merely to produce eggs, although it does so on a huge scale. Its farm near

Solapur is the largest hatchery in this part of the world, with 2,50,000 birds, and has the latest feeding and light and temperature control systems. In addition to making incubators and vaccines, or egg powder for European, Japanese and Russian spaghetti and biscuit manufacturers, Venkateshwara also produces and processes chickens: its factory near Lonavla can handle 4,000 birds an hour and supplies five-star hotels and fastfood outlets such as KFC, Domino's Pizza or Pizza Hut in Mumbai, Delhi, Bangalore and, obviously, Pune. Lastly, when business in the domestic market is slow, as it was following the 1996 broiler production surplus, the group does not sell one-day chicks but eggs, of which it exports up to 2 million a month to neighbouring countries.

Chicken

At the end of the 1990s, fewer than 5 per cent of the birds reared at battery farms in India were processed to make chicken pieces, sausages or frozen goods (and hardly any tinned goods or ready meals). As with fruit and vegetables, the market is dominated by fresh goods: small-scale poultry farmers set up near places where horticulture products are sold, and remove their distinctive white birds from their cages for slaughter as and when required (90 per cent of the total number of birds killed). Demand is growing: chicken is cheaper than lamb or goat meat, and is not taboo for most Hindus (although as chickens eat excrement in the farmyard, they are not considered entirely pure). Supplies trebled between 1986 and 1998 (5,40,000 tonnes, placing India eighteenth in the world, with Andhra Pradesh and Maharashtra accounting for 35 per cent), amounting to 12 per cent of the meat eaten in India (6 per cent in 1986), albeit in very small quantities per inhabitant: 500 g according to the FAO in 1998 (800 g according to the USDA), compared to a global average of 10.1 kg! The urban/rural split in terms of both production and consumption is still at least as marked as for eggs, although poultry farms tend to be located on the outer edge of towns and cities rather than actually in them. Here too, there is a long way to go before the production chain is in a position to offer a majority of Indian consumers an affordable product, or to move into the Middle Eastern or South-East Asian markets, which India—given its proximity and low labour costs—could supply in the long term, in the same way as Thailand, China and Brazil currently do. It will be a long and winding road in many respects, but as things stand, there is one major obstacle: animal feed (which accounts for 70 per cent of avicultural production costs on the subcontinent), whose scarcity and poor quality mean that chickens cost almost twice as much to rear in India than in Brazil.

Animal Feed

Even more than livestock rearing, animal feed is a sector that the Indian authorities had considerably underestimated and neglected until they realized in the late 1990s how important it was for the future of agrifood supplies in the country and in terms of development policy. The almost total lack of databases on the subject, as regards both quantity and quality, is sufficient proof of the extent of the problem: as a result, for cereals alone, based on an estimated animal consumption figure of 3.7 million tonnes in 1993, the forecasts of demand by 2020 vary by almost 400 per cent, from 13 million tonnes (P. Kumar, 1998) to 50 million (G.S. Bhalla and P. Hazell, 1999), assuming roughly 4 per cent growth in GDP. The second two authors' estimate is as much as 107 million tonnes assuming a 6 per cent increase in per capita income, i.e. almost 60 per cent of the cereals produced in India in 1998-9! However, the experts do agree on one point: production of maize, a crucial element at least in the case of poultry farms, increased from 7 to 10 million tonnes between 1980-1 and 2002-3, which is largely insufficient, particularly as yields are still very low (a national average of less than 1.7 tonnes). It is also generally suggested that the resulting high prices have been exacerbated by import restrictions, and the 1992 maize shortage drove 30 per cent of poultry farmers to shut up shop. However, import restrictions on animal feed were lifted five years later, as was the stipulation introduced in 1977 that such feeds (except granules) could only be produced by SSIs (whose size was limited by the government), resulting in far from satisfactory product quality. Even so, the Indian compound feed production sector is still badly organized. At the end of the 1990s, the members of the Compound Livestock Feed Manufacturers' Association of India (CLFMA, founded in 1967) accounted for just 60 per cent of the total output from the official sector, estimated at 7 million tonnes (Hindustan Lever, Godrej Agrovet, SKM), which itself represented 15 to 20 per cent of a total figure of 42 million tonnes. Demand is nearer 80 million tonnes, i.e. a 47 per cent shortfall. The dry fodder shortfall is around 33 per cent, as against 23 per cent for green fodder: the equivalent of around 88 million hectares of land.

Fish and Shellfish: Fishing for Currency

The Blue Revolution (MPEDA...)

Fish and shellfish production in India doubled over a fifteen-year period, from 1980 to 1995, and reached 6.4 million tonnes in 2003–4 (5.4 million in 1997–8, Figure 27), placing the country third in the world ranking for fish production and second for inland fisheries, which is the sector that has made the most progress (2.4 million tonnes in 1997–8), as it has throughout Asia (86 per cent of global aquacultural production). In 2002–3, inland fish production was 3.2 million tonnes, and had overtaken marine production (3.0 million). Between 1980 and 2003, the increase in annual per capita availability was just 52 per cent (reaching 4.7 kg in 2003 for a global average of 16.1 kg according to the FAO). The 'blue revolution' has primarily been revolutionary in terms of Indian agrifood exports. Since 1994–5, despite the excessive number of public supervisory bodies (the Ministries of Agriculture for inland fisheries, Food Processing Industries for processed fish and seafood, and Trade for exports),

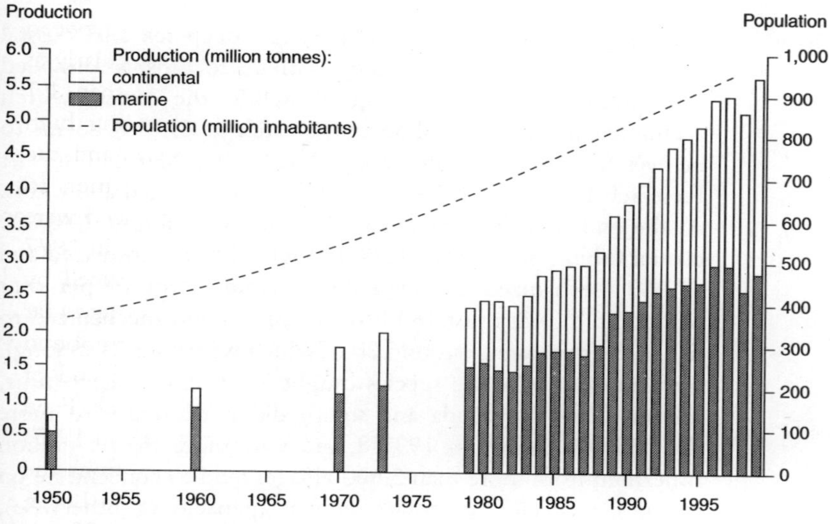

Source: Based on Ministry of Agriculture.

FIGURE 27: FISH AND SHELLFISH PRODUCTION (1950–1 TO 1999–2000)

annual foreign currency revenue has gone up, topping a billion dollars in 1997-8 (almost 400,000 tonnes of exports; $1.3 billion in 2003-4), compared to just 274 million in 1980-1 (less than 70,000 tonnes). Frozen prawns play a major role, and account for over two-thirds of turnover, with 1,30,000 tonnes exported in 2003-4. At the end of the 1990s India was the world's sixth largest fish and seafood exporter, to the delight of the Marine Products Export Development Authority (MPEDA), which controls some 3 to 4 per cent of Indian exports. The 60 or so countries that now buy these mainly frozen Indian products (including squid and cuttlefish) are headed by two heavyweights: Japan in value terms (India was the leading supplier of prawns to Japan in 1997-8), and China in volume terms, followed, in varying order depending on the year, by South-East Asia (Hong Kong, Singapore, Thailand), the European Union and the United States. With its 8,000 km of coastline, 2 million km^2 of economic exclusion zones, 1,70,000 ha of rivers and canals, and 2.5 million ha of tanks and reservoirs, India has room to develop the sector even further. According to some estimates, the total potential of sea fishing and aquacultural operations could be up to 8.4 million tonnes, including 3.9 million from sea fishing.

Fishing It is important to distinguish between deep-sea and coastal fishing, since the former could continue to prosper provided port infrastructures are adapted, while the latter, which accounted for a 2.95 million-tonne catch in 1997-8, seems to be over-fishing the available stocks. The Central Marine Fisheries Research Institute (CMFRI) is extremely concerned about this. At the end of 1996, the Indian fleet included almost 2,40,000 coastal fishing boats (only 32,000 of which were motorized and 47,000 mechanized, although they accounted for 70 per cent of the catch), with just 180 boats equipped and mechanized to fish in deeper waters (around 20 of which were over 24 m long). This explains why the species caught in offshore waters (tuna, lobster, shark, barracuda and squid) did not amount to more than 35,000 tonnes in 1997-8, and why more than a million fishermen from more than 3,600 villages tend to concentrate on sardines, mackerel, anchovies, prawns (penaeid or otherwise), perch, catfish, cuttlefish, bass and skate.

Over-fishing is particularly serious in Kerala, where the

situation is exacerbated by the choice of species with a high added value on the international market, but things are also far from rosy in Gujarat, where the whole of the catch comes from areas where the water is no more than 100 m deep; its value is particularly low. At the end of the 1990s, these two states still accounted for over 40 per cent, and along with Maharashtra and Tamil Nadu 70 per cent of Indian fish and seafood output.

Aquaculture

Fish farming (inland fisheries) is somewhat less concentrated, in so far as 70 per cent of the total volume comes from six rather than four states (West Bengal, Andhra Pradesh, Bihar, Uttar Pradesh, Orissa and Assam), although West Bengal is well ahead of the others (over 30 per cent, compared to 6 to 10 per cent for each of the others in 1998-9). Along with its sea fishing operations, West Bengal is the country's leading fish and seafood producer (although it still imports from states such as Andhra Pradesh in order to satisfy internal demand), followed by Kerala, which has made valiant efforts—using subsidies from the Fish Farmers' Development Agencies (FFDA)—to revitalize fish farming in paddy fields, as practised prior to the green revolution and its excessive use of phytosanitary products. This is a welcome initiative, since despite its advantages (fertilization, additional income), fish farming is not combined with other types of farming anywhere else in India, unlike in China, for instance. In fact, fish farmers in other regions—particularly in Tamil Nadu and Andhra Pradesh, where the largest fish farms are concentrated—tend to use tanks and cages to increase their productivity (2 t/ha/year in 1998) of carp, catfish and prawns (the main farmed freshwater species).

Freshwater fish production totalled 1.7 million tonnes in 1997-8, over 70 per cent of the total tonnage of farmed fish produced in India, although this was six times less than the amount produced in China. The brackish water production potential is still underexploited: only 8 per cent of the area available for fish farming was in use by the end of the 1990s. However, this type of fish farming is developing strongly now, notably through the expansion of penaeid prawn farming.

Prawn Exports

The popularity of prawn farming has rocketed: the total area covered by prawn farms in India doubled between 1992-3 and

1997-8, to almost 1,42,000 ha (primarily on the east coast), producing nearly 67,000 tonnes (47,000 in 1992-3). Production reached 1,15,000 tonnes in 2002-3. The efforts made by the World Bank, public research centres and the NABARD have been relayed by the private sector (large-scale farmers and firms), particularly along the low coasts of the Gulf of Bengal. There are some 150 spawn suppliers in Andhra Pradesh and 50 in Tamil Nadu, capable of supplying several billion eggs a year. Most farms (over 80 per cent) cover no more than 2 ha, but prawn farming should not be seen as a remedy for agrarian poverty in India (if only because farmers need to own land), and this apparently small size in fact requires substantial investment, at some risk. The 1995 cyclone along the east coast, and a subsequent virus outbreak led to a 15 per cent drop in Indian prawn production. Lastly, the production chain is largely dependent on the international market; in 1999, the crisis in Asia resulted in a significant drop in Japanese and Chinese purchases. In 1998, the United States denounced the use of fishing techniques that endangered marine turtles, and reported the matter to the WTO: its complaint was thrown out, but significantly hampered trade. Even more seriously, a cholera strain was detected in frozen Indian prawns in Denmark, and on 1 August 1997, as a result of various other health issues, the European Union decided to ban frozen marine product imports from India (and indeed from Bangladesh and Madagascar). The ban was lifted on 23 December, but under certain conditions: only companies approved by the Export Inspection Council of India (EICI), i.e. those that have been controlled and found to have a drinking water system, permanent electricity supply, effluent treatment plant, crushed ice-making equipment, cold storage facilities and an analysis laboratory are now allowed to export to the European Union. In 1998, the profession in India spent almost a billion rupees on improving standards, with support from the MPEDA. It has kept up its efforts since then, and by July 2000, ninety-eight companies satisfied European Union standards.

Abad, Al-Kabeer, Amalgam, Allana, Castlerock, Chirag & Co.

This is undoubtedly a step in the right direction, although here again, the financial investment required rules small-scale producers out of the sector. Fishing and fish farming are in fact suffering—and perhaps even more so than other food production chains—from the country's poor infrastructures and the lack of a cold chain. It is estimated that 20 per cent of the volume produced is lost during unloading and during transport, 50 per cent of the fresh fish sold locally fails to satisfy the minimum hygiene requirements laid down by the Indian authorities, and 10 per cent is actually rotten and is thus a real danger to the local population (this figure doubles during the hot season and the monsoon). Fortunately, almost 60 per cent of the fish and seafood produced is processed: half traditionally (sun-dried, salted or pickled in brine), and the remainder (tinned and particularly frozen) primarily for the export market, in urban centres near ports, such as Porbandar (Gujarat); Mumbai, Thane and Ratnagiri (Maharashtra); Panjim (Goa), Mangalore and Karwar (Karnataka); Kochi and Kozhikode (Kerala); Tuticorin, Mandapam and Cuddalore (Tamil Nadu); Vishakhapatnam (Andhra Pradesh); and Kolkata (West Bengal). In 1999, there were almost 390 processing units (50 per cent of them using a freezing process taking just 90 minutes), with an installed capacity of over 7,500 tonnes a day, plus some 400 cold storage warehouses with a daily potential of 7,000 tonnes, also largely under-used. All these units were private (the cooperative sector used to play a major role but is now non-existent), with some 20 operators leading the field: Abad, Al-Kabeer, Amalgam, Allana, Alsa Marine & Harvest, Amar Cold Storage, Amulya Sea Foods, Baraka Overseas Traders, Castlerock, Cham, Chirag, Crown Frozen Food, Falcon Marine Exports, Forstar Frozen Foods, Mangala, Naik Seafoods, Sawant Food Production, Yaduguri Seafoods, etc. It is these groups or firms that have launched technical and commercial operations with partners from the Philippines, Thailand (CP Group), Japan (Nissin, Higashimaru, Itochu, Mitsubishi, etc.), the United States and Belgium (via INVE) in recent years, to boost the development of a sector that still has good prospects.

The Natural Environment

While the development of inland fisheries has not aroused much criticism, particularly in the case of village irrigation ponds from which landless households can benefit, the same cannot be said for coastal operations. While its advocates claim that fish farming is far from being the main culprit behind the fact that a good 2 million ha of coastal agricultural land in India are now under threat from increased salt levels, it is obvious that it does nothing to remedy the situation. It also competes with rice growing, and some critics see it as a threat to national cereal self-sufficiency, or at the very least to job opportunities for labourers. Lastly, it also causes substantial pollution: excessive chemical use is a threat to both farmers and fishermen in the neighbouring area. The pollution control bodies in the various states have little control over this activity, for which operators do not require a licence. In 1991, five years after an environmental protection law was passed, the coastal strip within 500 m of the high tide mark was declared a Coastal Regulation Zone (CRZ), and in 1996, the Supreme Court ordered the destruction of all prawn farms in the zone, except for those using 'traditional or improved traditional' methods. Beyond the CRZ, prawn farms were also banned on agricultural land, salt marshes and village common land. However, this was all to no avail, as the rules were not applied. On the contrary, to the disgust of traditional farmers, an Aquaculture Authority was set up to look into the situation of existing fish farms, and fish farming was eventually authorized at distances of more than 200 m above the high tide mark. It is important to bear in mind that under the Constitution, fish farming is controlled by the provincial states rather than by the central government, which considerably restricts New Delhi's room for manoeuvre.

6. The Failure to Eradicate Poverty

Despite a range of impressive agricultural revolutions and poverty alleviation programmes, millions of Indians are still below the absolute poverty line. Slow economic growth, an accumulation of sometimes redundant and poorly designed operations, social inequalities and poor 'governance' are some of the reasons behind this depressing situation. The considerable grain stocks that the State has built up in certain years and the malfunctions observed in the Public Distribution System, which is supposed to subsidize food supplies to the poorest communities, make the nutritional deficiencies that affect a large proportion of the country's population all the more shocking. Despite having achieved cereal self-sufficiency, India still has not managed to ensure food security, because wheat and rice alone cannot guarantee food security.

A MULTITUDE OF POVERTY ALLEVIATION PROGRAMMES

The Hindu Growth Rate

The first half-century of the Indian republic was dominated by one overriding national concern and priority, on which everyone was agreed: alleviating poverty. This fundamental objective has endured, despite the various political and economic crises the country has been through, and has not stopped at good intentions, although it is true that the same fine words are often trotted out repeatedly during electoral campaigning. Is this Mahatma Gandhi's moral heritage? Gandhi did not see poverty as a curse, but as a positive system of values, by virtue of its underlying asceticism. This asceticism undoubtedly infiltrated the very specific national economic policies adopted, since it is only a slight exaggeration to say that until the 1980s, the objective was to make do with as little as possible and promote equality, in other words to raise the low overall standard of living among the population, at a risk of not exceeding the well-known 'Hindu growth rate' of 3.5 per cent per year. In a country where federal unity is under constant threat from disputes between communities and between regions, there is also a fear of accentuating the differences between economic classes, another trigger of division and violence. From the outset, these various factors led the State to play a dominant role in many production and consumption sectors, leaving the free market to operate on a small scale, within the country as well as with the rest of the world. This 'mixed', relatively 'closed' economy resulted in financial collapse in 1991 and a highly conventional IMF's Structural Adjustment Plan (see Chapter 8) was adopted. The recovery plan centred on the 'trickle down' principle, i.e. on the assumption that the benefits of economic activity 'upstream' would spread downwards, through the emergence and establishment of a middle class eager to consume goods and services that were previously inaccessible in India.

Poverty Alleviation Programmes (PAPs)

While waiting for this 'trickle' to reach the lowest levels of Indian society, there is another level on which the State can intervene: PAPs. Such programmes are not new in India, but like in many other regions worldwide in the throes of readjustment and liberalization, since the IMF reforms, they have also had to act as a safety net and absorb the impact of such reforms on the poorest families (redundancies, reduced support for production, increasing consumer prices). As a result, the proportion of total central government expenditure (both under and outside the Plan) by the so-called 'social services' (Figure 28) increased from 8.1 to 10.7 per cent between 1992-3 and 2000-1. Considerable efforts have clearly been made, particularly given that this figure does not include expenditure on the part of the various states (in 2003-4, expenditure on social services by Centre and states combined was 19 per cent of total expenditure and had peaked at 22 per cent in 2000-1), or subsidies paid to the public food distribution system (PDS—over $2 billion at the end of the 1990s). However, expenditure on social services under the Plan represented just 1.7 per cent of GDP in 2000-1 (1.3 per cent in 1992-3), and the authorities themselves seem to have lost track somewhat in their assessment of the situation: ministries have launched and supported a myriad of programmes: in Dharmapuri district in Tamil Nadu alone, the M.S. Swaminathan Foundation listed almost 50 development support projects in 1996! Even so, some have managed to emerge from the jungle of acronyms, primarily in rural areas, where the government is continuing to concentrate most of its operations in the hope of

Social services
6.85 billion dollars
(Plan and non-Plan)

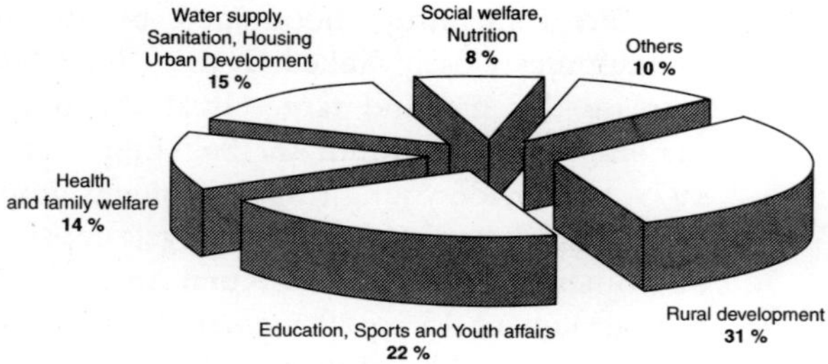

Programmes in rural areas
2.22 billion dollars
(Plan only)

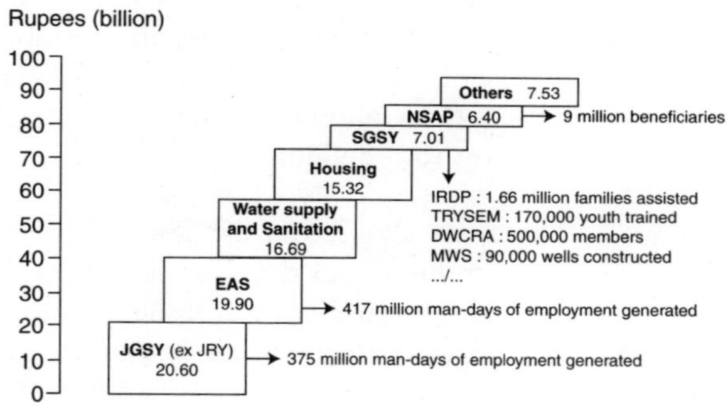

Source: Based on Economic Survey, 2001.

FIGURE 28: EXPENDITURES ON 'SOCIAL SERVICES' BY THE CENTRAL GOVERNMENT (1998-9)

discouraging people from moving to the slums of the country's cities.

Support of Rural Entre-Preneurs (IRDP, DWCRA, TRYSEM, SGSY)

The Integrated Rural Development Programme (IRDP), introduced in 1978 and managed by the District Rural Development Agencies (DRDA), set out to offer poor rural inhabitants small capital subsidies (30 per cent, or 50 per cent for Dalits and tribals) and low-rate loans to encourage self-employment in fields as varied as horticulture, fish farming, small-scale rural industry, trade, dairy farming and irrigation (the Million Wells Scheme (MWS), to encourage the boring of wells). There is increasing awareness that for want of land, rural areas can only be saved by diversifying employment, looking beyond the cereal farming encouraged by the green revolution. Programmes closely linked to the IRDP have been set up to increase this aid and target it at the poorest communities: Training of Rural Youth for Self-Employment (TRYSEM) in 1979, to provide young rural inhabitants with technical training in fields such as electronics or bicycle repair; and Development of Women and Children in Rural Areas (DWCRA) in 1982, to train groups of 15 to 20 women in weaving, fish farming and rope, broom and brick making. These various programmes were merged in 1999 to form the Swarnajayanti Gram Swarozgar Yojana (SGSY: Golden Jubilee Rural Self-employment Programme), funded by central government (75 per cent) and the states (25 per cent). It has the same poverty alleviation objectives, but also includes the possibility of lending money (with a 50 per cent subsidy) to Self-Help Groups (SHG) in villages or neighbourhoods, and even to groups of friends, rather than just to individuals.

Food for Work (JRY, JGSY, EAS, SGRY, NREGS)

There are also somewhat less ambitious 'food for work' type programmes under the Jawahar Rozgar Yojana (JRY) launched in 1989. The JRY was established to offer at least a hundred days of paid work to members of families living below the poverty line, through works on labour-intensive projects of benefit to the general public, such as water collection, soil conservation, public building projects, roads, and so on. As with the IRDP, priority was theoretically given to women, tribals and Dalits. Participants had to be paid the legal minimum wage, part-paid in grain (under Indira Gandhi, India adopted a 20-point poverty alleviation plan, including a largely unrespected Minimum Wages Act). Compared to the IRDP, funding was more centralized (New Delhi bore 80 per cent of the cost), but implementation was less so, as it is the village *panchayats* rather than the blocks that were in charge. However, DRDA supervision was still omnipresent. In 1993-4, the JRY's funds were split between three envelopes: 75 per cent to extend its operations to all Indian villages, 20 per cent to concentrate on pockets of unemployment or severe under-employment in 120 districts considered particularly deprived, and the remaining 5 per cent to prevent so-called 'distress' migration. Ten per cent of the funds in the first envelope were set aside for the Indira Awas Yojana (IAY) programme to build free housing, and 30 per cent for the MWS.

In 1999, the JRY was renamed the Jawahar Gram Samridhi Yojana (JGSY: Jawaharlal Nehru Programme for Rural Prosperity), but retained its counterpart in desert, mountainous and tribal regions, where the Employment Assurance Scheme (EAS) had been launched at the end of 1993. This latter scheme theoretically guaranted 100 days' work during the agricultural off-season to a maximum of two adults per poor family; it had gradually been extended to cover the whole of rural India, and thus apparently mirrored the JGSY. The Rs. 96.5 billion set aside in the 1999-2000 federal budget for the SGSY and other rural or urban employment programmes could no doubt be managed in a better way. In 2001 the JGSY and EAS were merged into the Sampoorna Grameen Rozgar Yojana (SGRY, Composite Rural Employment Scheme) funded at 75 per cent by the Centre. In 2003-4, Rs. 41.2 million and 5 million tonnes of foodgrain were paid for more than 760 million mandays of work generated (between April 1999-April 2004, SGSY benefited to 4.6 million households). Lastly, in 2006 was launched the National Rural Employment Guarantee Scheme (NREGS), funded by the centre at 75 per cent and by the states at 25 per cent: it promises a daily minimum wage of Rs.80 for at least 100 days of work per year to one member per family. It started in 200 districts, and should cover the whole country within five years. Will the potential 30 million beneficiaries be better served by this programme initiated under the National Rural Employment Guarantee Act passed by the Indian Parliament in August 2005? Its co-management by the local bodies (*panchayats*, *gram sabhas*) may hopefully increase its efficiency. In 2006-7 905 million mandays of work were provided of 21 million households.

Social Aid (ICDS, MDMS, NSAP...)

A multitude of more targeted, shorter-term nutrition and basic hygiene programmes have been launched since the start of the 1960s, notably to prevent deficiencies among women and small children in terms of calories and protein (SNP: Special Nutrition Programme), vitamin A (MDVAD: Massive Dose of Vitamin A Distribution), iron and folic acid (IFATD: Iron and Folic Acid Tablet Distribution) and iodine (ISD: Iodized Salt Distribution), and through the primary education system (MDMS: Mid-Day Meal Scheme, distributing free school meals). The Integrated Child Development Services (ICDS), set up in 1975, are one of the major country-wide programmes. Through the services, which are often entirely run by women via *Anganwadis*, a sort of crèche-cum-dispensary, mothers receive check-ups, vaccines, dietary supplements and training in the basic rules of childcare and feeding. Since 1975, mothers have also been supported by the National Social Assistance Programme (NSAP), which is entirely funded by the central government and which also aims to help poor elderly couples or families in which the head of the household has died.

Food aid (PL 480, PDS, WFP)

Lastly, to complete our nevertheless far from exhaustive picture, it is important to point out that while India benefited from considerable overseas food aid in the past, in the form of cereals prior to the green revolution (PL 480, see Chapter 3), powdered milk and vegetable oils prior to the white and yellow revolutions (see Chapter 4), it now only resorts to it in extreme circumstances (the October 1999 cyclone in Orissa, the February 2001 earthquake in Gujarat). By virtue of its improved agricultural productivity and PDS (see Chapter 3), in some cases backed up by regional programmes such as the costly '2 rupee-kilo of rice' operation launched in Andhra Pradesh in 1982 (Rs. 4 billion spent in 1993-4 alone), India considers it has the means to provide even its poorest citizens with a satisfactory basic diet. The United Nations World Food Programme (WFP) has therefore limited its operations in India to providing emergency aid and supporting national programmes aimed at at-risk women and children (such as the ICDS), or at tribals in forest areas: some $26 million were spent on average between 1996 and 1999, and grain often come from the national stocks.

Even so, in other areas such as agricultural development, food production and many others, India is still a major international aid beneficiary: over $3 billion a year in the 1990s, almost 90 per cent of which came from four sources: the International Development Agency (IDA), Japan, the Asian Development Bank (ADB) and the International Bank for Reconstruction and Development (IRDB), in decreasing order of their contributions. In 2004-5, India was the largest recipient of the World Bank's aggregate support (US $2.89 billion), as also of the IDA assistance (US $1.1 billion). However, most of these funds are not grants but loans (US $3,416 million out of 3,880 million of total utilized external assistance in 2003–4) which have to be repaid, albeit at low interest rates, leading to a net annual influx of less than a billion dollars, i.e. less than $1 per inhabitant per year.

CENTRALIZATION, BUREAUCRACY AND CORRUPTION

Bureaucracy (IRDP, SGSY)

The wealth of programmes bears witness to the authorities' concern about alleviating rural poverty, but also to a weakness: a clear lack of coordination and integration, which obviously carries a financial penalty and has an adverse effect on their efficiency. For instance, the IRDP was not really worthy of the name. It was originally based on an 'integrated' overall vision of development, involving functional integration of the various sectors (agriculture, industry, education and so on), and spatial integration, with overall plans drawn up for each block. However, it very rapidly became a simple direct aid programme, and SGSY still suffers from the same flaws: credit was distributed to beneficiaries based on more or less obscure criteria, with no real overview nor specific approach at block level (potential resources and main problems), and often without any diagnosis of the households concerned. As the question of infrastructures (roads and markets) was not really tackled and ecological, political and institutional issues such as the dominant position of community leaders and large landowners were barely looked at, little was in fact done to grab poverty by the roots. It is therefore not surprising that most of the loans remained agricultural: investment in trading or small-scale industry failed to tempt many people, except those who were craftsmen and traders by virtue of their caste (potters, weavers, peddlers). The fact that purchases of animals, large and small, never really took off is not surprising either, since no thought was given to providing enough resources to feed them (grazing and feed purchases) or care for them (veterinary services). The female buffaloes bought by the IRDP were often sold on a few days later to buy grain or clothing . . . or pay for a wedding.

Misappropriation (IRDP, SGSY)

IRDP credit was officially intended for production, but the poor had other priorities (consumption). Worse still, in order to repay the IRDP, they often had to resort to informal loans and usurers, which only worsened their situation. Loan recovery rates were still below 30 per cent, but in fact, it was the rich who proved to be the craftiest and thus who repaid the least. A fifth of the selected households in fact benefited illegally from these low-interest loans, while women and agricultural labourers were under-represented, as were isolated villages and the regions in greatest need. The adoption of a system that rotated annually so as to cover villages in turn largely failed to improve the situation, made it even more difficult to obtain loans in good time and compounded the random way in which beneficiaries were selected by itself selecting villages at random. In short, the IRDP was the perfect illustration of the weaknesses of Indian development programmes, and was a victim of the biased, excessively bureaucratic way in which it has been implemented, since for some civil servants, the obsession with fulfilling quotas has been combined with a temptation to divert funding. It is these disappointing results that account for the fact that the number of families helped by this programme fell by 50 per cent in ten years, from 3.4 million in 1989-90 to under 1.7 million in 1998-9.

Dependence on Aid (JRY, ICDS...)

With the JRY and following food-for-work programmes, the choice of beneficiaries has been less biased (there are not many takers for road workers' jobs, which are not very highly considered), but administrative costs are still high and fraud is common (misappropriation of funding or of grain). It has been estimated that in order to transfer Re. 1 to a truly deprived person, the programme has to start with Rs. 4.35. The grain distributed has almost certainly had an anti-inflationary impact on a local scale, but quantities vary: only 2,65,000 tonnes of wheat and rice were distributed in 1993-4, i.e. 0.2 per cent of national output, while in 2003-4, 5 million tonnes were paid, plus 6.6 million released to calamity-affected states, i.e. more than 7 per cent of the output. The wages paid are undoubtedly a lifeline for the poor during the agricultural off-season, but the JRY was generating just 375 million days' work by 1998-9, compared to 896 million in 1995-6. In comparison, the severe drought in 1987 is assumed to have led to the loss of 1.4 billion days. In short, the benefits have often only been temporary, and the results of the work of only limited use: how many latrines have been built and never used (and rapidly ruined by fraud on the part of the entrepreneurs), how many saplings have been eaten, and how many wells have collapsed or been dug too far away from potential users?

The food-for-work programmes, which are theoretically structural development programmes, have in fact proved to be too much like a simple aid programme, like the ICDS, whose educational role is in reality somewhat limited. Here again, its administrators are poorly paid, and often take an excessively bureaucratic view of their work, preferring to distribute contraceptive pills, IUDs and vitamins rather than taking the time to talk to the women involved, who are often illiterate. Moreover, the programme does not cover the whole of India. However, in places where the ICDS has been combined with the Mid-Day Meal Scheme (MDMS), it has played a crucial role, both in increasing the number of children in school and in reducing the birth rate. It has almost undoubtedly been partly responsible for the reduction in illiteracy in India (48 per cent of population in 1991, 35 per cent in 2001), although this figure is still high, with a considerable difference between the sexes (24 per cent of men and 46 per cent of women).

Populism (PDS...)

The same degree of ambiguity surrounds the largest aid programme in India, in terms of the number of people concerned: the PDS. As we have seen, its charitable aspect (see Chapter 3) in fact hides its considerable indirect role in bolstering agricultural prices. This ambiguity is the system's main weakness, given that it claims to simultaneously alleviate poverty, encourage agricultural production, and guarantee low prices for consumers and high prices for producers. This is an open door for all sorts of populism, and it is not surprising that there have been numerous malfunctions, primarily on a financial level. Between 1966 and 1997, the so-called 'food' subsidies set aside to fund the system represented 0.3 of GDP on average, and 2.4 per cent of central government expenditure. The figure was Rs. 258 billion in 2003-4, or 0.93 per cent of GDP. Although the PDS cannot be criticized for this, in view of the population's requirements, many observers are concerned, since these subsidies cover not only the difference between the price at which the PDS buys goods from producers and that at which it sells them on, but also the cost of managing and redistributing stocks, two operations that are the subject of heated debate.

Wastage (PDS...)

In response to calls from the increasingly well-organized cereal sector, the State initially determined and fixed a relatively high procurement price each year, which meant a roughly proportional increase in PDS prices, so as not to increase the budgetary burden too heavily, and to discourage private trading in favour of public purchases. In 2000-01, the FCI bought 16 million tonnes of wheat and 19 million of rice, i.e. 23 per cent of total output, which were added to its existing stocks. By June 2002, these stocks had peaked 65 million tonnes: over a third of global wheat exchanges and the equivalent of all global rice exchanges, and obviously well over the 17 million tonnes considered to be a satisfactory figure at that time of year. With an estimated Rs. 230 million of storage costs per day, this meant a hefty bill, amounting to almost a quarter of the 'food' subsidy. Worse still, to prevent stocks from rotting and empty its warehouses, New Delhi decided in 2000 to sell wheat to domestic and international traders at the price granted by the PDS to people living below the poverty line. This morally debatable operation (why not subsidize consumption among the poor more generously, rather than export?) also proved to be commercially ineffective: grain quality was poor and India had problems finding outlets. Even without planning hiccups (stocks were running at 36 million tonnes in 1995, but two years later, India had to import 2 million tonnes of wheat, despite the fact that the harvest had not been particularly poor), India will find it difficult to export large quantities as this would drive world prices down and it would thus make less profit on its 'surpluses'. Moreover, if it were to export much more, it would also expose its input subsidies to widespread criticism on the international stage, where people would be quick to see them as indirect export subsidies. And if input subsidies have to be cut, procurement prices will have to be raised, or else the verdict in the streets and polling booths will be merciless: in this case, matters really have come full circle (Figure 29).

Corruption (PDS...)

Distribution also places a considerable financial burden on the PDS. A sack of grain travels some 1,500 km on average: cereal surpluses mainly come from the north (Punjab), while the states best served by the PDS are in the south (due to the 'social' policies of the states concerned) and the Himalayas (thanks to a strategic drive on the part of New Delhi to favour its peripheral

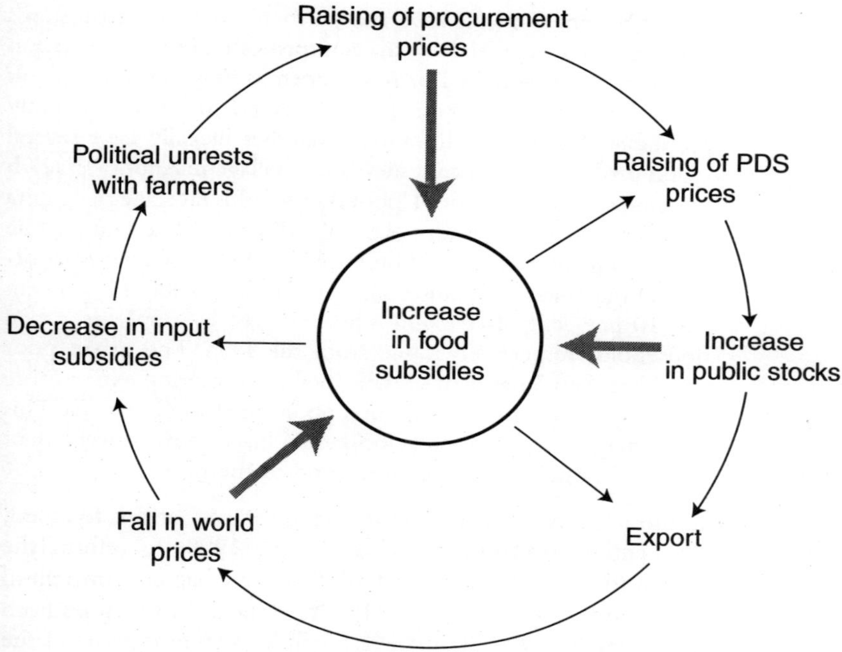

FIGURE 29: THE VICIOUS CIRCLE OF FOOD SUBSIDIES (1998-2003)

states). In addition to transport costs, there are 'leaks' from FCI warehouses to those of the Civil Supplies Corporations in the various states, and from those warehouses to the PDS' Fair Price Shops (FPS). It seems that the number of trucks leaving the warehouses is sometimes greater than the number that arrives at the desired destination. It also appears that further down the chain, FPS managers, who are poorly paid based on the volumes sold, are often tempted to forge ration cards so as to sell the goods obtained in the open market, or to add sand to grain, tamper with weighing equipment, fail to apply the official price in isolated areas, give more to some customers and less to others. In all, according to a 1997 survey by Tata Economic Consultancy Services (TECS), 55 per cent of the oil, 36 per cent of the wheat, 31 per cent of the rice and 23 per cent of the sugar allocated to the PDS do not reach the intended buyers, 'losses' that cannot all be put down to the relatively perishable nature of the products concerned. Moreover, how many isolated villages do not benefit from the PDS (not to mention some urban slums that are not recognized by the authorities)? How many ration shops are never supplied or never open as they are too difficult to reach, or have a customer base deemed to be insufficiently profitable? Conversely, how many families illegally have several ration cards? For instance, a survey of a village in Andhra Pradesh revealed that 60 per cent of 'poor' households (average per capita monthly income of under Rs. 182) did not have cards, while 63 per cent of 'non-poor' households had at least one! According to the National Sample Survey, in 1999-2000 12 per cent and 10 per cent of rice and wheat bought by rural and urban households respectively came from the PDS. The urban poor saved less than 3 per cent of their total consumption expenditure through the system, and the rural poor less than 6 per cent. This is not negligible, but it costs more than Rs. 6 to the government to transfer one rupee's worth of food to the poor.

Centralization (PDS...)

In the hope of targeting and reducing the cost of this food aid, the central government decided in the 1990s to reform the system (the RPDS and then the TPDS, see Chapter 3), which in effect led it to exclude Above Poverty Line (APL) families from the system: in 1999-2000, these families saw wheat prices at the FPS double in less than 15 months. This change of policy was a shock, as until then, APL families had bought more cereals (10.3 million tonnes in 1998-9) than Below Poverty Line (BPL) households (7.2 million). It resulted in a drop in purchases from the PDS, despite the doubling of the allocation to BPL households—viz. 20 kg per month—at 50 per cent of the price quoted to APL households. Wheat purchases fell from almost 8 million tonnes in 1998-9 to less than 5 million the following year. The drop in rice purchases was less marked: the main consumers (the southern states) opted to shoulder some of the burden of the price increase imposed by New Delhi. At the start of 2001, BPL households in Tamil Nadu could buy a kilo of rice for Rs. 3.50, whereas the federal price (CIP) was Rs. 5.65. These same households also saw their allocation of cereals double (from 10 to 20 kilos/month) in 1998, well before the central government issued its instructions in 2000. In Tamil Nadu and elsewhere, questions were also asked about the poverty line applied by the central government, which considered 25 per cent of households in Kerala to be BPL, whereas the state put the figure at 42 per cent. In view of the central government's inflexibility, the Kerala state government decided to subsidize the difference. However, this has proved to be a huge financial burden, and has still failed to resolve the overall crisis (prices that are too high for APL households, abysmal grain quality, and so on): unsold stocks have been left to rot and shop managers are facing bankruptcy.

Instant Socialism

Kerala still has the largest PDS in India, with 97 per cent of its population buying from the system in 2000. There is even a second subsidized circuit, Supplyco Maveli, outside the FCI chains. This situation has resulted from the reduction in the area sown with rice in favour of plantation crops, which is both a cause and a consequence of New Delhi's decision to encourage expansion of the PDS. However, it is not the only explanation. This southern state was also characterized by an active social policy well before the Communist Party's electoral wins, which has put it ahead of the field with respect to numerous human development indicators. In short, in India, the PDS and many other programmes have developed more in areas where people have traditionally been literate and where villagers are in the habit of making themselves heard politically, without relying on large landowners or the authorities. Conversely, they are much less well established or efficient in areas where—ironically—they are most needed, in tribal zones or areas with wide social gaps such as Bihar, in rural areas with an explosive political and social situation and in regions where the commercial infrastructures and level of education are still marginal.

Without a true political will, both the SGSY and the PDS tend to be nothing more than machines distributing subsidies, and although they provide the poor with instant relief and are sociopolitically painless, they do nothing but increase reliance on aid. The authorities have been content to fight the most noticeable consequences of poverty, rather than actually fighting the roots of poverty themselves. As a result, like M.L. Dantwala, some have used the expression 'instant socialism', as it dissolves rapidly, just like coffee.

CHRONIC POVERTY AND UNDER-NUTRITION

The Poverty Line

With a gross national per capita income of $620 in 2004 (US $3,100 allowing for purchasing power parity or PPP), despite the progress made over the years, India is still a poor country (the French average is US $30,090 and the global figure US $8,280, according to the World Bank), much more so than China ($1,290 or US $5,530 allowing for PPP). The change in average incomes is a criterion in assessing the new economic policy introduced in 1991, but also in encouraging or discouraging foreign investment, on which its success largely relies. However, there is also the change in the number of people living below the absolute poverty line. There is widespread agreement that the figure fell significantly between the end of the 1970s and that of the 1980s (from 320 million people, a stable level since 1972-4, to around 300 million, Figure 30), despite steady population growth. However, in 1994, there was heated debate among high-ranking civil servants and other experts about the two primary estimation methods used, which gave contrasting results (17 and 36 per cent of the total population), and consequently prompted radically different conclusions as to the impact of the economic reforms. The Planning Commission eventually opted for the more pessimistic figure: 320 million

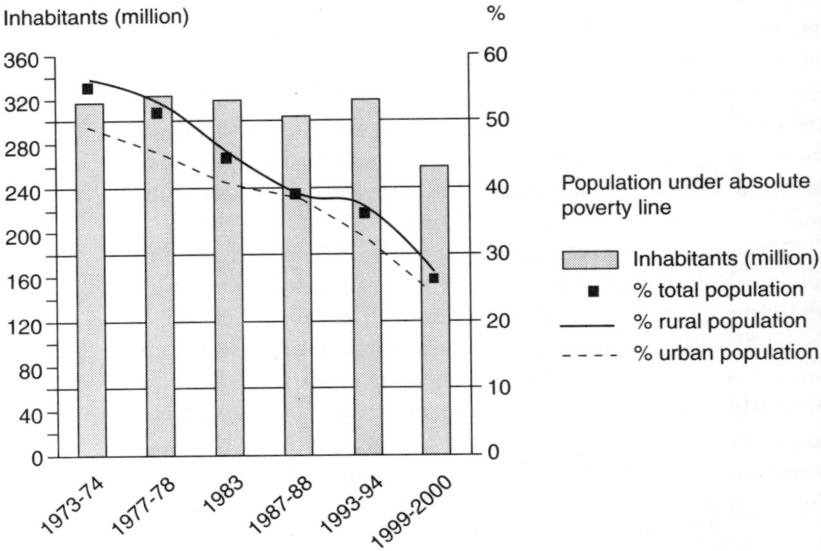

Source: Based on Economic Survey 2001.

FIGURE 30: POPULATION BELOW ABSOLUTE POVERTY LINE (1973-4 TO 1999-2000)

people were assumed to have an income so low that they cannot have a daily diet providing them with 2,400 kilocalories in rural areas and 2,100 kilocalories in urban areas. The National Sample Survey Organization (NSSO) consumer survey had estimated a figure of 26 per cent of the total population in 1999-2000, although the methodology used meant that this figure was not directly comparable with those calculated from 1973-4 to 1993-4. Taking an annual income threshold of Rs. 5,496 per person in urban areas and Rs. 3,936 in rural areas (less than US $7.66 per month) in 1999-2000, it was calculated that the number of people living under the absolute poverty line had dropped by 60 million in six years, at last falling below the 300 million mark, where it had been stuck for at least three decades.

Poverty and Disparities

During the 1990s, other indicators apparently showed clear signs of progress, although again, the changes in methodology over the years meant that it is important to take care when comparing figures (Table 3). Infant mortality had fallen to 66 per thousand live births in 2001 (half the 1951 figure), life expectancy at birth had risen to 65 years (32 years in 1951), and the literacy rate had leapt to over 65 per cent of the population in 2001 (18 per cent in 1951). Bearing in mind that the population has trebled in 50 years, these are impressive figures. Even so, they cannot erase the

TABLE 3: INFANT MORTALITY, LIFE EXPECTANCY AND LITERACY (1951 TO 2001)

Infant mortality (%)	1951	1961	1971	1981	1991	2001
- Rural areas	-	-	13.8	11.9	8.7	7.8
- Urban areas	-	-	8.2	6.2	5.3	4.2
- Mean	14.6	-	12.9	11.0	8.0	6.6
Life expectancy (years)	**1951**	**1961**	**1971**	**1981**	**1991**	**2001**
- Male	32.5	41.9	46.4	50.9	58.6	63.4
- Female	31.7	40.6	44.7	50.0	59.0	66.9
- Mean	32.1	41.3	45.6	50.4	58.7	65.1
Literacy rate (%)	**1951**	**1961**	**1971**	**1981**	**1991**	**2001**
- Male	27.2	40.4	46.0	56.4	64.1	75.9
- Female	8.9	15.3	22.0	29.8	39.3	54.2
- Mean	18.3	28.3	34.5	43.6	52.2	65.4

Source: Census of India, Economic Survey (2001).

really shocking destitution millions of Indians still live in or fall into each year. At the end of the 1990s, it was estimated that half the under-nourished people in the world lived in India, and that more than half of the children under five years old in India were still suffering from varying degrees of malnutrition. Moreover, there are still huge differences between the sexes, and the gaps between the different regions are continuing to widen. For instance, in Bihar, Uttar Pradesh and Rajasthan, more than half of the women were unable to read and write at the turn of the twenty-first century. It is in these states, along with Orissa and Madhya Pradesh, that almost one child in ten dies shortly after birth, and the fertility rate is most out of control. Lastly, it is often in rural areas of these states that pockets of poverty become concentrated and deepen. In 1999-2000, officially 44 per cent of the population in Bihar and 48 per cent in Orissa were BPL, whereas Punjab and Haryana had a low figure of 6 and 7 per cent, thanks to their productive farming systems. West Bengal reached a figure of 32 per cent, in spite of social reforms and the boom in rice growing.

From fish farming to informatics, India is now one of the most dynamic countries in the world, with a growing middle class eager to be seen in fast food outlets, nightclubs and at the wheel of air-conditioned cars. But between January and July 2005, the Government of Maharashtra has also admitted that 2,814 children, mainly from tribal areas, had died of starvation. Both there and elsewhere, physical and mental handicaps, anaemia, suicide and infanticide are rife, and the press has long been tired of reporting on these symptoms of human misery, as the causes are only too obvious: lack of education and of drinking water, insalubrious living conditions, pollution, unemployment or under-employment, starvation wages, etc., along with another factor that has been more difficult to accept since the green revolution: insufficient consumption of protein, fats and other nutrients.

Calories

Are malnutrition and under-nutrition a chronic problem? India's agricultural nutrition profile in relation to the rest of the world, which can be established using FAO statistics, shows some very distinctive characteristics (Table 4). The first is its still modest daily calorie availability: 2,473 kcal per person per day in 2003 (about 2,150 as per the National Sample Survey for 1999-2000),

TABLE 4: AGRO-NUTRITIONAL PROFILES (1999)

	India		China		France		World	
	kg/yr	kcal/d	kg/yr	kcal/d	kg/yr	kcal/d	kg/yr	kcal/d
Cereals, Roots, Tubers	180.0	1,476	268.3	1,869	181.6	987	221.7	1,505
Fruit, Vegetables	100.9	91	226.7	164	214.3	167	156.9	140
Pulses	12.8	122	1.1	10	2.3	20	5.9	57
Fish, Seafood	4.6	9	25.1	36	28.7	42	15.8	28
Meat, Offal, Eggs	6.7	28	66.4	466	125.8	644	48.1	248
Milk (excl. butter)	65.1	113	7.7	16	265.2	373	78.7	122
Vegetable oils, Animal fats, Nuts, Oilseeds	20.8	292	18.6	319	42.0	736	23.0	377
Sugar crops, Sweeteners	39.0	259	6.6	64	41.0	385	31.1	249
Alcohols, Stimulants, Spices and Others	-	28	-	99	-	219	-	83
	Total	2,417		3,042		3,575		2,808

Source: Based on FAO (July 2001).

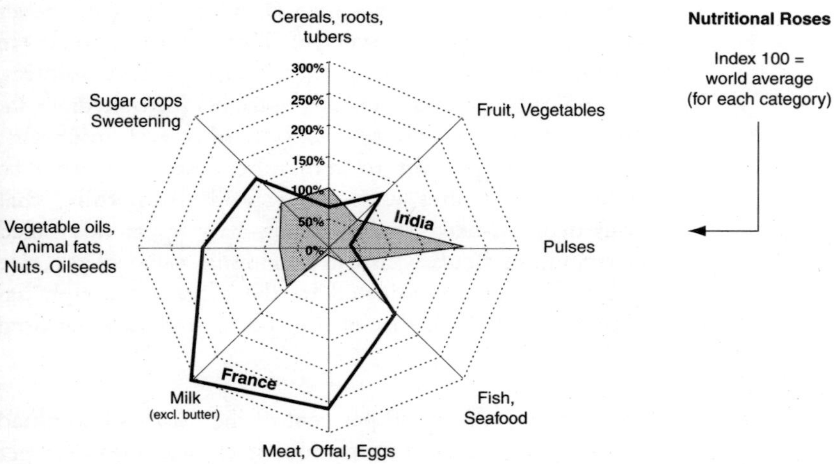

compared to 2,669 for developing countries as a whole (2,940 in China) and 2,809 for the world as a whole (3,623 in France). Human energy requirements obviously vary from one country to another, particularly depending on the climate, but this national average is still very close to the minimum levels quoted by the Indian Council of Medical Research (ICMR): between 2,425 (sedentary activity) and 3,800 kcal per day (high activity) for a 60-kg man and between 1,875 and 2,925 for a 50-kg woman (the authorities base themselves on a figure of 2,400 kcal in rural areas and 2,100 kcal in urban areas). This is not counting the variations masked by a national average: some people consume more calories than necessary, while others consume fewer (two-thirds of Indians in 1993-4, 52 per cent in rural areas and 15 per cent in urban areas, i.e. more than the number of people estimated to be BPL based on their incomes). Daily calorie availability has increased by more than 400 kcal per inhabitant since the end of the 1970s, partly as a result of the green revolution. But this revolution failed to help diversify production and food consumption systems: public support was massively centred on wheat and rice (HYVs, procurement prices, input subsidies, PDS), and India is still, just as it was at the time of Independence and just like most developing countries, a 'traditional cereal-based agricultural country'. In 2003, with 159 kg per person per day, cereal availability in India was among the highest in the world (118 kg on average in South America, 146 kg in Africa) along with China (158 kg) and many other Asian countries (162 kg on average). These cereals, which are more evenly distributed among the population than calories, help to supply the necessary energy, nutrients (carbohydrate, fat and protein) and micronutrients (vitamins and minerals). However, it is important to remember that it is vital to supplement such a diet with other foods (something that numerous decision-makers and advisers have apparently failed to understand), particularly as the nutritional value of the rice and wheat varieties disseminated by the green revolution has proved to be lower than that of the species and varieties used previously.

Fats

In 1999 (Table 4), almost 60 per cent of the calories consumed in India came from particularly carbohydrate-rich cereals (56 per cent in China), while oils, fats and nuts provided just 10 per cent, despite their high lipid content. However, fat provides twice as much energy as the other two types of nutrients (8 kcal/g, compared to 4 for carbohydrate and protein). More generally, India is characterized by its very low fat availability in relation to the rest of the world: 53 g per person per day in 2003, compared to 68 g for developing countries as a whole (96 g in China) and a global average of 80 g (168 g in France). Fat is also the most unevenly distributed nutrient: in the mid-1990s, NSSO consumption surveys per income group revealed that as fats are concentrated in the most expensive foods (vegetable oils, animal products, dairy products, etc.), two-thirds of the Indian population (80 per cent of rural dwellers and 20 per cent of urbanites) had a diet seriously lacking in fat: fat accounted for just 15 per cent of total calorie intake. This latter percentage is the minimum quoted by the ICMR, FAO and WHO for adult men (Table 5, with a figure of 20 per cent for pregnant women and 50 per cent for newborn babies). One particularly dramatic consequence of this shortfall is that 16 per cent of Indians (5 per cent of urbanites and 19 per cent of rural dwellers, concentrated in Orissa, Assam, West Bengal and Bihar) were not covering their essential fatty acid requirements in 1993-4, whereas it is fatty acids that govern normal development in foetuses and subsequently in humans, who cannot synthesize these unsaturated vegetable fats (oils). Conversely, in prosperous areas such as Punjab, fat intake is more than satisfactory, and indeed very often excessive, which can stimulate the worrying development of obesity and cardiovascular diseases, like in many other regions of the world (especially amongst poor people who migrated from rural to urban areas).

The yellow (oilseeds) revolution, which served to increase annual per capita vegetable oil availability in India by 2 kg in ten years (7.7 kg in 1996 compared to 5.5 kg in 1987, i.e. an extra 50 kcal per person per day on average) was apparently of greatest benefit to the upper classes, who also buy the most meat, offal and eggs, products that are not yet widely eaten in India despite their high fat content (these foods provide 50 per cent of dietary fat in China) and, obviously, their high protein content.

Protein

There is a third way in which India differs from other countries in terms of diet: its animal protein consumption was 3.5 times (fish and seafood) to 7 times (meat, offal and eggs) lower than the global average in 1999 (Table 5). Indians cook 50 times less pork, 15 times less poultry and 10 times fewer eggs than the Chinese. However, it is important to remember milk, which is also a good source of protein: availability in India has more or

TABLE 5: NUTRITIONAL AVAILABILITY AND RECOMMENDATIONS (1999)

			India	China	France	World	WHO standards	
							Min.	Max.
Availability (national average)	Energy	(kcal/day/person)	2,417	3,042	3,575	2,808	-	-
	Carbohydrates	(g/day/person)	450.9	516.2	448.7	477.5	-	-
	Protein	(g/day/person)	58.4	83.1	115.9	75.3	-	-
	Fat	(g/day/person)	47.5	80.6	164.6	74.6	-	-
Contribution to total energy	Carbohydrates	(4 kcal/g)	75 %	68%	50%	68%	55%	75%
	Protein	(4 kcal/g)	10%	11%	13%	11%	10%	15%
	Fat	(8 kcal/g)	16%	21%	37%	21%	15%	35%

Source: Based on FAO, July 2001.

less doubled since the white revolution (68 kg per person per year in 2003, compared to 32 kg in 1970). Even so, the figure is still lower than the world average—81 kg—considerably dragged down by China (almost 17 kg in 2003, and less than 9 kg in 1999 according to FAO's estimates). Crucially, high-protein vegetable consumption (peas, lentils and other pulses) in India is twice the global average, but even so, this taste for pulses is not enough to compensate for the Indians' low animal protein consumption, which stems as much from economic factors (animal protein is expensive to produce) as from socio-religious factors (Hinduism and Islam). Total daily protein availability was less than 60 g per person in 2003 (35 g from cereals and 7 from milk), whereas the global average (including India) exceeded 75 g (82 g in China and 117 g in France). Those 60 g provide some 240 kcal per day, i.e. 10 per cent of the minimum average daily intake recommended by the WHO and the ICMR. The NSSO statistics for 1993-4 gave slightly higher results (11 per cent), which moreover were uniform irrespective of income group, due to the relative security of access to cereals (and thus to the proteins they contain, except for lysine). Even so, at the time, some two-thirds of the population had an insufficient energy intake, and as a result, some Indian nutritionists opted to use a set figure rather than a percentage in relation to energy value, viz., 60 g of protein per day. Some 60 per cent of people (those with the lowest incomes in 1993-4) were below that figure (45 per cent in rural areas and 15 per cent in urban areas). As the Green Revolution did not include pulses, their availability has fallen by half since its launch (12 kg per inhabitant per year in 2003, compared to 23 kg in 1961, according to the FAO). Prices have rocketed since 1993 in particular (see Chapter 8), despite the fact that pulses have traditionally been a vital protein supplement to cereals, for want of cheaper substitutes (the number of calories of vegetable origin required to produce one calorie of animal origin goes from 3 to 7 or more).

Food Security

The fourth and last major characteristic is that India consumes only small amounts of fruit and vegetables (38 and 69 kg per person per year respectively, compared to a global average of 62 and 118 kg in 2003). These foods are not only a source of water (which makes up two-thirds of the human body, and which is of increasingly dubious quality in India, whether drawn from wells or from the tap), but also of vitamins and minerals, micronutrients which are just as essential for physical and mental development in humans. This low fruit and vegetable consumption, combined with low or insufficient consumption of other foods, is reflected in particularly widespread and marked vitamin and mineral deficiencies among young children and pregnant women, particularly in terms of vitamin A (slow growth, visual deficiencies, reproductive difficulties and low immunity), iron (anaemia), and iodine (goitre and physical and mental disorders). In short, while India is proud to have achieved cereal self-sufficiency, it is still far from achieving food security, and even nutritional security: nothing like all its inhabitants have access to the food they need to lead a healthy and active life, irrespective of their income and circumstances. This sorry situation is compounded by another, more recent phenomenon: increasingly Americanized consumption patterns among those who can afford them. Like many other western food patterns, the 'American way of life' is far from providing the perfect example of a balanced diet. Above all, for the time being, it cannot be transposed to India without rendering the diet eaten by the country's poorest inhabitants even more inadequate, since it is based on calories and nutrients that are expensive to produce: the agricultural production required to feed an American consumer is currently five times that required for an Indian consumer.

7. The Sacking of Natural Resources

Like most South Asian countries, India is exploiting intensively its natural resources, not without substantial wastages and risks of ecological catastrophe. This is particularly true for water, drawn from dams, wells or village ponds, which is now not only used in vast quantities for demanding subsidized crops such as rice and sugar cane, but also more and more coveted by a wide range of activities other than agriculture. Besides this increasing and competing use of water, its runoff or stagnation has led to soil degradation, just like deforestation and over-grazing which are also widespread. In short, population pressure on natural resources has resulted in an energy and ecological stress that looks likely to jeopardize the Indian development model in the medium term. The problem is not peculiar to India, but is undoubtedly showing how deep and worrying is the trap. Amongst closely related causes for concern is not only the erosion of biodiversity but also the patenting of living organisms, towards which India is currently heading along with the other signatories of the GATT intellectual property agreements. There seems to be little legislative or political room for manoeuvre, between the protests from anti-imperialist NGOs and pressure from multinationals, between the wish to develop a national biotechnology sector and the fight against biopiracy.

THE WATER WAR

Cereal self-sufficiency in India is largely reliant on irrigation, since almost three quarters of the total cereal crop is currently grown in irrigated cropping systems. There is a price to pay for this. In 1997–8, agricultural irrigation represented 83 per cent of the country's total water consumption (compared to 12 per cent in France, according to the World Bank), with rice alone using 45 per cent, alongside sugar cane, which is also highly water-intensive (on average, it takes 200 tonnes of water to produce 1 tonne of sugar cane). Counting other uses (household, industrial, energy generation, and so on), which will inevitably

Water

intensify in the coming years (Table 6), the subcontinent probably used 629 km^3 of fresh water that year, when the monsoon was normal. The enormity of this figure is not as dramatic as it may at first appear: of the 4,000 km^3 of rainfall in India each year (see Chapter 3), some 1,086 km^3 (690 km^3 of surface water and 396 km^3 of groundwater) could be used without any ecological risk, according to the National Commission for Integrated Water Resources Development Plan. The World Bank, for its part, quoted around 1,900 km^3 of available fresh water in 1998, which in relation to the population is far from critical compared to the situation in many other countries. However, water is probably the most crucial and sensitive issue that India will have to resolve in the twenty-first century. The first question is supply, since the usable resource (1,086 km^3) represented barely 1,100 m^3 per inhabitant in 1997-8 (barely more than the 1,000 m^3 below which a country is considered to be under 'stress'), and availability is set to fall as the population continues to grow. The other main factor is distribution: current consumption figures do not provide any pointers as to the differences in supply over time (seasonal and annual variations) or space (the Brahmaputra Basin alone accounts for 32 per cent of the available resource), or to effective use of the resource within both the economy and the population, in either quantity or quality terms. India has very serious problems on these various levels, which have resulted in veritable 'water wars', proof, if proof were needed, that the situation is already giving cause for concern.

TABLE 6: WATER CONSUMPTION PER SECTOR (1997-8) AND FORECAST (2025)

	1997-8		2025	
	m^3 (billion)	%	m^3 (billion)	%
Total	629		784-850	
- Agricultural use (irrigation)	524	83.3	561-618	72.1
- Industrial use	30	4.8	67	8.2
- Domestic use	30	4.8	55-62	7.2
- Energy generation	9	1.4	31-33	3.9
- Others	36	5.7	70	8.6

Source: A.D. Mohile, *Central Water Commission*, February 2000.

Reservoirs (Narmada, Tehri...)

The war began with the reservoirs, which were supposed to capture and distribute an unpredictable and unevenly shared resource more efficiently (see Chapter 3). In 1998, 147 'major projects' (to irrigate over 10,000 ha), launched 15 years previously, had still not been completed. Administrative delays and errors of appreciation on the part of the authorities (dispersal of funds, underestimation of the constraints and of the resources required to maintain the installations and build and operate irrigation canals) have been largely, but not wholly, responsible for this costly situation. There is also active opposition to such schemes, which have various types of consequences: human (population displacement), economic (flooding of rich valleys), ecological (ecosystem destruction), and even health (proliferation of malaria) and seismic (some experts would have it that the weight of the stored water increases the earthquake risk). The considerable benefits of such schemes may thus be offset by some equally significant drawbacks, which moreover are generally borne by people or areas that do not receive anything in return. For instance, for several decades now, three states in the west of the country have been fighting over the waters of the Narmada, under an ambitious hydroelectric programme launched in the early 1960s. Of the 165 'major' and 'medium' projects planned, many have seen the light of day, and the conflicts of interest or of opinions are now focusing on the Sardar Sarovar main dam project. One camp comprises industrialists and supporters of agricultural productivism, but also Gujarat state, which is the main beneficiary as it accounts for the major share of the 1.8 million hectares scheduled to be irrigated. Their opponents are Madhya Pradesh state, upstream of the dam, which accounts for 80 per cent of the villages that would be flooded by the project, supported by the NGO Narmada Bachao Andolan, which is protesting about both the ecological impact of the project and the conditions imposed on the 40,000 families due to be displaced. Those conditions have shocked even the World Bank, which has withdrawn the funding it initially promised. Construction of the Sardar Sarovar dam was halted from 1995 to 1999, but subsequently resumed, despite the fact that the Madhya Pradesh and Maharashtra governments acknowledged that those people who had already been displaced had not received all the land they were promised as compensation.

Demand for water and electricity (estimated at 1,450 MW) is such that the future of a few tens of thousands of tribals carries little weight.

The Tehri dam, on a tributary of the Ganges in the Himalayan Uttarakhand, is another highly controversial project. Under the original 1972 plan, it was to be over 260 m high, the highest in Asia, and was to produce 1,000 MW. It was due to be built in a zone highly liable to earthquakes, and was designed to resist quakes of over 8 on the Richter Scale. The town of Tehri has been rebuilt on higher ground, and Tehri Phase 1 started in 2006 in spite of the efforts of its opponents (notably hunger strikes by the Gandhian leader S. Bahuguna), who have questioned its solidity and denounced the dubious amount of compensation promised to the 20,000 families due to be displaced. There have also been complaints from Hindu nationalist groups about interfering with a river as sacred as Mother Ganga. Given the circumstances, it is highly unlikely that the Ganges Basin, which alone accounts for 36 per cent of India's surface water and 40 per cent of its groundwater, will ever be fully equipped.

Water Sharing (Kaveri, Krishna...)

This leaves the existing installations and irrigation schemes. However, in view of the various problems that the Green Revolution served to highlight (access to water governs the use of HYVs, fertilizers and electricity, and thus productivity and income), it is clear that any conflict in this respect will be just as violent. Alongside disputes between communities, which sometimes end in bloodshed at the village level, there are numerous quarrels between states, since they are responsible for water supplies under the Constitution. In the case of basins stretching over several states, New Delhi does have the power to act as arbitrator (Inter-State Water Disputes Act, 1956), but it has always struggled to enforce court decisions. For instance, every drought year, Karnataka is reluctant to release the amount of water from the Kaveri to which Tamil Nadu is entitled, despite the fact that it is under a legal obligation to do so. This further complicates production conditions for Indian farmers: not only do they have to deal with climatic uncertainties, they also have to cope with political ones!

More generally, it is extremely difficult to make basins with surplus water (Indus, Brahmaputra, Narmada, Mahanadi,

Godavari) release water to structurally deficient basins (Kutch, Pennar, Kaveri, and so on). The National Water Development Agency (NWDA), founded in 1982, is supposed to support and manage such operations, but is still finding it difficult. Its plan of river-linking across the subcontinent is debatable for technical, economical and ecological reasons, as well as political ones. For instance, the Telugu Ganga, a diversion of the Krishna (a river in Andhra Pradesh) towards Chennai (capital of Tamil Nadu), was hotly disputed by the farmers of Telangana through whose land it flows: they were furious at having to supply a neighbouring state with water while they themselves were in a semi-arid zone. However, they eventually won their battle for a share of the precious water.

Canal Irrigation

Even if it is available, is this precious resource distributed fairly? Unfortunately not, in most cases, with some consumers using vast quantities and leaving just a few drops for the weakest or most isolated consumers, in some cases even selling them at the best possible price. On average, the completed reservoirs are only irrigating 30 to 40 per cent of the planned area. The government has tried to remedy the many possible reasons for this situation, albeit with little success (see Chapter 3). Those reasons include poor pipe design (45 per cent of the total volume of water is apparently lost due to infiltration) and over-irrigation of crops in relation to their actual requirements (a loss that is estimated to amount to 15 per cent of the total volume). However, it is important to remember that as soon as they are in a position to irrigate their land, it is also in the interests of Indian farmers to switch to crops that are heavily subsidized by the authorities despite being very water-intensive (rice and sugar cane in particular), which further reduces the possibilities of sharing the available water with neighbouring areas. Those same authorities also seem to condone a system that maintains insufficiently drained areas alongside others suffering from water stress: the Ministry of Water Resources is determined to maximize water availability without worrying about efficient use, while the Ministry of Agriculture is aiming for intensification without giving much thought to the direct and indirect costs generated by the varieties and techniques it is promoting, and there is little contact between these two ministries and the one (Revenue Department) in-charge of collecting the fees paid by irrigating farmers. In any event, those fees are ridiculously low, due to the farming lobbies' political clout: water prices have not been increased for 30 years in Tamil Nadu, and water was declared free in Punjab in 1997. For want of sufficient revenue, the state is reluctant to invest in new installations or even maintain the existing ones, which obviously does little to help cut wastage and even less to reduce the considerable inequality of access. In short, there is a lack of bodies such as the Water Agencies in France: basin-based institutions capable of managing surface as well as underground water from A to Z, in a—as far as possible—democratic and responsible way.

Irrigation by Tanks, Pats, and Surangams

There is also a cruel lack of attention to and support of certain collection and application techniques in India. Such techniques may be modern, like sprinkling (just 1.3 per cent of the irrigated area) or drip irrigation (about 3,50,000 ha in 2003, including half in Maharashtra for vines and bananas), but also traditional. The country already has ingenious systems that world famous militant environmentalists such as the late Anil Agarwal among others have been trying to rehabilitate since the end of the 1990s. These systems are not always very old, but have often been abandoned despite the fact that they could irrigate using negligible amounts of equipment. In Jhabua district (Madhya Pradesh), for instance, the Bhil tribals divert the tributary torrents of the Narmada using small mud and stone dams that raise the water level upstream by 30 to 60 cm. The water flows into a diversion channel (*pat*) that runs above the level of the river to transport water up the slope through mini-aqueducts made from hollow tree trunks. Relatively high-lying plots can be irrigated in this way without pumping water, and above all can be cultivated during the dry season. However, *pats* are still a collective system: they have to be rebuilt every year, and it is up to the family irrigating its plot on a given day to carry out any maintenance required. The same goes for the tip of the Indian peninsula, north of Kerala, with the *surangams*, which are horizontal tunnels used to transport groundwater to the bottom of a slope, like the ancient *qanats* in the Middle East. The largest are up to 300 m long, and require vertical ventilation shafts. These techniques have declined sharply as a result of competition from new irrigation methods (which are nevertheless more costly in both economic and ecological terms), and of the break-up of rural societies. Unfortunately, it has been more or less the same story for the often architecturally remarkable tanks that are one of the oldest irrigation systems in India. They have often been abandoned by the state, which has been responsible for them since the British colonial period, or by villagers in the case of the smallest ones, and are gradually being filled in. As a result, their crucial function in restoring groundwater levels is no longer fulfilled, despite the fact that the green revolution centred on large-scale use of groundwater, and this veritable plundering of resources will almost inevitably mean ecological suicide at some stage in the future.

Well Irrigation

The state in which Indian groundwater reserves have been left is shocking in many respects. Access to this common good is restricted to individual landowners, since they enjoy the usufruct of subsoil. The lack of water meters, and more generally of any form of collective regulation, has led landowners to use this common resource at will, hampered only by the power of their pumps and the length of their pipes and hoses. Lastly, since the 1970s the State has been encouraging the sinking of new tube wells (see Chapter 3), and while it has scaled down the incentives since the 1990s (restriction of NABARD loans, imposition of a minimum distance between wells, bans on connection to the electricity grid, and so on), it has maintained its heavy subsidies of the electricity required for pumping (in 2000-1, the average charge was Re. 0.28/kWh, i.e. 9 per cent of the unit cost of supply), or even to supply it free of charge, for instance in Punjab and Tamil Nadu. With population growth, this has naturally led to over-exploitation of the available resource, a trend that is now both accelerating and becoming increasingly concentrated: in 2000, of 673 blocks/taluks using more than 100 per cent of the annual recharge capacity of their groundwater, 57 per cent were concentrated in the six states quoting—but for how long?—the best rice or wheat yields in the country (Tamil Nadu, Karnataka, Rajasthan, Gujarat, Haryana and above all Punjab): 59 per cent of the tehsils in Punjab (and 8 per cent of the blocks/taluks in India) are considered to be 'over-exploited' (Map 10). Between 1980 and 1998, while several large aquifers remained unused for want of funds or electricity, for instance in Bihar or eastern Uttar Pradesh, almost 30 per cent of Indian districts saw the level of their groundwater reserves drop by at least 4 m (48 cm per year since 1974 in Kurukshetra district, Haryana).

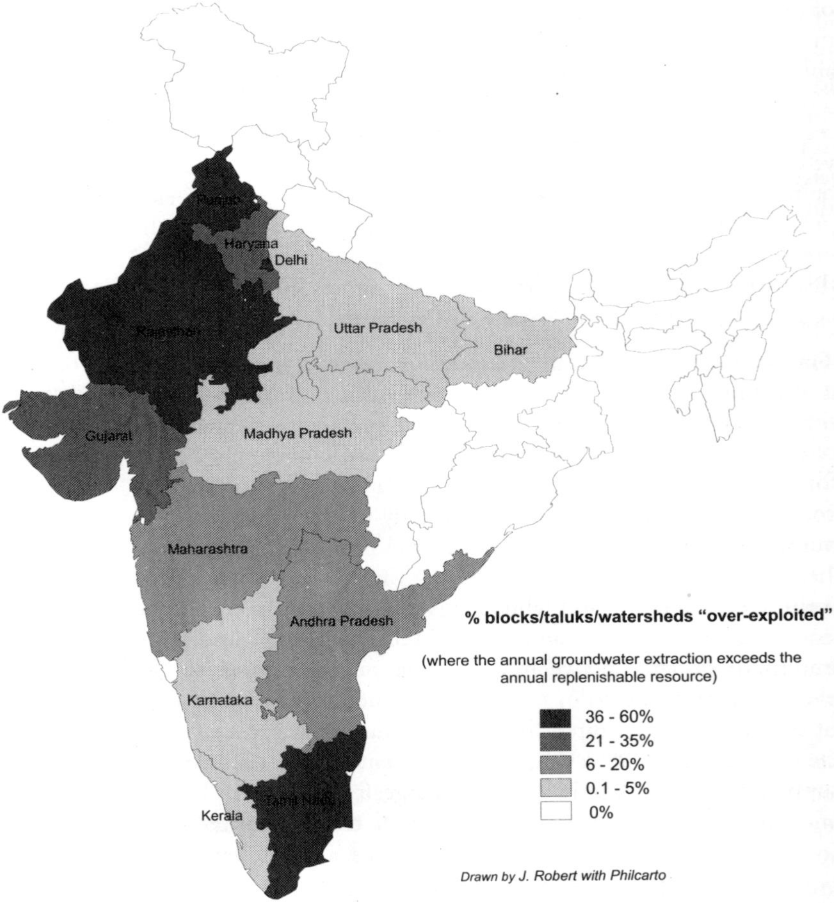

Source: Based on Central Ground Water Board.

MAP 10: FALLING WATER TABLES (2003)

Social inequalities have also worsened. Small-scale farmers no longer have the means to invest in sufficiently deep wells to reach an ever-deeper water table, particularly in the crystalline bedrocks of the Deccan Plateau. The new legislation on minimum spacing has meant situational advantages for some: in Gujarat, for instance, well owners can prevent any new wells being bored within an area of up to 144 ha. These various factors account for the development of a parallel water market (40 to

60 per cent of the water drawn in Gujarat is estimated to be sold in this way), which has increased not only the social dominance of the waterlords, but also the profitability of pumping, whereas the increasing cost of extraction had previously been one of the last remaining safeguards against the dangerous mortgages being taken out on the future of India's aquifers.

ENVIRONMENTAL DAMAGES

Degraded Soils (Salinization, Waterlogging, Erosion...)

The race for groundwater, which has also affected urban areas engendering the risk of eventual subsidence, has already resulted in fresh water pollution with arsenic (Bengal), fluoride (Gujarat and Rajasthan) and on a larger scale with salt, not just in coastal areas as might be expected, but also in arid environments where it is now necessary to bore such deep wells that saltwater aquifers are being reached. The resulting soil salinization, which eventually rules out any form of crop farming, is not a new phenomenon in India, but is accelerating: fewer than 4 million hectares were affected in 1950, compared to very roughly 11 million in 1997. This problem is combined with another that has been markedly exacerbated by the green revolution and its disastrous management of irrigation systems: waterlogging, which has practically multiplied by ten the area of asphyxiated land that could otherwise be used to grow rice: around 1.4 million hectares in 1950, compared to 13 in 1997 or thereabouts. This begs the question of how many irrigation projects were designed without drainage systems and involving excessive water applications. Moreover, these factors are combined with other far from negligible obstacles: north of the Ganges, for instance, most of the tributaries and canals flow north to south, and water evacuation runs up against roads and railways, which are mainly east to west. Lastly, when there are large quantities of water and consequently runoff, this causes erosion, which removes not only soil but also tonnes of nitrogen, phosphorus and potassium nutrients (the Indian government puts the figure at 5.8 to 8.4 million tonnes a year, which is apparently a conservative estimate). This means less for crops, but more in reservoirs, which lose between 1 and 2 per cent of their storage capacity each year as a result of silting up. This is compounded by wind erosion, particularly in the far west of the country, and the area suffering from erosion in 1997 was estimated at almost 167 million ha, compared to around 110 million in 1950. These estimates are very rough, but in all, salinization, waterlogging and other factors (lower soil fertility due to monoculture or over-frequent slash-and-burn, flooding, opencast mining, etc.) can be estimated to have resulted in some 200 million ha of more or less degraded land in India by the end of the 1990s (Figure 31), at least 80 million more than in 1950, representing 60 per cent of the official geographical area of 329 million ha. The Energy Research Institute (TERI) put the agricultural production shortfalls or losses resulting directly from this situation at Rs. 89 billion to 232 billion in 1997, or 30 to 75 per cent of the total value of oil imports, India's largest item of overseas expenditure.

Deforestation and Over-grazing

Water and wind erosion of the soil is exacerbated by deforestation and over-grazing, which also reduce the possibilities of aquifer regeneration. In the name of conservation, the state has taken over most of the forests, but also substantial amounts of village (common) land, which is far from being a solution in itself. Even if they still have access to the land,

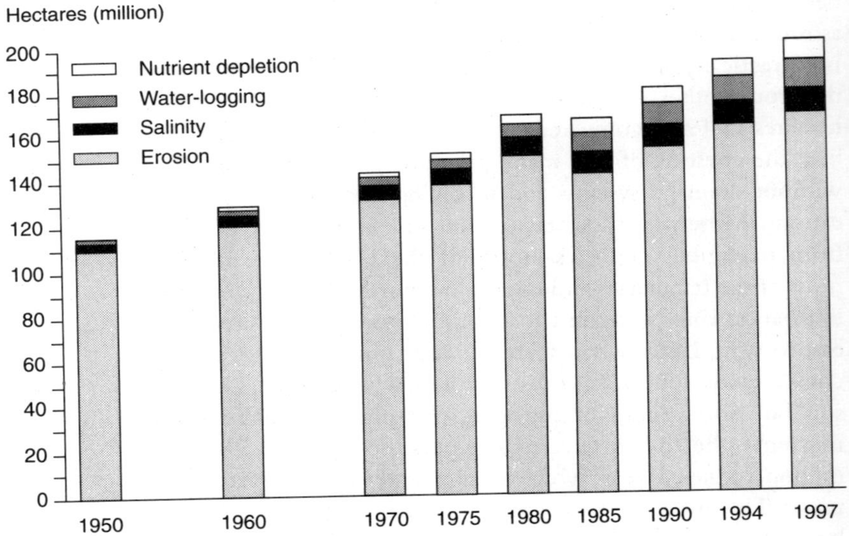

Source: Based on Tata Energy Research Institute, 1998.

FIGURE 31: SOIL DEGRADATION (1950 TO 1997)

dispossessed villagers tend to make even more excessive use of a resource for which they are no longer responsible. However, combined with active reforestation on the part of forestry services, it has helped to keep the forest cover rate in India at 21 per cent (including open forest, in 2003). Better management on the part of some communities that have been made more aware or reminded of the importance of their environmental capital may also have played a part, especially since the implementation of Joint Forest Management in the 1990s that gives to local people some duties and rights on (mostly) degraded forest previously managed by the State Forest Departments only. Also positive are the effects of planting trees on farms. The success of non-native species is very important in this respect, for instance eucalyptus on good land or mesquite (*Prosopis juliflora*) in more difficult areas. Similarly, in Tamil Nadu, casuarina is increasingly being grown in former paddy fields, as it takes just five years and hardly any work to grow and then fetches a good price when sold as scaffolding timber or firewood for use in cities. These new plantings are a threat to food production, and to the labourers who have traditionally worked in the rice plantings, but farmers do not care when offered the opportunity to profit from new markets and reduce their production costs. There are similar problems with eucalyptus, which is highly water-intensive and whose leaves tend to sterilize the surrounding land.

The area of forest in India is no longer falling, but in 2003 almost 42 per cent of forest had a canopy cover density of less than 40 per cent, and at least 10 per cent was in reality encroached with illegal crops. Shifting slash-and-burn cropping in Orissa and the Himalayas is continuing to degrade a million ha or so each year, as a result of shorter fallow periods (down from 20-30 to 3-6 years) necessitated by population growth. Demand for timber or industrial wood (brick and paper manufacture) is also growing, and demand for pasture even more so: the number of goats has doubled in 30 years (see Chapter 5), and as far as larger livestock species are concerned, there is now only 0.15 ha of land per head (including unreserved forests, but excluding fallow). It would take 88 million ha just to make up the fodder shortfall (see Chapter 5). These problems are compounded by the demand for firewood, which is huge due to the lack or excessive cost of other sources of energy.

Fuel

In 1992-3, an NCAER survey revealed that an average rural household consumed 2.5 kg of firewood per day, while in urban areas, firewood still provided 33 per cent of the energy used for cooking, although 50 per cent came from gas (LPG) and paraffin (kerosene). The State subsidizes kerosene through the PDS, but obviously not sufficiently, particularly in rural areas, where it accounts for less than 5 per cent of household energy consumption. People prefer dried cow dung (17 per cent) and crop residue (13 per cent) (which could otherwise be used to fertilize their fields), and particularly logs (32 per cent) and branches (29 per cent). In order to save firewood, and also to reduce smoke emissions, which can cause serious lung diseases (according to the TERI, 90 per cent of rural and 35 per cent of urban households are exposed to such pollution inside their homes), the government is also promoting more ecologically sound stoves than the traditional *chulha*. Similarly, it is facilitating the installation of *gobar gas* household digesters, which mix animal manure and water to make methane and fertilizer. Lastly, for a long time now, it has been encouraging non-conventional energy generation (notably wind and solar power), albeit without making it a budget priority. Conventional electricity generation uses by far the major part of the energy budget and is the greatest cause for concern, in addition to the constantly growing oil import bill ($30 billion in 2004-5, or 27 per cent of India's imports bill).

Electricity

Of the 587 billion kWh generated in 2004-5, 83 per cent came from primarily coal-fired thermal power stations (14 per cent from hydroelectric stations and 3 per cent from nuclear). India has considerable coal reserves, but the coal is of poor quality, which has two consequences. The first is severe air pollution: 15 million tonnes of emissions (suspended particles, nitrogen oxides and sulphur dioxide) in 1997, according to the TERI, 50 times more than in 1947 and 5 million tonnes more than the equally worrying pollution caused by the various modes of transport (carbon monoxide, nitrogen oxides, hydrocarbons, and so on). The second is its inability to satisfy the ever-growing demand for electricity, particularly as losses within the distribution system officially amounted to over 20 per cent of output in 1999 (and over 40 per cent, according to some experts), due to the poor state of repair of the distribution grid and numerous illegal connections. The shortfall at peak times was estimated at 24 per cent in 1999 (and much more in some regions), even though 40 per cent of the Indian population still does not have access to electricity! This shortfall at present means frequent power cuts, or at best rationing of the supply to industry in favour of agriculture or vice versa, which is a very serious handicap for production operations and which forces producers to buy costly generators and the fuel required to run them.

The financial situation of the State Electricity Boards (SEB) is catastrophic. Till recently they had triple responsibility—to produce, transmit and distribute electricity. They have long been controlled by local political leaders, heavily subsidizing the electricity supplied to farmers (see Chapter 8), who primarily use it for irrigation (31 per cent of total consumption in 1998-9, compared to 34 per cent for industry and 21 per cent for households, etc.). In some states, this electricity is entirely free, again in the name of the fight against poverty (35 per cent of tube well owners have less than 2 ha of land). This encourages wastage on their part and unpaid bills and fraud on the part of other users due to the differences in charge rates (particularly in industry, which is taxed). This means that most of the SEBs are heavily in debt to both the private and public sectors. These SEBs have been undergoing restructuring since the end of the 1990s as part of the gradual liberalization of the sector, which is now even open to overseas investment. However, despite the Electricity Act, 2003, which provides a framework for privatization and competition, it is not hard to understand the lack of enthusiasm to date on the part of the private sector, given the particularly low charge rates granted to the politically sensitive agricultural sector.

Pollution (Fertilizers, Pesticides...)

The Indian agricultural sector is a heavy consumer not only in terms of electricity, but also hydrocarbons, via fertilizers (see Chapter 3), which too are heavily subsidized (see Chapter 8). This results in yet more wastage that is just as harmful as excessive water consumption. In Mahendragarh district (Haryana), for instance, over-use of cheap chemical fertilizers has resulted in nitrate levels in water of up to 1,310 mg/litre (the WHO maximum is 50 mg), not counting heavy metals (lead, cadmium, zinc, copper), which are found in particularly high concentrations in phosphate fertilizers. The same problem occurs a little further north, in Punjab, where cancer is now the fourth largest cause of death, after heart attacks, malaria and respiratory disease; pesticide residues in water and plants are among the prime suspects. True, pesticide consumption is relatively low in India as a whole (540 mg/ha in 2000-1), and as a consequence of the adoption of a bio-intensive Integrated Pest Management Programme, the national consumption of pesticides has come down by 28 per cent between 1994-5 and 2001-2, reaching 43,600 tonnes. Nevertheless, it is sometimes considerable locally (about 1,500 mg/ha in Tamil Nadu). Above all, it is important to bear in mind that in 1985, 70 per cent of the pesticides in common use in India had already been banned or were subject to strict restrictions in developed countries due to their toxicity. They included DDT or hexachlorohexane (HCH), which had been banned in Europe by then but was still being applied on the subcontinent by workers without gloves, and often too close to harvest time (HCH, an organochlorine compound, has a half-life of 80-110 days). Moreover, it is these products that cotton growers in Andhra Pradesh, Maharashtra or Karnataka take to commit suicide as they are unable to pay their suppliers for the costly (often adulterated) insecticides they had ordered, to which parasites are in any event becoming increasingly resistant. By the late 1990s, it was estimated that a quarter of the cotton crop was being lost each year as a result of this resistance, despite the fact that cotton accounts for 55 per cent of the pesticides used by Indian farmers.

More insidiously, in addition to hormonal imbalances in the human body, pesticide residues also apparently inhibit folic acid absorption and may thus be responsible—according to Indian doctors such as S.G. Kabra in Jaipur—for the 8,000 or so babies born each year in Rajasthan with neural malformations. Most die within a few months of birth, and those who survive are handicapped for life. If we add to this the reports of fluorine (Rajasthan, Gujarat) and arsenic pollution (Bengal), and also the cases resulting from the increasingly common application of sludge or compost produced from urban or agro-industrial waste, the ecological track record of the intensive agriculture practised in India is far from positive. Nothing is spared, be it the soil, water or air. However, the international community's main concerns about Indian agriculture and its effects on man and the environment are on a much higher plane altogether.

Greenhouse gases

It is now widely acknowledged that carbon dioxide, water vapour, methane and other gases such as freons (CFCs) trap some of the thermal radiation produced by the Earth within the atmosphere, resulting in a 'greenhouse effect' and subsequently in global warming, which could have catastrophic consequences. India is already one of the world's leading methane producers with its rice fields and the manure produced by its livestock. Due to deforestation and above all due to increasing fossil fuel consumption (in New Delhi, the number of cars is growing by 15 to 20 per cent per year since the late 1990s), the subcontinent is also unfortunately a major producer of carbon dioxide (908 million tonnes in 2000, compared to 675 million in 1990, according to the World Bank), and its often outdated factory technologies and equipment only make matters worse. In short, India is one of the world's largest greenhouse gas producers (ranking fifth for CO_2 in 2000, after the United States, China, Russia and Japan). However, we obviously cannot overlook the fact that eradicating its rice fields and livestock would mean starvation for millions of people, or that India in fact produced just 1.0 tonne of carbon dioxide per inhabitant in 2000, compared to a global average of 3.9 tonnes (2.7 in China, 6.1 in France and 20.2 in the United States). Nevertheless, we can unequivocally denounce the planting of rice monocultures in the deltas, or strict monsoon paddy/winter wheat rotations in Punjab. These modes of intensive agriculture contribute to overconsumption of both water and other agricultural inputs whose disastrous impact on the environment and human health are well known. They also play a part in eroding animal and plant biodiversity in these regions where, moreover, the increase in yields has begun to slow down over the years.

ENDANGERED BIODIVERSITY

Biodiversity

Hot on the heels of the greenhouse effect and acid rain, biodiversity erosion was acknowledged as a global environmental problem in the 1987 Brundtland Report, and above all at the 1992 Rio de Janeiro Earth Summit. India is known to be a major global reservoir of animal and plant diversity (see Chapter

1), and well before the 1990s, parks and reserves were already trying to protect that diversity, albeit with some difficulty. The tiger population alone shrank from 40,000 in 1900 to roughly 1,800 in 1972 (and 3,642 in 2001-2, two-thirds of them outside reserves). However, safeguarding only the wild flora and fauna is just one factor in maintaining biodiversity. There is also a need to preserve the diversity of plants that have been cultivated for centuries, along with the associated know-how (cropping, cooking and medicinal techniques). The green revolution's excessively productivist rationale pushed small-grain cereals (millets) in particular into the background. The areas sown have continued to fall, whereas these cereals used to play an essential role in feeding semi-arid central India, as did pulses, for which the areas planted and the yields obtained rose by just 25 per cent between 1950-1 and 1995-6 (see Chapter 3). More generally, dozens of indigenous species and varieties that were very common at the time of Independence have been overwhelmed by a movement now supported by the boom in contract farming.

This threat is as much the result of the production methods recommended at the start of the chain as of the distribution system introduced further on. In 2005, for instance, if the local ration shop had been properly managed, poor families in Andhra Pradesh could have bought buy 35 kg of rice per month through the PDS, at Rs. 5.50 per kilo: for farmers in Telangana with just a few acres of non-irrigated land, it is no longer either worthwhile or profitable to grow sorghum, pearl millet, red gram or horse gram. In some areas land is therefore gradually being abandoned, whereas these crops used to provide fodder for animals, plant cover for soils that are otherwise subject to erosion and, above all, a much richer, more nutritious diet than the rice varieties now sold.

Decentralized PDS

In order to reduce high costs and malfunctions inherent to the current PDS (see Chapter 6), eight states were experimenting in 2003-4 with a decentralized management of the PDS (Tamil Nadu, Uttar Pradesh, Uttarakhand, Madhya Pradesh, Chhattisgarh, Gujarat, Orissa and West Bengal). The State Civil Supplies Corporations would buy grains and build stocks while the Food Corporation of India would supply the missing quantities only when the local procurement could not meet the local demand.

This decentralized management could be a way to protect or reintroduce the local diversity of crops if procurements were not focused on a few high yielding varieties of rice and wheat. It could also help to fight other perverse aspects of a centralized system. During the 1990s, in Medak district (Telangana region of Andhra Pradesh), thanks to the NGO Deccan Development Society, Dalit women (mainly) set up associations (*sangams*) to denounce how the PDS was endangering their nutritional (anaemia), economical (abandoned land, loss of labourers' jobs), social (disappearance of women's role in weeding, harvesting and seed selection) and even cultural life (decline in traditional agricultural festivals and ceremonies). After a long campaign, they succeeded in obtaining central government funding to set up a 'local PDS', for sorghum alone. However, the battle with the authorities was not yet won in 1997-8: local civil servants, no doubt fearing for their prerogatives, managed to delay payment. Nevertheless, the movement has had remarkable results since then: women were lending money to a hundred landowners in more than 30 villages in the district to encourage them to replant their fallow land, and subsequently buying the crop before storing it for resale to the poor at an attractive price (Rs. 2/kg), based on a monthly quota system. In all, a good thousand ha of fallow land have been replanted, resulting in 800 tonnes of sorghum. That translates into 2000 days' paid work, fodder for 6,000 bovines, a staple food for 3 million meals, soils regenerated by organic manure, a return to a complex crop range via subtle intercropping with sorghum, seed banks with a large number of varieties and, perhaps above all, a sense of independence for people who had previously been increasingly controlled by their economic and administrative environment.

Such movements are fortunately not that rare in India: other non-governmental initiatives are being launched to defend crop and cultural biodiversity, sometimes hand-in-hand with international organizations such as the International Crops Research Institute for the Semi-Arid Tropics (ICRISAT in Hyderabad: 24,000 samples of millet varieties grown worldwide and more than 670 wild *Pennisetum* species) and national centres such as the National Bureau of Plant Genetic Resources (NBPGR, in New Delhi: 12 regional *ex situ* species conservation centres) or the Indian Institute of Science (IIS, in Bangalore: an inventory of agricultural knowledge in terms of biodiversity).

Environmentalists (Vandana Shiva, M.S. Swaminathan, Anil Agarwal, KRRS...)

The geneticist Suman Sahai and her NGO Gene Campaign are fighting for Indian farmers to be respected and recognized not only for their varietal selection and breeding work over the centuries, but also for their current role in this field, as they still produce most of India's seeds (70 per cent of seeds are produced on-farm). Along the same lines, Vandana Shiva and her Research Foundation for Science, Technology and Ecology (RFSTE, New Delhi) are denouncing Indian farmers' increasing submission to the capitalist logic of the multinationals, in the seed sector and many others (agricultural research, phytosanitary products, credit). However, while this campaigner has long been critical of all the hidden defects of the green revolution, it is ironically one of the fathers of that very revolution who has now taken centrestage as the defender of biodiversity and, more generally, of sustainable development as a whole. M.S. Swaminathan (see Chapter 3) and his eponymous research foundation (MSSRF, in Chennai) admittedly know how to use simple, seductive slogans. Through their 'pro-poor, pro-women, pro-environment' policy, they are aiming to launch an 'evergreen revolution' (a concept similar to that of the 'doubly green revolution' used by Michel Griffon from CIRAD). It is supported by four main pillars: ecology, economy, employment and education. The experiments undertaken in the field are also appealing, for instance the setting up of 'community gene banks', both *ex situ* and *in situ*, by tribal populations. There are also the famous 'bio-villages', which have admittedly so far been limited to popularizing new sources of income around Pondicherry: fish farming by women in village ponds, mushroom growing by landless families using rice straw sacks hung from the ceiling, tethered rearing of one or two goats, cooperative jasmine cultivation, household waste recycling using earthworms to make compost, etc. The outcomes were eventually very limited. From remote sensing to molecular mapping, via biotechnologies, the MSSRF has not hesitated to make use of the latest techniques, including genetic modification.

On this last point, Anil Agarwal, another well-known Indian scientist (who died in 2002), was more reticent: with his Centre for Science and Environment (CSE, New Delhi), his internationally-read fortnightly publication *Down to Earth*, his regular articles on the state of the environment in India and his highly professional website, he was able to back up his various political campaigns with scientific fact. This has not always been the case with the other 'green' movements that have flourished in recent years in India—NGOs or agricultural unions that are in fact sometimes verging on the 'red'.

GMO

In 1992, the KRRS trade union (see Chapter 1) ransacked the head office and factory of the American seed producer Cargill in Karnataka. In 1999, genetically modified cotton trials in Andhra Pradesh were destroyed, for fear of seeing in India what a Canadian NGO has dubbed the 'Terminator' gene, a technology developed by the American giant Monsanto, which produces sterile seeds to force farmers to buy new supplies each season. In the same year, campaigners from the KRRS travelled to France to join the Confédération paysanne in destroying a GM rice planting at CIRAD in Montpellier. The international 'anti-globalization' movement has a foothold in India, but like anywhere else, the often self-appointed poor farmers' spokespeople in fact sometimes serve as a front for wealthy farmers who are skilful at combining ecologism and third-worldism with populism, nationalism and protectionism. In any event, it is true that genetically modified organisms (GMO) provide major hopes of obtaining high yields with limited pesticide, fertilizer and water consumption, hence ensuring national food security in future while preserving the natural resources that are currently under threat, particularly for developing countries such as India. But it is also true that their impact on the environment (mutation of insects or plants) and on human health (food safety) has not yet been elucidated, hence the need to exercise considerable caution. Moreover, these GMOs are primarily produced by multinationals whose monopolistic situation and profit-oriented views are not bearable on such key issues, even if some Indian companies are now producing and selling legally or illegally some Bt cotton (the only GM crop today authorized in India), and if many farmers have succeeded in crossing GM seeds with cotton hybrids. These multinationals have also the power to hijack the genetic heritage of some countries—and in some cases their ancestral indigenous knowledge—to develop products that they then patent, i.e. from which they get the exclusive right to profit for a given number of years. This is at least a conclusion which was drawn in India after what has happened with neem and turmeric, making the country acutely aware of the complex issue of natural and cultural heritage ownership ever since.

Neem

Neem (*Azadirachta indica*), of the family *Meliaceae*, has given rise to many place names, as it is one of the seven sacred trees in the Vedas scriptures. It has been worshipped since time immemorial (it is an offence to fell a neem tree), and reliquaries are placed in the tree, its fruits and seeds serve as daily offerings to the gods and goddesses, and its particularly bitter leaves are eaten with sugar during Hindu New Year festivities to symbolize the best and worst that people expect to face during the coming year. It is not very demanding in terms of soil type, is rumoured to purify the air (studies have shown that its daytime oxygen production rate is much greater than that of other trees), and is common throughout India at the entrance to villages and temples, or under windows. However, its popularity also stems from its many other uses. Large numbers of Indians use neem twigs as toothbrushes and chew them at certain times of day, and the twigs are often an ingredient in toothpaste produced by small rural firms and even modern manufacturers (Godrej). The seeds yield a non-edible oil (around 83,000 tonnes were produced in 1997) used to condition and darken the hair or to make soap. The by-product of this operation, oilcake (around 30,000 tonnes), has traditionally been used by farmers who have long known about its fertilizing and prophylactic properties, which explains why official networks have also been marketing it as a fertilizer and biopesticide.

Of the sixty or so useful substances in neem, which Indian traditional pharmacy has often been using for considerable time, one in particular has proved to be a very powerful insecticide: azadirachtin A (200 insects are susceptible to it). India isolated the substance in the 1960s and has since produced various forms of it. The snag is that India has registered very few patents (and Indian farmers even fewer), unlike foreign companies, which in this 'organic' age have been quick to realize the potential benefits of using plants such as neem to produce agricultural, pharmaceutical, cosmetic and hygiene products. In 1993, for instance, an Illinois-based firm, Floss Products Corp., was granted a US patent (5009886) for a neem root- and wood-based toothpaste. Similarly, in 1994, US patent 5397571 was awarded jointly to the multinational W.R. Grace and the United States Department of Agriculture (USDA) for a pesticide containing neem seeds. The innovative aspect acknowledged under this patent is in fact a new procedure (Indians had already come up with others) for stabilizing azadirachtin to make it more transportable and storable, i.e. also exportable. It took several years of campaigning on the part of Vandana Shiva (RFSTE), backed by a good many other NGOs, the International Federation of Organic Agriculture Movements (IFOAM) and Magda Aelvoet (the Belgian Environment Minister) to convince the European Patent Office to revoke this American licence in May 2000. An appeal to the revocation by the EU was dismissed in 2005. However, as of 1 June 2001, in the European Commission database listing patents registered with the various national or international bodies, there were 178 that specifically mentioned neem, including 46 in the United States and just eight in India.

Turmeric

According to Indian law on agricultural and pharmaceutical products, not everything is patentable, since it acknowledges the common ownership of certain types of knowledge or practices and also the work already done by generations of anonymous researchers. This applies to neem, and also to turmeric (*Curcuma longa,* also known as Indian saffron), a monocotyledon of the family *Zingiberaceae* whose rhizome is used as a spice. The orange root has also long been used in ayurvedic medicine to treat sprains and inflammation and heal wounds. However, in 1995, two American scientists (of Indian origin) at the University of Mississippi were granted US patent 5401504 for having 'discovered' a substance that healed external wounds, whereas they claimed that traditional Indian medicine had only previously used turmeric to treat various types of sprains and inflammatory conditions. Luckily, the Indian Council of Scientific and Industrial Research (CSIR) was able to supply a multitude of documents written prior to the patent that proved otherwise. Faced with this overwhelming body of evidence, the United States Patent and Trademark Office was forced in 1997 to reject the six patent applications concerned. If it had not done so, Indian firms would have been unable to market turmeric as a healing agent in the United States. By extension, however, the tightening of patent systems worldwide, including in India, could eventually make it illegal to market turmeric in its birthplace. Even now, as with neem, local communities can already be seen as victims in so far as the price inflation generated by demand from foreign firms has reduced their access to the resource and has also jeopardized small- and medium-scale industry in India.

UPOV and CBD

As a result, there has been considerable criticism in India of these patents and rights that have served to give foreign multinationals a monopoly and to push up the price of local products. However, India has been involved from a relatively early stage in the move towards globalized intellectual protection, launched in March 1883 (Paris Agreement for the Protection of Intellectual Property). As long ago as 1928, it signed the Bern Convention for the Protection of Literary and Artistic Works and after Independence, the Universal Copyright Convention (and the 1971 revised version), the Geneva Phonograms Convention (1971) and the Washington Treaty on Intellectual Property in Respect of Integrated Circuits (1989). However, like many other countries, it feels that this type of private protection has its limits. The 1970 Indian Patent Act decreed that products and processes affecting the health of humans, animals and plants and processes that increase their economic value or that of their products were unpatentable. The aim was not only to acknowledge the existence of collective rights over these resources, but to encourage the multiplication and low-cost distribution of products considered to be of public benefit, such as medicines or the green revolution's high-yielding seeds. For the same reasons, despite considerable international pressure, the subcontinent refused to sign the 1978 version (or the following version) of the Union for the Protection of New Varieties of Plants (UPOV) Convention, although it was more favourable to farmers than the 1991 version, which explicitly condemned what is called the 'farmers' privilege' (using some of their crop for seed). It was not until 2002 that the government announced that India was to sign the 1978 UPOV Convention. Along with 156 other countries meeting in Rio, India did sign the United Nations Convention on Biological Diversity (CBD) in June 1992 (and ratified it in February 1994), as its stated aim was 'the conservation of biological diversity, the sustainable use of its components and the fair and equitable sharing of the benefits arising out of the utilization of genetic resources . . .' (Article 1). However, in addition to the vagueness of some of the terms used (for instance, what exactly does 'fair and equitable sharing' mean?), the Convention also includes two principles that apparently run counter to certain Indian concepts. The first is the affirmation of national sovereignty over natural resources (Articles 3 and 15), a principle strongly defended by developing countries to prevent industrialized countries from pillaging those resources, but which at the same time rejects a notion that lay at the very heart of the International Undertaking on Plant Genetic Resources negotiated some ten years previously at the FAO: that of a common heritage of humanity. Hence the International Undertaking was renegotiated to bring it in harmony with the CBD, and was renamed in 2001 as a treaty which was eventually ratified by India. Secondly, and this time egged on by industrialized countries, the CBD surreptitiously encourages the affirmation and extension of intellectual property rights (patents, copyrights, trademarks) over resources and techniques liable to be used in biotechnologies (Article 16.5): a door which was pushed open even wider a few years later during international talks more explicitly linked to trade.

TRIPS

In late 1994, after eight years of talks, the GATT Uruguay Round (see Chapter 8) culminated in a new General Agreement on Tariffs and Trade, which India signed as it had in the past. The agreement in fact took the form of a series of more or less hotly debated texts, such as the Agreement on Trade-Related Aspects of Intellectual Property Rights (TRIPS), which according to some NGOs, was submitted at the last minute by a small—but powerful—group of interested parties. In fact, the United States—led by its pharmaceutical industry—wanted to use this round of trade talks to introduce intellectual property rights (IPR), and also to ensure protection of those IPRs by patents in each and every technological field, a move opposed by most developing countries. However, there was one major obstacle: the European Patent Convention excludes plant varieties and animal races, along with the essentially biological processes used to produce them. After much persuasion (the royalties being lost by industrialized countries were estimated at some $200 billion a year), the two protagonists finally struck a compromise in article 27.3(b) of the TRIPS agreement, which authorizes signatories to exclude from patentability 'plants and animals other than micro-organisms, and essentially biological processes for the production of plants or animals other than non-biological and microbiological processes'. 'However', it also stipulates that 'Members shall provide [by the year 2000 in the case of developing countries] for the protection of plant varieties either by patents or by an effective *sui generis* [UPOV-type] system or by any combination thereof'.

Intellectual Property

In all evidence, it was in order to satisfy the conditions of this last clause that two projects were submitted to the Indian Parliament in December 1999: an amendment to the 1970 Patent Act and above all the Plant Varieties and Farmers' Rights Bill. The latter, which was passed in August 2001 but was notified only in December 2006, guaranteed the rights of inventors, under certain conditions (rights limited to a 15- or 18-year period, lack of protection for anything relating to public health or 'Terminator'-type technologies, etc.), but confirmed farmers' right to reuse or sell their seeds, except those marked as branded. The Second Patent Amendment Act was passed in 2002. It continued to ban patents on 'agrochemical' and pharmaceutical products, but authorized those on procedures intended to increase plant resistance or economic value. It banned patents on 'discoveries', but not on 'inventions' (except for those derived from the 'traditional knowledge' of 'indigenous communities'). It also decreed that 'plants and animals in whole or any part other than microorganisms but including seeds, varieties and species and essentially biological processes for production or propagation of plants and animals' were not patentable. Later, the Patent (Third Amendment) Act was passed in 2005: it authorizes patents on agricultural and pharmaceutical products. This has obviously triggered considerable debate and controversy, as some people feel that the country would be 'shooting itself in the foot'. The last clause in article 27.3 of the TRIPS agreement was due to be re-examined in 1999, and as it was not, nobody can be expected to adhere to it (in fact, there has been considerable international confusion over the issue ever since).

In the other fields covered by the TRIPS agreement, India is near the top of the class (Table 7). In December 1998, it at last opted to sign the Paris Convention for the Protection of

TABLE 7: COMPLIANCE WITH TRIPS OBLIGATIONS (JANUARY 2000)

TRIPS obligations	Indian law	TRIPS deadline	Comments
Patents			
Product protection	No protection	01/01/2005	-
Marketing rights for new molecules	Law modified in April 1999	01/01/1995	Complies
Import authorized to exploit patent	Law modified in April 1999	01/01/2000	Complies
20-year protection period	7 years for pharmaceuticals sector,14 years for other sectors	01/01/2000	Law under study
Defender to provide proof	Holder to provide proof	01/01/2000	Law under study
Brands			
Commercial brands protected	Law modified in December 1999	01/01/2000	Complies
Seven-year protection period	10-year protection period	01/01/2000	Complies
Obligation of use: at least once every 3 years	At least once every 5 years	01/01/2000	Complies
Copyright			
Computer programs protected	Protection granted	01/01/2000	Complies
Minimum protection: 50 years after death of artist	Minimum 60 years' protection	01/01/2000	Complies
Geographical indications			
Geographical indications protected	Law adopted in December 1999	01/01/2000	Complies
Designs			
10-year protection period	5-year protection period, renewable twice	01/01/2000	Law being drafted
Plant varieties			
Plant varieties protected	No protection	01/01/2000	Law under study

Source: Nouvelles économiques de l'Asie du Sud, issue 11, French Embassy in India, New Delhi.

Industrial Property, and a year later, it agreed to grant exclusive marketing rights (EMR) for five years to holders of patents registered in other countries, even if those patents concerned processes or products (pharmaceutical, agricultural and otherwise) that could not be patented under Indian law. This has obviously not done anything to motivate local researchers. In 1999, India also adapted its trademark law, and voted a new Geographical Indications of Goods Registration and Protection Act (GIGA). By early 2007, 30 indications had been registered (Darjeeling tea was the first). In future, the act should prevent confusion between aromatic Indian basmati rice and the Texan rice cunningly called 'Texmati'. Conversely, it also confirmed the obligation to stop calling 'champagne' the sparkling wines produced in India. Nevertheless, these various legislative changes, which were intended to protect, reward and encourage innovation in all its different forms, have not solved the thorny issue of 'fair and equitable sharing of the benefits arising out of the utilization of genetic resources' (CDB, 1992). On the contrary, they have complicated matters still further: the more the exclusive property system encouraged by the TRIPS agreement is extended, the less countries—however sovereign—will be able to control access to and sharing of their resources and knowledge, since those resources will become non-shareable private property!

Biodiversity Act

Pending the eventual international resolution of this major contradiction, the Indian government is advancing on both fronts: after tackling TRIPS in 1999, it had passed the Biological Diversity Act in 2002 in the hope of giving 'communities' a degree of power, although the term 'communities' is somewhat vague and masks the heterogeneities within local society. The Act includes setting up, beyond State Biodiversity Boards, local Biodiversity Management Committees to take charge of conserving the diversity of species. They are authorized to levy taxes on the collection of biological material and associated knowledge. Officially, the newly born National Biodiversity Authority (NBA) has to consult the local committees before making any decisions on the use of Indian biological resources (patent applications, the fight against biopiracy, etc.). In reality, the rules notified in 2004 by the Ministry of Environment and Forests vest very little power to the local committees. The NBA receives royalties for the use of those resources, which it can then pass on to the individuals or groups concerned, if they are identifiable, or can otherwise pay into the National Biodiversity Fund. From local to national scale, and from nation-states to the multinationals' assumed or real greed, the trend now is towards a system of interlinked political controls over resources. The next step is to test this new mode of collective action, which is based on practices that already exist in India, for instance at the Thiruvananthapuram (Trivandrum) Botanical Garden. Since 1995, the garden has been paying 50 per cent of the royalties it receives from the manufacturer of a tonic to the Kani tribe which discovered the properties of the plant used by the firm. It is nevertheless worth pointing out that it is not the tribe that holds the relevant intellectual property rights, as one might expect, but the Botanical Garden.

8. Market Liberalization

The 1990s proved to be the death knell for the interventionist policies implemented since Independence. The 1991 Structural Adjustment Plan committed India to unprecedented liberalization of its economy, and the agricultural sector was not spared, as India also signed the GATT Agreement on Agriculture in 1994. However, the reforms were limited in this latter field, due to domestic electoral pressure and also due to the relatively weak international constraints: with agricultural products being net taxed due to low domestic prices, input subsidies could be maintained to a large extent despite the financial burden they represented and their various perverse effects. Indirect support of agricultural exports has increased from year to year, but is still out of all proportion to the American or European ones. Access to the Indian food market, for its part, was apparently facilitated by the removal of non-tariff barriers in April 2001, but in practice, those barriers have often quite legally been replaced by high customs duty. In view of internal demand, which is both growing and becoming more diversified, it looks almost inevitable that India will become a leading food importer within the next 20 or 30 years, unless there is a major change of direction that transforms its current agricultural landscape. That is not beyond the realms of possibility: India has already proved in the past that it can win what might look like lost causes.

THE JUMP INTO FREE-MARKET ECONOMY (1991)

Mixed Economy

In the fourth century BC, King Chandragupta Maurya's minister Kautilya's *Arthashastra* raised the question of the ambiguous relations between *artha* and *dharma*, economics and policy. Similarly, in 1947, the intellectuals leading the Congress party agreed not on an economic growth target, but on a two-way dogma. The first aim, on a global level, was to assert national independence through an original development model: the famous third way, or non-alignment. The second, a domestic version of the first, was the institution of a mixed economy, i.e.

one in which the State had varying degrees of control over markets. This had one sovereign objective: social equity, which was considered to govern the unity of a country that was proving complex to construct (due to multiple, marked identities centring on religion, caste, region, language, etc.). The ingredients of this issue were listed in Jawaharlal Nehru's famous *Discovery of India*, which never left his daughter Indira Gandhi's side, and it was not until 1959 that a political party, Swatantra Party, dared to call openly—albeit unsuccessfully—for economic liberalization. In short, State intervention was not only accepted but considered necessary in India. Some saw it as a bastion against speculators, usurers and monopolies and others, particularly the big industrial groups (Bajaj, Birla, Godrej and Tata), as a means of protecting the domestic market. For several decades, this State-controlled capitalism steadily asserted itself and expanded onto various levels: industrialization and five-yearly development planning (see Chapter 3), import and foreign capital barriers (see infra), nationalization of certain spheres of activity such as banking (see Chapter 3), and production under licence and quota fixing in other fields (agrifoods, textiles, etc.) so as to encourage small-scale industry and trade, and thus provide jobs.

Agricultural Policy

In terms of agriculture, the Green Revolution (see Chapter 3) obviously fitted in with the mixed economy and the target of endogenous development (self-reliance). The State acted to balance supply and demand (disseminating new techniques, subsidizing some inputs and controlling prices both upstream and downstream), but also encouraged commercial agriculture, and farmers became increasingly dependent on the markets for both product sales and input purchases. The State served to foster and support this profound change in production practices, whereby unlike subsistence farming systems, some regions and some farmers were required to provide others with foodstuffs as essential as rice and wheat. However, it is important to bear in mind that the Green Revolution was just one stage in a longer movement. Depending on political power shifts, that movement has taken alternate steps towards concentrated, polarized development aimed at improving productivity on the one hand, and homogenization and perequation in the hope of ensuring social equity on the other.

Just after Independence, agrarian reforms and experiments with 'community development' triggered an initial period of homogenization in the name of social justice, egalitarianism and progress throughout the country. This trend was then reversed with the advent of the Green Revolution, when the government reacted to the emergency in the 1960s by concentrating its efforts and investment on a limited number of regions, crops and social groups. The hope was that development would spread, both vertically (improved living standards for the poor) and horizontally (spread of progress to the most disadvantaged, non-irrigated regions), but this 'trickle effect' was a long time coming, and a new homogenization policy was drawn up in the late 1970s in an attempt to redress the balance in favour of crops, regions and social groups that had previously been neglected (Table 8).

TABLE 8: THE MAJOR AGRICULTURAL POLICY PHASES (1940 TO 2000)

PRODUCTIVISM (concentration and polarization of development)	SOCIAL EQUITY (homogenization, perequation)
1940s	
• 'Grow More Food' campaign (1942-51)	
1965-75 (Green Revolution)	1950s
• Strict canalization of imports	• Land reforms, rural credit cooperatives (PACS), community development (Panchayats), etc.
	1975-90
• Crop polarization (wheat, rice)	• Launching of millet HYVs, 'White (dairy) Revolution', 'Yellow (oilseeds) Revolution', etc.
• Regional polarization (Punjab, etc.)	• Aid to extend irrigation (CAD, MWS, watershed development, etc.)
• Social polarization (enterprising, well-off farmers)	• PDS extension to rural areas, extension of poverty alleviation programmes (IRDP, TRYSEM, JRY, etc.)
1990s	
• Decontrol of some sectors (seeds, credit, etc.) • Attempts to reduce input subsidies • PDS targeting, development of futures markets, etc.	

There was another switch in 1991, with gradual deregulation of the sector, under an overall reform of the economy that marked the abandoning in India of a model that set out to be both original and generous, but which after four decades was showing serious signs of running out of steam in terms of adapting to the changes in its environment.

Rajiv Gandhi and Middle Classes

The change initially came from within, with the emergence in the early 1980s of a middle class resulting from the 'Indian socialism': prosperous post-Green Revolution farmers, bosses of family firms, senior staff and managers in large companies, traders, civil servants or workers protected by powerful trade unions. This class was keen to consume and frustrated at being unable to do so, as it was bridled by principles, be they Gandhian (increased material well-being robs the majority in favour of the few) or Nehruvian (encouraging people to save rather than consume so as to develop a strong public investment capacity). The fear was also that very marked differences in income would feed the religious and social fire. However, this 'Lakshmi's India' (Lakshmi being the goddess of wealth, beauty and elegance) was also the most visible sign of economic progress: the subcontinent had at least partly ceased to be the symbol of global poverty, and was beginning to be seen overseas as a hive of opportunity. For Rajiv Gandhi, the young prime minister with modern managerial practices, educated in Britain and married to an Italian, this new economic strength was an opportunity to revitalize the private sector and loosen administrative procedures and red tape. He lowered import barriers, as his mother Indira had begun to do on her return to power in 1980, to enable the production of fans, food processors, refrigerators, motor scooters, televisions and many other goods that were then being consumed in unprecedented quantities. However, this did nothing to improve the trade balance: the record deficit seen after the second oil crisis in 1979 barely improved at all during the 1980s (Figure 34), particularly as imports (arms, fertilizers, cooking oils, etc.) were generally on the up and the country still did not have any concerted export strategies for spearhead products. Moreover, the cost of external financial resources was growing, as the opening up of China, followed by some less developed countries and then the Commonwealth of Independent States (the former USSR) meant that foreign aid and concessionary credit were increasingly hard to come by. Debt servicing increased, and to reduce the budget shortfalls at the Central and state government levels, public companies were encouraged to look elsewhere for funding, in other words to incur debts on the domestic market by making optimum use of domestic savings (issuing stock certificates at very attractive interest rates and/or offering tax advantages). This in return resulted in a marked increase in overseas debt among the private firms pushed out of the domestic market. Public and private domestic and overseas debt rapidly steered the country as a whole into bankruptcy.

Structural Adjustment Plan (SAP)

In the late 1990s, the economic journal of Indosuez Bank published an article that effectively summed up the critical nature of the situation: 'to avoid a major financial crisis, India has to choose between massive administrative restrictions on imports, which would be a big step backwards in relation to the country's opening up in the 1980s, or resorting to IMF funding, which it has previously turned down due to the conditions attached'. In a tense political climate (Rajiv Gandhi was assassinated during the election campaign in May 1991), India opted for the second solution in July, by which time overseas debt amounted to more than \$70 billion, inflation was running at almost 17 per cent and foreign currency reserves were not able to sustain more than three weeks of imports. For the first time in its history, India pawned part of its gold bullion stock in the Bank of England. It subsequently received a \$6.7 billion loan from the World Bank Aid Consortium and an initial payment of \$2 billion from the International Monetary Fund (IMF). This was not the first time that the IMF had lent money to India, since it had provided almost \$6 billion in 1981, but this time, there was no question of failing to follow its recommendations, i.e. its famous Structural Adjustment Plan already implemented in South America, Africa and South-East Asia: devaluation to boost exports, deregulation of the private sector and submission to foreign competition so as to increase its productivity, control of budget deficit by restricting public expenditure, privatization of public undertakings. In short, it was an admission of the failure of the previous system and a switch to a market economy, a move that probably could not have been made prior to this major crisis.

The new government headed by P.V. Narasimha Rao set out to implement radical reforms. For instance, the 1969 Monopolies and Restrictive Trade Practices Act was relaxed, enabling large industrial groups to develop their assets without prior authorization. However, the government also showed considerable restraint, as have its successors (the Congress party's domination over several decades had eventually given way to a series of somewhat precarious coalitions). The 'Licence Raj', for example, was not abandoned immediately, since in 18 sectors (including sugar, animal and vegetable fats, tobacco), it was a long time before entrepreneurs could set up and expand without prior authorization from the authorities (and such approval is indeed still required in some areas). Similarly, for several years, foreign shareholders could not own more than 50 per cent of Indian companies, except in 34 priority fields (such as fertilizers or agrifoods).

Prices (WPI, CPI...)

However, it was probably agriculture that saw the most moderate reforms, except in the fields of seeds and credit where private firms emerged on a big scale (see Chapter 3). An attempt was made to limit fertilizer subsidies (see Chapter 3), but the measures imposed with difficulty each time largely failed to slow the growth in expenditure (see infra). The equally delicate question of electricity was not raised until the late 1990s, and has since become bogged down (see Chapter 7). Lastly, the issue of water rates remains to a large extent a topic for seminars. In short, the price of these three crucial agricultural inputs has remained more or less stable in the 1990s, which in view of the inflation rate means that the government has increasingly been subsidizing farmers, or at least those who use large amounts of these inputs.

Further down the production chain, the successive reforms of the PDS (see Chapter 3) have in the end been more radical, but have resulted in a transfer of responsibility to the different states and in the accumulation and wastage of public stocks (see Chapter 6). Since these reforms, silos have been full to overflowing, yet cereal prices have rocketed, whereas they had previously followed the Wholesale Price Index (WPI, which is more commonly used as a reference in India than the Consumer Price Index) (Figure 32). Cereal price inflation has nevertheless remained much less significant than for most other agricultural

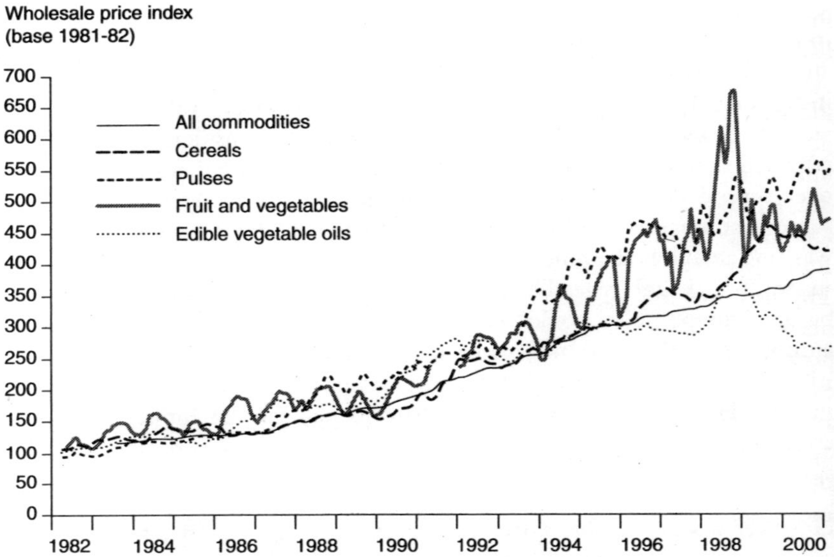

Note: Since May 1994, 1981-2 based indices are here deducted from the new 1993-4 based series. This creates a slight bias (regarding fruit and vegetables particularly) since the basket compositions and weightings were more or less modified.

Source: Based on Ministry of Industry.

FIGURE 32: MONTHLY WHOLESALE PRICE INDICES (APRIL 1982 TO MARCH 2001)

products, which have for some considerable time now been much more variable, with the exception of vegetable oils that are re-imported in huge quantities like they were at the start of the 1980s (see Chapter 4). The government has maintained its market intervention (procurement, storage and redistribution) in both the cereal and sugar production chains, as much to guarantee producers a minimum price as to control spatial and temporal price variations for consumers. However, for other goods, the lack of such a system, even a not entirely satisfactory one, is now being cruelly felt within an increasingly free-market, diversified economy. To help producers guard against the current volatility and instability, the government has decided, encouraged by the World Bank and other organizations, to reinstate the futures markets it more or less abolished 50 years ago.

Futures Markets

Primarily thanks to dynamic Marwari brokers from Rajasthan, India had futures markets as long ago as the start of the twentieth century, for cotton (Bombay), groundnut and castor (Gujarat, Punjab), jute (Calcutta), wheat (Uttar Pradesh, Punjab) and pepper, turmeric, sugar, etc. However, a law passed in 1952 imposed a three-tier structure to prevent speculation: at the top, the Ministry of Civil Supplies, then the Forward Markets Commission (FMC), which in turn supervised the associations authorized to manage trading in a list of clearly defined products. This list was very limited: until 1998, the only authorized futures markets were for jute, black pepper, *gur* (unrefined sugar), potatoes and turmeric, and forward markets only officially existed for cotton fibre and jute. The numerous FMC restrictions and controls meant that those markets obviously lost their dynamism and significance; some were also operating illegally, albeit in line with international standards, for instance for cotton and groundnut or rapeseed oil.

However, trade and industry deregulation under the 1991 reforms increased the risk of price instability, and the central government relaxed and broadened the measures intended to enable operators to guard against uncertainty. There was still a ban on forward markets for foodgrains (cereals and pulses) and sugar (along with flax, various spices, gold, silver, copper, zinc, etc.), irrespective of whether they were organized or informal. However, since 1999, it has been possible to trade in the main oilseeds and oilseed products through futures markets (for instance, a copra market was opened in 2002). While in 2000 futures trading was allowed for only eight commodities, their number was eighty in June 2004. In 2002, the National Multi-Commodity Exchange of India Limited (NMCE) was created in Ahmedabad, followed by the National Commodity and Derivatives Exchange Limited (NCDEX) and the Multi-Commodity Exchange of India Limited (MCX) in Mumbai in 2003. The older organizations (Cochin Oil Merchants Association, East India Jute and Hessian Exchange, Coffee Futures Exchange of India Limited, Bombay Oil Seeds and Oil Exchange, Soyabean Processors Association of India) have been encouraged to modernize. It is true that they stand to gain from opening up to foreign operators, and from strengthening their often too fragmented, under-funded brokerage structures: some exchanges still operate as the strongholds of local trade barons.

THE GATT AGREEMENTS ON AGRICULTURE (1994) AND AFTER

GATT, WTO

In 1991, India launched economic reforms primarily aimed at liberalizing trade and industry. Three years later, it embarked—much more determinedly this time—upon a relatively long-term agricultural liberalization process. In 1994, it signed the Agreement on Agriculture in Marrakech that concluded the Uruguay Round (URAA) of talks, the last and longest cycle of international talks under the General Agreement on Tariffs and Trade (GATT). There were two main reasons for signing. Firstly, India had become the world's second largest food producer, but its share of international trade was still below 1 per cent (all products combined), an isolation exacerbated by the development of major integration and free trade zones from which it was excluded (EU, NAFTA, MERCOSUR, ASEAN, etc.). As a founder member of the GATT (1947), it was in its best interests to strengthen and extend the powers of what was to become the World Trade Organization (WTO) as of 1 January 1995. Secondly, India is a developing country, and like many others, it felt that it could benefit more from world agricultural trade if rich countries in Europe or the United States did not protect their domestic markets so much with import barriers, and did not distort international prices so much with their production and export subsidies.

The URAA was the first agreement in the history of the GATT that dared tackle these various types of restrictions or trade distortions in the field of agriculture. According to certain Indian experts, the agreement should have been signed a long time ago, and the conditions should have been even stricter. But India itself subsidized its farmers, closely protected its food market, and was increasingly encouraging its agricultural exports. Might it not risk having to give back with one hand (decreasing its support to agriculture) what it had received in the other (greater opening up to its exports on the part of other countries)? In fact, this was not really an issue in 1994, given its modest support compared with that of other countries, and also the exemptions or specific regimes granted to the developing countries.

Domestic Support: A Missed Opportunity for Domestic Reform

Domestic Subsidies (AMS)

In fact, during the URAA talks, it transpired that India would not have to cut its domestic support of agriculture (–13 per cent over ten years for developing countries, –20 per cent over six years for industrialized countries). Indeed, the total Aggregate Measure of Support (AMS) did not exceed the limit set for developing countries of 10 per cent of agricultural product value (the threshold was 5 per cent for industrialized countries), particularly as public funding such as that allocated to PDS operations could be excluded from the aid categories subject to restraints, like those generally placed in the 'green box'. India's Notification sent to the WTO in mid-1998 confirmed, for the 1995-6 season (Table 10), that the internal support subject to restraints (electricity, fertilizer and irrigation subsidies) came to less than \$5.8 billion, or 7.5 per cent of Indian agricultural product value that year. This was without even considering paragraph 2 of Article 6 of the URAA, which authorizes agricultural input subsidies for producers in developing countries with low incomes or limited resources: if the WTO considered these producers to be farmers with four hectares or less, 60 per cent of the input subsidies paid in India would be exempt (90 per cent for a figure of 10 ha). However, above all, the notification reaffirmed another point: overall, Indian agriculture appears to be heavily taxed, since at least \$29.6 billion of (product) 'specific' AMS can be deducted from the sum of 'non-specific' support (\$8.2 billion). Most Indian crops are indeed sold at prices below—and often well below—those on the world markets, which also confirms the impression that India has a clear comparative advantage in the agricultural sector. The total AMS would therefore be –26 per cent of Indian agricultural product value in 2000 (Table 9). In short, India can easily encourage the WTO to severely reduce domestic support in other countries, while for its part continuing to subsidize its own farmers, as it is so important for the local political power on a subcontinent where farmers make up the main vote banks.

TABLE 9: AGGREGATE MEASURE OF SUPPORT AS PERCENTAGE OF PRODUCTION VALUE (1987 TO 2000)

Year	Specific AMS (%)	Non-specific AMS (%)	Total AMS (%)
1987	–33.2	4.2	–29.0
1988	–24.7	5.2	–19.5
1989	–29.8	5.0	–24.8
1990	–32.8	6.2	–26.6
1991	–27.6	5.9	–21.7
1992	–57.5	7.5	–50.0
1993	–46.6	6.8	–39.8
1994	–51.1	5.7	–45.4
1995	–38.6	6.8	–31.8
1996	–39.3	7.9	–31.4
1997	–40.7	7.5	–33.2
1998	–33.2	6.9	–26.3
1999	–39.7	6.0	–33.8
2000	–32.8	7.2	–25.6

Source: A. Gulati and S. Narayanan, *The Subsidy Syndrome in Indian Agriculture*, New Delhi, Oxford University Press, 2003.

TABLE 10: OFFICIAL DOMESTIC SUPPORT OF AGRICULTURE (1995–6)

'Green Box' programmes (million dollars) 2,195		
Public stockholding for food security purposes		1,570
Domestic food aid		n.a.
General services	⇒ Research	163
	⇒ Marketing and promotion services	105
	⇒ Provision for livestock health facilities	105
	⇒ Other (CAD, pest and disease control, training services)	25
Relief from natural disasters		125
Structural adjustment assistance	⇒ Dry land farming, etc.	59
Environmental programmes	⇒ Soil conservation, watershed management, control of shifting cultivation	33
Income insurance	⇒ Crop insurance scheme	11
Development programmes (million dollars)		**254**
Subsidies to low income producers	⇒ Agricultural input subsidies	149
Investment subsidies	⇒ Field channels, land levelling, shallow wells, etc.	105

Non-product-specific support (million dollars)		5,772
Subsidy on electricity		2,437
Fertilizer subsidy		1,864
Irrigation subsidy		1,345
Credit subsidy (1994-5)		102
Subsidy on average supply of seeds		24
Product-specific support (million dollars)		-29,619
Sugar cane	⇒ (12.7 - 11.64) $/t × 174 million tonnes	184
Tobacco	⇒ (605.43 - 912.82) $/t × 0.59 million tonnes	-181
Soya bean	⇒ (191.35 - 229.77) $/t × 4.99 million tonnes	-192
Jute	⇒ (146.5 - 417.55) $/t × 1.43 million tonnes	-388
Rapeseed and mustard toria	⇒ (257.12 - 513.37) $/t × 6.59 million tonnes	-1,689
Pulses (gram, urad, moong and tur)	⇒ (231.71 - 345.66) $/t × 14.97 million tonnes	-1,706
Groundnut	⇒ (269.08 - 514.58) $/t × 7.37 million tonnes	-1,809
Cotton	⇒ (343.83 - 1292.64) $/t × 2.22 million tonnes	-2,106
Coarse cereals (bajra, jowar, maize and barley)	⇒ (89.69 - 238.57) $/t × 30.43 million tonnes	-4,530
Rice	⇒ (168.923 - 262.51) $/t × 80.96 million tonnes	-7,577
Wheat	⇒ (113.61 - 264) $/t × 64 million tonnes	-9,625

Source: Based on the Delegation of India's Notification to the WTO dated 17 June 1998.

Agricultural Competitiveness

Nevertheless, there are many possible reservations about the above calculations and conclusions. Firstly, the classification of costly public procurement, storage and redistribution operations in the 'green box': in addition to the fact that the PDS has long benefited people who are not really poor (see Chapter 6), it also has to be recognized that as with food aid programmes in the United States, such operations constitute indirect production incentives, above all for wheat, rice and sugar cane. Secondly, as certain Indian economists have observed, the imprecision as to how non-specific AMS are calculated has resulted in considerable laxity in developed countries. This is also true for India. For instance, what about the significant energy subsidies upstream of fertilizer production? The occasional but very considerable writing off of farmers' debts, as for instance in the early 1990s? The different forms of public aid for sinking wells? Are not the almost total absence of charges for water and the non-taxation of agricultural income a form of disguised subsidy? Thirdly, as the same economists have observed, to further highlight the competitiveness of Indian agricultural products, in practice, the calculation of specific AMS used world prices of the 'reference period', i.e. 1986-8, and not for the current year, whereas those prices had generally increased since, at least for a time. But the same can also be said for input prices, which are not part of the specific AMS calculations, whereas India subsidizes heavily their production and use. These so-called 'non-specific' subsidies for electricity, fertilizers and irrigation do not benefit all products, as one might assume, but primarily wheat, rice and sugar cane since they are very water-intensive. If these subsidies are added to the price of Indian products, it is clear that those products are not as competitive in the international market as they might seem, and that in any case, their competitiveness is largely overestimated in the case of foodstuffs such as rice (Table 11). On a domestic level, these subsidies have also resulted in wastage and in situational advantages in privileged agricultural zones (Punjab, Haryana, western Uttar Pradesh, the deltas), often leaving other regions and their farmers unable to benefit from these important public transfers to agriculture.

Input Subsidies

It is difficult to assess what Indian agriculture actually gains from a complex system of input subsidies, or to pinpoint the benefits per crop or per state (cross-sector subsidies, missing or inaccurate statistics, etc.). However, even conservative calculations (i.e. excluding the cost of capital investment in irrigation, including 'non-technical' electricity losses) give enlightening results. First, the main three types of input subsidy (irrigation, electricity and fertilizers) increased sharply from 1980-1 to 1995-6 (mean growth rate of 12 per cent per year in constant rupee terms), reaching about Rs. 220 billion in 1995-6 (Figure 33), i.e. almost $6.6 billion (5.6 according to India's declaration to the WTO). This last amount represents 8.6 per cent of agricultural GDP (2.2 per cent of overall GDP), whereas the figure in 1980-1 had been just 2.7 per cent (0.9 per cent of overall GDP). This increase was primarily due to electricity and fertilizers, since the volumes consumed increased more than tenfold in that 15-year period. In terms of per hectare of gross cultivated area, it amounted to Rs. 1,178 in 1995-6, i.e. just over US $35. However, this is just an average, since in the field, at least 60 per

TABLE 11: PRICE COMPETITIVENESS IN WORLD MARKET (1980-1 TO 1994-5)

APPARENT COMPETITIVENESS (%) — (domestic price – world price) / world price

	1980	1981	1982	1983	1984	1985	1986	1987	1988	1989	1990	1991	1992	1993	1994	Average
Groundnut	-43	-29	-21	-33	-23	-15	1	-1	-30	-20	-37	-34	-45	-43	-35	-36
Rice	-10	1	31	24	39	66	6	-4	-19	-12	-29	-28	-21	-15	-8	-19
Barley	-25	-19	-2	-17	11	15	27	10	-16	-18	-9	-29	-31	12	-23	-16
Wheat	-5	2	11	-5	5	17	41	17	-13	-14	-3	-22	-12	3	-23	-12
Maize	10	30	21	-17	10	35	44	25	4	-11	-4	-13	-31	-6	-4	-11
Cotton	-2	-5	-9	-13	-16	-15	16	-5	-8	-29	-17	-15	-11	21	1	-8
Sugar cane	-3	23	21	15	30	31	41	23	6	-1	-5	-4	19	20	11	7
Rape/M.	58	32	46	33	19	43	113	43	8	31	33	11	33	27	27	27
Average	-6	2	17	7	18	37	25	7	-14	-12	-16	-22	-16	-5	-10	-13

REAL COMPETITIVENESS (%) — (domestic price + input subsidies – world price) / world price

	1980	1981	1982	1983	1984	1985	1986	1987	1988	1989	1990	1991	1992	1993	1994	Average
Groundnut	-42	-28	-20	-32	-21	-13	5	1	-27	-17	-34	-31	-42	-40	-32	-33
Rice	-7	6	35	30	47	77	14	3	-12	-4	-22	-21	-14	-6	1	-11
Barley	-19	-10	6	-8	22	31	48	26	-2	-6	4	-16	-17	33	-9	-2
Maize	13	36	24	-13	17	44	58	35	13	-2	6	-4	-22	4	7	-2
Cotton	1	0	-4	-8	-10	-5	29	4	1	-20	-8	-4	1	31	10	2
Wheat	1	11	19	5	16	32	62	34	2	2	14	-7	3	20	-7	4
Sugar cane	0	28	25	21	38	39	52	34	15	9	6	9	32	33	23	19
Rape/M.	62	37	51	39	26	53	125	53	19	41	45	24	49	42	43	41
Average	-3	8	23	13	26	48	37	16	-5	-2	-6	-12	-6	6	2	-3

Notes: 1. Domestic price = Wholesale price (Ministry of Industry)/official exchange rate rupee versus US $ (Ministry of Finance)
2. World price = Fob value of total world exports in US $/worldwide quantities exported (FAO)
3. Input subsidies = Irrigation + electricity + fertilizers (Dorin et Jullien)
4. Annual average = Average weighted by the gross cropped areas (Ministry of Agriculture)

Source: Dorin and Jullien (2004).

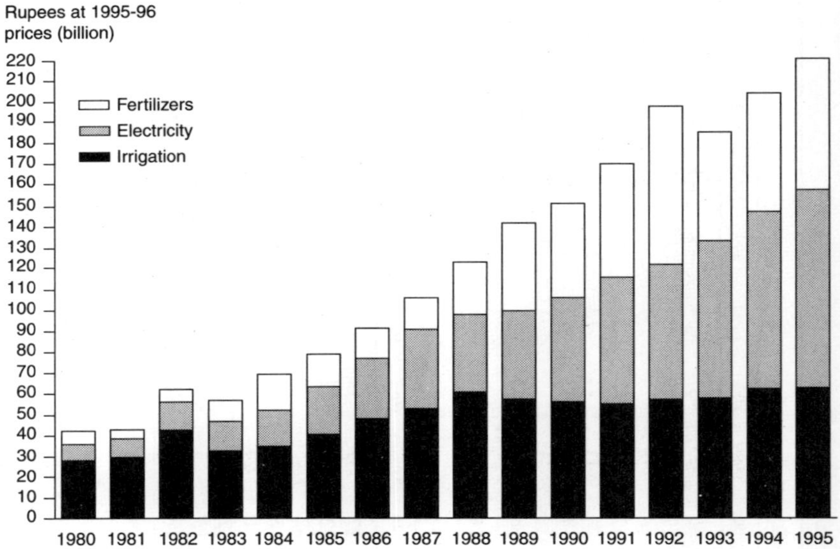

Source: Dorin and Jullien (2004).

FIGURE 33: AGRICULTURAL INPUT SUBSIDIES (1980-1 TO 1995-6)

cent of the subsidies went to rice ($1.95 billion dollars), wheat ($1.65 billion) and sugar cane ($430 million), leading to an unofficial support of these crops to the tune of $45, $66 and $104 respectively per hectare cultivated (Table 12).

The regional inbalance was also important (Table 13): in 1995-6, farmers in Orissa received the equivalent of $14, whereas the state's GDP was one of the lowest in the country ($214/inhabitant), while in Punjab, which has the highest incomes in India ($554/inhabitant), the figure was $188. This last figure is still much lower than in the United States, European Union or Japan, and India may continue to denounce subsidy levels in other countries. But it could also use the WTO platform to restructure its own agricultural subsidy system that suffers from serious malfunctions and which is unsustainable in terms not only of equity, but also natural resources (see Chapter 7) and nutritional security (see Chapter 6).

The task is indisputably a hard one. Unlike the European Union or the USA, for instance, which support more and more their relatively low number of farmers with direct payments

TABLE 12: INPUT SUBSIDIES PER CULTIVATED HECTARE (1980-1 TO 1995-6)

	Rupees at 1995/6 prices															
	1980	1981	1982	1983	1984	1985	1986	1987	1988	1989	1990	1991	1992	1993	1994	1995
Maize	170	166	250	189	247	283	367	410	468	557	553	630	820	684	664	818
Groundnut	134	125	192	199	261	250	308	458	442	464	610	624	799	694	804	899
Barley	395	379	527	439	512	586	681	824	914	923	943	1,064	1,192	1,135	1,192	1,272
Cotton	255	243	365	315	420	499	549	776	804	996	996	1,098	1,421	1,275	1,287	1,370
Rape/M.	200	205	306	311	479	482	577	771	925	950	1,000	1,139	1,182	1,186	1,320	1,464
Rice	340	348	504	448	547	621	716	803	950	1,076	1,121	1,212	1,444	1,302	1,411	1,520
Wheat	594	588	849	730	881	999	1,141	1,320	1,504	1,619	1,694	1,859	2,131	1,963	2,080	2,210
Sugar cane	813	823	965	962	1,223	1,472	1,627	1,871	2,137	2,413	2,651	2,958	3,377	3,143	3,280	3,493
INDIA	245	243	360	316	392	444	518	616	680	778	812	934	1,063	993	1,081	1,178

Source: Dorin and Jullien (2004).

TABLE 13: INPUT SUBSIDIES PER CULTIVATOR (1980-1 TO 1995-6)

	Rupees at 1995/6 prices															
	1980	1981	1982	1983	1984	1985	1986	1987	1988	1989	1990	1991	1992	1993	1994	1995
Orissa	195	180	249	228	254	205	247	241	253	359	334	411	505	475	430	470
Bihar	172	178	263	244	302	412	483	596	647	735	693	668	759	602	591	585
Madhya Pradesh	213	203	264	260	297	273	295	325	374	445	609	675	799	860	999	1,104
West Bengal	451	405	534	540	595	489	508	549	668	869	973	1,042	1,226	1,008	1,021	1,150
Uttar Pradesh	468	446	602	549	633	657	715	842	1,002	1,193	1,186	1,303	1,526	1,274	1,344	1,382
Rajasthan	441	466	691	559	594	739	775	919	837	874	950	978	1,255	1,245	1,321	1,479
Kerala	662	614	862	843	931	936	1,119	1,219	1,420	1,709	1,896	1,792	2,123	1,670	1,803	2,075
Tamil Nadu	649	687	943	885	971	1,101	1,130	1,198	1,289	1,618	1,727	1,797	2,257	2,017	2,210	2,278
Karnataka	585	621	863	742	899	1,144	1,231	1,270	1,412	1,532	1,726	1,877	2,168	2,068	2,247	2,519
Andhra	675	717	1,061	942	1,159	1,260	1,407	1,131	2,218	1,982	2,192	2,401	2,760	2,492	2,826	3,174
Maharashtra	568	623	905	738	960	1,205	1,303	1,560	1,754	2,074	2,234	2,407	2,614	2,379	2,803	3,210
Gujarat	733	666	939	842	1,024	1,086	1,650	3,384	3,256	3,094	3,002	3,654	4,157	4,096	4,113	4,647
Haryana	1,305	1,562	2,303	1,736	2,221	2,423	2,852	3,252	2,821	3,683	3,575	4,669	5,491	5,281	6,174	5,009
Punjab	1,385	1,248	1,876	1,822	2,,722	2,926	3,679	4,537	5,047	6,158	6,026	6,080	7,807	6,657	6,261	6,272
INDIA	465	466	662	593	709	793	905	1,027	1,174	1,327	1,388	1,538	1,756	1,625	1,760	1,874

Source: Dorin and Jullien (2004).

decoupled from the output produced, India can hardly afford to reward in that way the 'multi-functionality' of its agriculture (biomass production for food and non-food uses, but also provision of many other current or potential services, like rural employment, landscape building, ecosystem maintenance, soil and water conservation, disease controls, and so on). Indeed, with several hundred million farmers, transaction costs (administration including controls) would be unbearable, not counting the social tension this would trigger in a country where the current system of positive discrimination (affirmative action) is already problematical.

Export Support: On the Offensive

Imports and Exports

India's concentration on its domestic market since Independence has placed it firmly on the margins of international trade, and its preferential trade agreements with the Soviet Union did nothing to help it escape from that position. Even in this new era of liberalization and globalization, it is still exchanging relatively little with other countries: in 2003, all products combined, the country with the second largest population in the world accounted for just 0.8 per cent of global imports, and above all only 0.9 per cent of exports ($63 billion out of a total of 7,370, according to the United Nations), with just three products having an international market share of over 10 per cent: tea and mate (10.9 per cent), pearls and precious or semi-precious stones (13.9 per cent), and rice (12.5 per cent).

Since the 'Rajiv Gandhi years' and above all the 1991 reforms, the Indian business sector has been increasingly active, although it has had to realize that having international ambitions is no guarantee of finding international customers. Agriculture has not been left out either. The share of 'agricultural and allied products' in total exports has been divided by four since the Green Revolution (44 per cent in 1960-1, 11 per cent in 2004-5 or $8.5 billion, see Figure 34), but the sector's trade balance has become comfortably positive since the mid-1980s, despite the decision to import cooking oils, which replaced cereal imports from the late 1970s onwards.

The key to this success is diversification. Traditional export products—coffee, tea and spices—are now merely one of four major exports (excluding cashew nuts, which are mostly imported raw and re-exported processed) (Figure 35). The Green

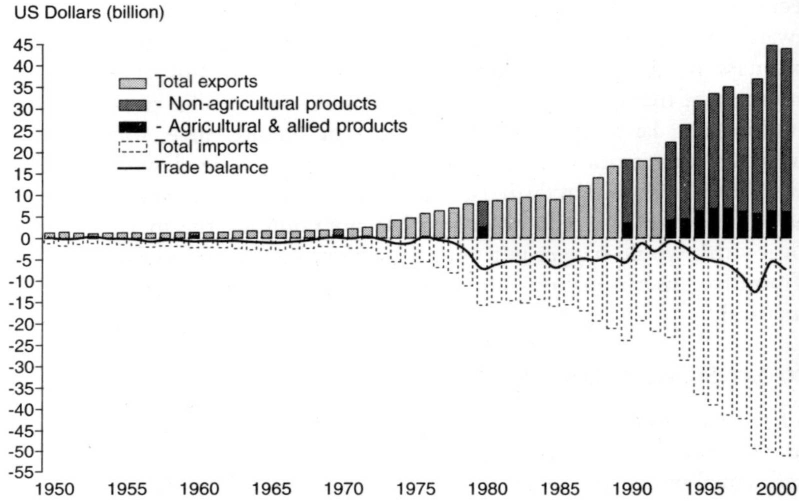

Source: Based on Economic Survey (2002).

FIGURE 34: IMPORTS, EXPORTS AND TRADE BALANCE (1950-1 TO 2000-1)

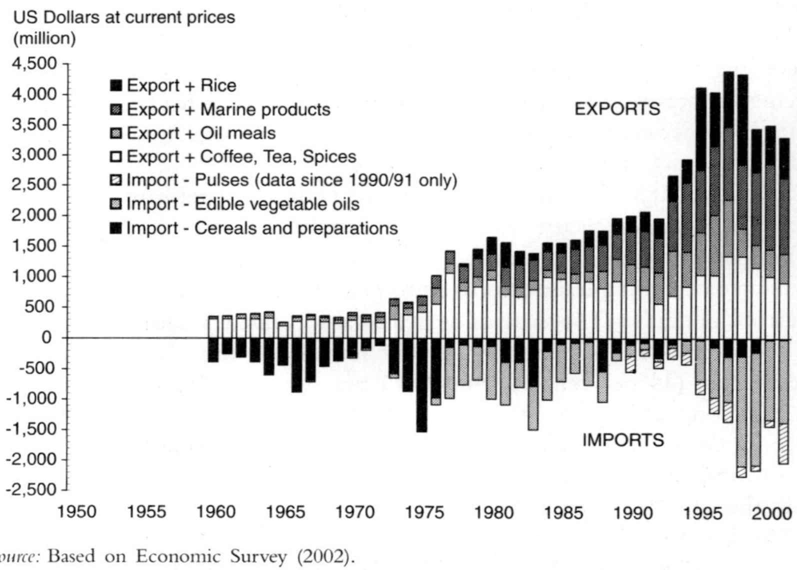

Source: Based on Economic Survey (2002).

FIGURE 35: AGRICULTURAL MAIN IMPORTS AND EXPORTS (1960-1 TO 2001-2) (cereals) Revolution has enabled basmati rice to be now produced for export, the blue (fish and shellfish) revolution has dedicated a significant share of its output to foreign markets (see Chapter 5), and the more recent yellow (oilseeds) revolution (see Chapter 4) has primarily served to boost exports of soyabean oilcake, which the domestic animal production sector is not yet able to use or promote very efficiently. However, the white revolution has not been involved in the increase in exports, despite the fact that India is now the world's leading milk producer: domestic demand for both milk and milk products is still huge. The Indian government is aware of this, and is only cautiously lifting or gradually relaxing the various restrictions on food product exports imposed over several decades. It is also well aware that the country does not really have the necessary infrastructures (energy, roads, railways, ports or airports) to become a major supplier of perishable goods to the international market. Until it is able to tackle these major bottlenecks, various indirect export subsidies are doing a good job.

Export Subsidies

India does not give exporters direct subsidies, but it is—increasingly—using indirect incentives to support them: tax exemption on export revenue (since 1961); allowing exporters to import goods that are otherwise subject to restrictions; import duty reductions or exemptions (EPCG, DEPB); free trade zones and enterprise zones specializing in exports (Agri-Export Zones, FTZs, EPZs and, since 2000, Special Economic Zones (SEZ); low-rate loans (set by the Central Bank of India and administered by commercial banks obliged to devote at least 12 per cent of their net loans to exports); special insurance via a public undertaking (ECGC); fund to promote Indian brands; and so on. According to the daily the *Economic Times*, these various forms of aid represented a loss in revenue of Rs. 155 billion in 1998-9, or $3.7 billion. However, for many agricultural products, these measures have had only a limited impact, since exports are still heavily regulated. Exports of some products are banned (some wildlife and wild flowers, exotic birds, tree roots and bark, sandalwood, beef, skeletons, tallow and animal fats and/or oils except fish oil). Others are subject either to special licences (90 tariff lines in the 1999-2000 budget: pulses, paddy/rice, rice bran, vegetable oils, some seaweed, certain types of oilcake, fodder), or are 'canalized' by State or parapublic bodies often specializing in the export of goods collected or produced by tribal communities in the forests (23 tariff lines in the 1999-2000 budget: karaya gum, onions and so on). Other products are also covered by export quotas (wheat and wheat products, coarse cereals and cereal flours, milk, including powdered milk and baby milk, sugar, brown seaweed and agarophyte in 2000), as they generally receive substantial domestic production support. Lastly, depending on world prices, some goods may sometimes be exported at a minimum price, as it was for instance the case for wheat and wheat products in 2000.

Indo-European Trade

Public export incentives, which were theoretically categorically banned under the GATT, have been subject to relatively clear conditions since the URAA: budget expenditure has to be cut (–36 per cent within six years for industrialized countries and –24 per cent within ten years for developing countries), as do corresponding product volumes (–21 per cent and –14 per cent respectively). Nevertheless, in 1994, it was considered that the support system established in India was neither wide-ranging nor significant enough to force the country to reduce that aid. While it has not notified the WTO of all its new measures since then, it has to be said that the aid bears no relation to the systems in place in the United States or the European Union, which are considered as artificial agricultural exporters: this is what India has always tried and will continue to try to hammer home, accusing rich countries of pushing down world commodity prices, thus robbing poor countries like itself of export revenue. While this is a more or less honest opinion, it does mask a reality: with economic liberalization, India is importing increasing volumes of processed products from these countries, and to compensate for this, it needs to boost its exports in sectors where it feels it has the greatest comparative advantages. The European Union is not only India's leading supplier, but also its biggest customer: a quarter of Indian exports were sent to Europe in 1997 (about 22 per cent in 2004-5), which represented, according to UNCTAD, almost $11 billion of expenditure for the EU. Of those $11 billion, almost 15 per cent (1.6 billion) were imports of 'agricultural products' (in the GATT sense of the term), including nine tariff lines amounting to over $50 million, headed by coffee (unroasted), cashew nuts, rice (brown and basmati) and black tea. European imports of Indian agricultural products have grown steadily since 1994, resulting in a trade balance in favour of India of virtually $1.2 billion in 1996 (Table 14). Whether or not this is a direct effect of the URAA, some observers feel that the trend is likely to continue unless Europe introduces increasingly stringent sanitary barriers on imports.

Market Access: A Comfortable Reform

Import Barriers

The European Union has long been India's biggest customer and also its leading supplier, albeit overall, as agricultural products are an exception. In 1996, for instance, of $2.1 billion worth of agricultural imports (in the GATT sense of the term), just 5 per cent came from the European Union, while 9 per cent came from North America (United States and Canada) and almost 22 per cent from the four main countries in the Cairns group (Argentina, Australia, Brazil and New Zealand). Agricultural imports, which in the late 1990s centred on four categories amounting to over $100 million (palm oil, cashew nuts for re-export, peas and occasionally wheat), now represent just 6 or 7 per cent of total imports into India. In this sector more than in any other, there are still numerous very stringent import barriers, despite the 1991 reforms and the URAA in 1994. In the year 2000, there were still three non-tariff barrier (NTB) systems alongside the Open General Licence (OGL) allowing for free imports (Table 15). The various tariff barriers (duty and taxes vary from one budget to the next, see Table 16 for the 1999-2000 figures) are among the most stringent in the world. In addition, there are anti-dumping measures, and others imposed by the various states in the Union, which are allowed to levy duty on a range of products (notably alcohol). There are some exemptions or reductions, notably under the 1975 Bangkok agreement (Bangladesh, Korea, India, Laos, Papua New Guinea and Sri Lanka) and the South Asian Free Trade Area (SAFTA) that came into force in 2006 after the ten-year experience of South Asia Preferential Trade Agreement (SAPTA). The latter was ratified in 1995 by the seven countries of the South Asian Association for Regional Cooperation (Bangladesh, Bhutan, India, the Maldives, Nepal, Pakistan and Sri Lanka) and provided tax rebate to neighbouring countries (less than $5 million in 1996 on $50 million of Indian imports) since India exports more to its neighbours than it imports from them.

TABLE 14: AGRICULTURAL PRODUCT IMPORTS BY THE EUROPEAN AND INDIAN UNIONS (1991 TO 1997)

		1991	1992	1993	1994	1995	1996	1997
European imports								
• All origins	US $ (million)	53,365	57,100	50,752	58,711	66,807	65,312	68,993
	6-digit lines	694	694	694	693	691	702	703
• Indian origin	US $ (million)	842	853	882	1,088	1,167	1,283	1,601
	6-digit lines	204	218	230	245	250	257	267
• IU's market share	%	1.6	1.5	1.7	1.9	1.7	2.0	2.3
Indian imports								
• All origins	US $ (million)	669	–	1,032	2,219	2,064	2,106	–
	6-digit lines	232	–	304	334	352	361	–
• European origin	US $ (million)	32	–	69	160	106	106	–
	6-digit lines	150	–	178	221	247	253	–
• EU's market share	%	4.7	–	6.7	7.2	5.1	5.0	–
Trade balance (IU-EU)	US $ (million)	+811	–	+813	+928	+1061	+1177	–

Source: Based on from UNCTAD (2000) and Dorin (2004).

TABLE 15: NON-TARIFF IMPORT BARRIER REGIMES (1999)

PROHIBITED	Import of products under this regime is totally prohibited in order to protect, for instance, certain wild species, or for security reasons linked to religion, such as beef tallow.
CANALIZED	Products under this regime can only be imported through State Trading Enterprises (STE) whose role consists of monitoring, supervising and intervening in markets for the generally proffered motive of food security: • FCI – Food Corporation of India (cereals and, from time to time, other PDS items) • STC – State Trading Corporation (cereals, pulses, edible oils, fertilizers...) • NAFED – National Agriculture Co-operative Federation of India (PDS products) • STCL – Spices Trading Corporation (spices) • NSC – National Seeds Corporation (seeds) • NDDB – National Dairy Development Board (milk and milk products and, from time to time, edible oils, fruit and vegetables...) • HVOC – Hindustan Vegetables Oils Corporation (edible oils)
RESTRICTED	For a variety of official reasons, the import of these products is only possible after obtaining a licence or a notification, which cannot be transferred to a third-party and is only valid for one transaction (precious or semi-precious stones, consumer goods, products whose manufacture has been reserved for the Small Scale Industry, etc.).
SIL	However, the Special Import Licences (SIL) are also included in this 'Restricted' regime. They are issued for specific products to exporters by way of a bonus, worth 2 to 5 per cent of the value of exports realized in foreign exchange,* and can be transferred to third parties against payment of a premium that ranged between 6 and 12 per cent in 1999.

Note: * While India does not officially apply quantitative restrictions in the form of fixed quotas, these limits nevertheless constitute an implicit form.
Source: Dorin (2004).

TABLE 16: IMPORT DUTY REGIMES (1999-2000)

BCD	The Basic Custom Duty can take the form of high tariff peaks for certain products
SCD	The Special Custom Duty was announced in the 1999–2000 budget in the form of a 10 per cent surcharge on the basic duty
ACD	The Additional Custom Duty has been in force for the past several years
SAD	The Special Additional Duty amounts to 4 per cent since the 1998–9 budget (2 per cent and later 3 per cent in preceding years); it is aimed at compensating taxes imposed on the sale of domestic products

Source: Dorin (2004).

Quantitative Restrictions (NTB)

Six years after Marrakech, India was thus still protecting its borders in many ways, despite its agreement in April 1994 to totally dismantle its non-tarrif barriers (NTB) and convert them into customs duty, as stipulated in the 'Market Access' schedule of the URAA, which allows for just one exception to this condition: the 'Special Treatment' that India ruled out. However, the promise made in Marrakech was not entirely sincere. Since the 1991 Structural Adjustment Plan, the country had divided the number of products on its 'negative list' (almost 11,000 lines at the time) by four, but in 1994, it was determined to maintain most of its remaining NTBs in line with article XVIII:B of the GATT, a concession in favour of developing countries that India had regularly called upon since 1957 in order to safeguard its balance of payments and ensure sufficient reserves to be able to implement its economic development programme. The *status quo* was thus maintained until 1997, when the plot thickened, as the Reserve Bank of India itself admitted that its monetary reserves had reached $29.9 billion on 14 August (including gold and SDRs), or the equivalent of seven months of imports and thus much more than would normally be considered sufficient (three months of imports). Most developing countries accepted the nine-year dismantlement plan proposed by India, but some disagreed. In November 1997, India submitted a new programme based on the lists of specific interests presented by the various members, this time spread over six years (from 1 April 1997 to 31 March 2003), in three phases (three years, two years and one year), for 2,714 product lines. The European Union, Switzerland, Canada, Japan and Australia agreed, even though the lifting of NTBs on sensitive products was not scheduled until the final phase.

Dispute with the United States

However, the United States refused, and called upon the WTO Dispute Settlement Body (DSB) to impose a more rapid lifting of restrictions on these lines, 710 of which were agricultural (26 per cent). In April 1999, the DSB ruled against India. Nevertheless, in its voluminous report, the panel appreciated 'the courage and sagacity with which India has carried out its economic reform programme', particularly the extensive liberalization of foreign trade and financial transactions, the unification of the exchange rate and the introduction of current account transactions convertibility. For its part, India remained convinced of the significant contradictions between the obligations of financial rigour imposed by the IMF under the Structural Adjustment Plan and the rapid opening up of markets recommended by the WTO. It attempted to have the 15 months the United States had allotted it to conform to the decision extended, while continuing to lift its restrictions on imports of various product lines as proof of its goodwill. At the end of 1999, an agreement was reached on the dismantlement of the remaining NTBs on 1,429 eight-digit lines: 715 were to be lifted by 31 March 2000 and the remaining 714 by 31 March the following year. This was done within the allotted time, and with a 35 per cent customs duty generally imposed on the lines that had not been bound in 1994 (see below). Except that India maintained various quantitative restrictions in the name of Articles XX and XXI of the GATT (health and national security reasons) for instance, or of biodiversity.

In 2001-2, cereal, copra and urea imports were thus still 'canalized', i.e. subject to a monopoly on the part of State Trading Enterprises (STE), while other products (sugar cane, beetroot, onions, potatoes, medicinal herbs and most seeds and fertilizers) were covered by other types of restrictions. More generally, all agricultural imports were subject to prior authorization on the part of the authorities, and almost 300 'sensitive' products were being monitored by a 'war room' to prevent 'abnormal' floods of imports and with a view to reintroducing quotas if necessary. It was planned to relax some of these measures in future, provided India was allowed to up its tariffs on the lines it bound at excessively low rates in 1994.

Tariff Binding

Since Marrakech, it has also been compulsory to bind customs tariffs for all agricultural products. With a few exceptions (for instance, the URAA 'Special Safeguard Clause' authorizes the temporary imposition of additional levies under very specific conditions), rates (or average rates, depending on the case in question) can no longer be increased in response to political or economic circumstances. When converting NTBs into customs duty rates, the bound tariffs must not exceed a figure corresponding to the difference between domestic and international prices over the 'base' or 'reference' period (1986-8), unless countries opt for 'ceiling binding', like many developing countries and India in particular, which had not really bound their tariffs, if at all, in the past. In this last case, a ceiling is set for each product line (and not per group of products), not necessarily with any link to existing protective measures, the only obligation being to maintain, on arithmetic average, the same level of market access allowed by the basic customs duty rates applied during the reference period. This is restrictive, since it does not allow for any subsequent 'tariff play'. However, it does exempt countries from having to reduce their tariffs (–36 per cent within six years for developing countries and –24 per cent within ten years for developing countries) and from minimum access criteria (between 3 and 5 per cent of domestic consumption for industrialized countries), two other URAA conditions that consequently were not to concern India until 2005. However, India did bind 3,374 six-digit product lines in 1994 (67 per cent of tariff positions, while only 6 per cent had been bound prior to the URAA), including 673 lines for agricultural products. Nonetheless, this agricultural binding was a somewhat soft option, as the arithmetic average of the tariffs applied in 1986–8 (the reference period) was 114 per cent: apart from 100 lines set at under 100 per cent (including 11 at 0 per cent), the rate for the others was generally set at 100 per cent for primary commodities, 150 per cent for processed products and 300 per cent for vegetable oils (Table 17).

Customs Duty

The customs duty actually imposed on agricultural products has not generally reached these levels (the average figure in 2004–5 was 37.5 per cent to be compared with 113 per cent in 1990–1),

TABLE 17: SUMMARY OF BINDING RATES FOR AGRICULTURAL PRODUCTS (1994)

0%	Rice, common wheat, sorghum, maize, millet, milk and cream in solid form
10%	Vegetable seeds, bulbs, tubers, roses, trees and plants with roots
25%	Skins and leathers
35%	Animal feed products
40%	Milk products, including butter, casein, cheeses
45%	Olive, soya and rape/mustard oils
55%	Soups and vegetable preparations
60%	Concentrates for non-alcoholic drinks, dessert powders
85%	Fruit juices
100%	Living animals, fresh, frozen, deep-frozen or dried meat, certain fruits and vegetables, durum wheat, barley, rye, oats, edible nuts, sugar, chocolate and chocolate-based preparations, plant seeds
150%	Coffee, tea, spices, bakery products, many processed food products, drinks, tobacco
300%	Edible oils and animal fats with a few exceptions (olive, soya, rape/mustard)

Source: Dorin (2004).

but has in some cases, to replace the NTBs abolished in April 2001. Except for a few products (milk, cereals, soyabean and rapeseed oils, etc.) that were consolidated at very low levels, India could thus quite easily continue to restrict access to its domestic market, which peaked at 2.5 per cent in the mid-1990s (Table 18). Customs duty is also a major source of revenue: over $16 billion in 1997-8 all products and taxes combined, or 27 per cent of total central government revenue. In that budget year, basic duty on palm oil alone brought in more than $187 million. This illustrates another facet of Indian foreign trade, which is controlled by powerful lobbies: some imports are not only a vital and expected source of revenue for the central government and the semi-public organizations in charge of channelling purchases, but also a source of high profits for corrupt civil servants and/or industrialists who may—sometimes in collusion, sometimes not—divert domestic subsidies based on those imports (see the case of vegetable oil in Chapter 4). In short, the tariff weapon will no doubt continue to be used for some time in India, particularly as the country is not keen to sign an agreement at the end of the current cycle of WTO talks that would reduce the rates bound in 1994. For India—and it was very clear at the Doha submit in 2001—the main concern is to apply the decisions made in Marrakech effectively, as it feels that industrialized countries have largely dodged these decisions thanks to the degree of 'play' allowed in both rate binding and reduction. Similarly, India is firmly against linking environmental or social issues with trade issues, as it feels that this would lead to introduce disguised NTBs that poor countries would be unable to overcome, alongside other obstacles that have already developed at their expense in recent years (phytosanitary issues, packaging and labelling standards, protection of trademarks and origins, etc.).

A HUGE MARKET TO SATISFY (UP TO 2030)

Food Projections

For most foodstuffs, India barricades its borders to provide it for its own population: a basic right. However, within the next 20 to 30 years, will it not have to import massive volumes that its farmers will be unable to produce in sufficient quantities and quality when it will have almost 1.4 billion inhabitants? Even now, the subcontinent is unable to ensure the nutritional security of a population that still generally makes do with very little. In

TABLE 18: FOOD MARKET ACCESS (1991 TO 1996)

			1991	1993	1994	1995	1996
Agricultural product imports		US $ (million)	669	1,032	2,219	2,064	2,106
PFCE*	- Food, drink, tobacco	US $ (million)	86,236	86,550	98,633	101,887	110,544
	- Food only	US $ (million)	78,471	78,595	89,369	90,709	98,064
Access	- Food, drink, tobacco	% (import/cons.)	0.8 %	1.2%	2.2%	2.0%	1.9%
	- Food only	% (import/cons.)	0.9%	1.3%	2.5%	2.3%	2.1%

Note: *PFCE = Private Final Consumption Expenditure

Source: Dorin (2004).

future, that population will probably not only be larger and more urbanized, but also—and this is both to be hoped and worked for—more demanding, as it will be wealthier. According to the World Bank, India is already the world's fourth largest economy in purchasing power parity terms, behind the United States, China and Japan (its adjusted GNP was $3,347 billion in 2004). The National Council of Applied Economic Research (NCAER), for its part, has estimated the very richest population sector with access to the most costly consumer goods at a million households or 6 million people in 2000. As for the middle class, with two or three consumer durables (car, colour television, microwave oven, and so on) and capable of purchasing at least one other, it is considered to include 30 million households, or 150 million individuals (India's mobile subscribers crossed 100 million in May 2006). In addition, at least 50 million households were just beginning to buy goods such as black and white televisions or sewing machines. All these families are also changing their eating habits: by 2030, if annual growth in per capita GDP is of 5.5 per cent on average, the Indian Council of Agricultural Research (ICAR) has estimated that demand for meat, eggs and fish could more than treble in relation to the 1995 figure (Figure 36), with that for vegetables, fruit and milk

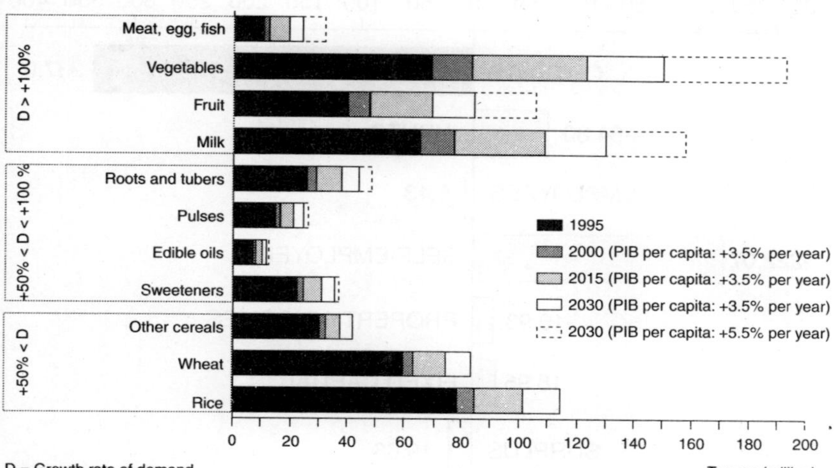

Source: Based on Paroda and Kumar (2000) in Dorin (2004).

FIGURE 36: PROJECTIONS OF THE DEMAND FOR FOOD (2000, 2015, 2030)

not far behind (+180, +166 and +142 per cent respective growth since 1995). Conversely, demand for cereals is unlikely to exceed 234 million tonnes (240 with a GDP growth rate of 3.5 per cent), since the growth in demand (+39 per cent since 1995) will be led more by the need to feed animals than humans. As ICAR concludes, if India's past record in terms of agriculture is anything to go by, the country is much better equipped to cope with these challenges than its South Asian neighbours (where the trends are expected to be similar). However, in view of the recent past, it is also quite clear that it is not the technical progress of the green (cereals) revolution that will ensure the necessary gains in productivity.

Productivity From 1980–1 to 1995–6, Indian agricultural surplus accounts demonstrated a particularly modest increase in productivity gains (technical progress): in constant rupee terms (1980–1), the overall cumulated surplus of productivity over this 15-year period was no more than 20 billion (Figure 37), i.e. less than 3 per cent of agricultural GDP in 1995–6. On average, the annual increase in productivity ('instant surpluses') did not exceed 0.25 per cent of

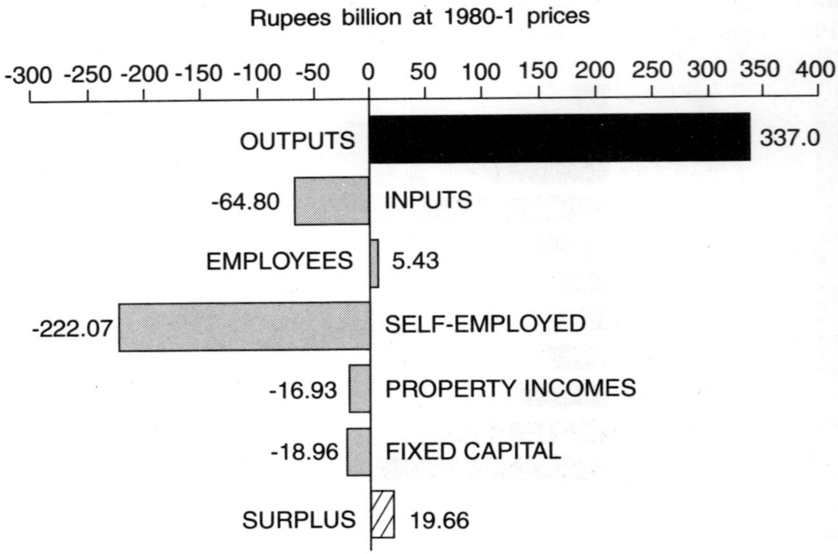

Source: Dorin et al. (2004).

FIGURE 37: CUMULATED SURPLUSES OVER 15 YEARS (1980-1 TO 1995-6)

agricultural GDP. However, agricultural production did grow significantly over the same period (in quantity terms, the 15-year increase was equivalent to 337 billion, including 33 per cent from animal production). Obviously, and at least for crops, the gains in India are neither 'progressive' (production growth without an increase in costs) nor 'recessive' (stable production but reduced costs) as observed in European Union countries between 1968 and 1986, for instance. They are rather 'intensive': the strong growth in production is almost entirely offset by a significant increase in the use of certain production factors. Those factors correspond to the inputs subsidized by the government since the Green Revolution (primarily fertilizers and energy for irrigation), but also and above all, the work brought by the growing number of farmers. In other words, the increase in family labour primarily boosted production that served to sustain the people involved. In this food economy where it is very difficult to substitute capital for work, any gains in productivity are thus largely down to the land (with a risk of exhaustion) and to paid labour (which decreased proportionally over the period in question). In short, for Indian crops, the formation of

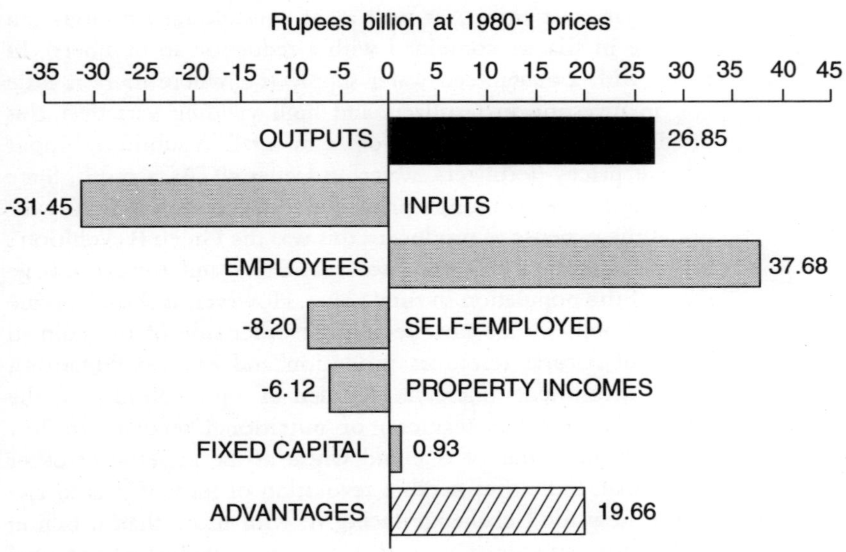

Source: Dorin et al. (2004).

FIGURE 38: CUMULATED ADVANTAGES OVER 15 YEARS (1980-1 TO 1995-6)

productivity gains did not seem to go beyond the Green Revolution recipe, and it is easy to imagine the dead end of this model which can no longer produce more without using ever greater amounts of water and fertilizers. Research seems to be resting on its laurels, whereas it needs to be twice as active and imaginative, particularly in order to adapt to regions with the greatest potential for marginal productivity gains (arid or semi-arid areas, isolated zones with low levels of education, and so on). In view of the challenges it faces, it should also broaden its fields of investigation, which are unfortunately still focused on wheat and rice.

Distributed Surpluses

That said, the legacy left by the Green Revolution of the 1960s does not boil down to a now obsolete model of increased cereal production. It can be shown by studying the distribution of agricultural surpluses or, in other words, the 'advantages' or 'disadvantages' derived from positive or negative price variations (Figure 38: by convention, for products, relative price variations are preceded by a minus sign). For the period considered, overall distribution in real terms was in favour of consumers (thanks to crop products, and particularly the fall in relative cereal, oilseed and sugar cane prices) as well as of agricultural labourers (an increase in salaries combined with a reduction in numbers). In zones with a guaranteed water supply (i.e. where there is little risk in investing in fertilizers and high yielding varieties), this disadvantage for growers was offset by a fall in subsidized input relative prices (fertilizers, water and energy). As a result, State subsidies for low consumer prices for certain basic foodstuff were not at the expense of producers: this was the Green Revolution's biggest success, as it served to sedentarize and sustain a large share of the population in rural zones. However, as shown before in this book, we are now seeing the other side of the coin in terms of natural resources (pollution and over-exploitation), public investments (increasing burden of input subsidies to the detriment of other services) or nutritional security (policy primarily in favour of rice and wheat at the expense of other foodstuffs). India thus needs a revolution of ideas if it is to rise to the new food challenge facing it: with more than a billion people, we can at least assert that it has the intellectual potential to succeed, and that this potential will no doubt be spurred on by the huge pressure the country is currently under.

9. Conclusion

India is a land of exceptional human and natural resources (Chapter 1). Under British rule, it was a leading producer and exporter of cotton, spices, tea and other tropical foodstuffs. It kept this leadership after its Independence in 1947 (Chapter 2), and also became self-sufficient in cereals within fifteen years, thanks to the Green Revolution launched after the death of Nehru in 1964 (Chapter 3). The dark forecasts of the early 1960s proved wrong: India did not become a land of famine, despite the formidable growth in its population. This great success left its mark on Indian leaders: the green revolution has shown the world the modernity of this young republic as well as its ability not to rely on foreign aid and power for its basic needs.

However, since the 1980s, India seems to have been resting on its laurels. It has not managed to capitalize on its success by breaking free of a model that is now clearly showing its limitations, but that is still influencing a good many decision-makers. Without caricaturing it too much, this model can be summed up through the five following equations:

(1)	food	=	wheat + rice
(2)	productivity	=	irrigation + fertilizers
(3)	food security	=	public procurement + redistribution
(4)	employment	=	small firms
(5)	subservience	=	imports + foreign capital

The first equation, 'food = wheat + rice', merely sums up the foodstuffs on which public efforts and funding have focused for the first forty years after Independence, under the Indian food policy: wheat and rice, on which international research has also capitalized a lot. This preferential treatment did not prevent other agricultural revolutions taking place in India, such as the white (dairy) revolution or the yellow (oilseeds) revolution (Chapter 4). However, the former was primarily the fruit of the labours of one man, V. Kurien, and of the network of cooperatives he fostered by dealing skilfully with the central authorities in New

Delhi. As for the yellow revolution, it began only in the mid-1980s when India had become the world's leading vegetable oil importer, and it did not last long since it disturbed certain ministerial departments, business circles and also wheat and rice production: massive vegetable oil imports resumed just ten years later. Other foodstuffs that the green revolution passed by, such as pulses, fruit and vegetables, could also be imported massively to satisfy the nutritional needs of the Indian population. However, between imports and domestic price inflation, India has tended to opt for the latter, which, after all, has helped the development of horticulture and animal production since the 1980s, albeit primarily for the benefit of wealthy households or foreign markets (Chapter 5). Democracy is sometimes the only way of giving the poorest better access to foodstuffs other than wheat and rice, like in October 1998: rocketing onion prices almost brought down the government of the Union and helped the opposition to victory in four states where elections were held simultaneously.

The second equation, 'productivity = irrigation + fertilizers', dates back fifteen years before the green revolution, since the First Five Year Plan in 1951 already saw agricultural production as a mathematical function to be maximized with two variables: water and fertilizers. Since then, it has worked very well, but every possible step has been taken to make this the only equation: high-yielding varieties (HYV) cannot express their potential without sufficient quantities of water and fertilizers, whose use is in turn truly cost-effective only with (rice and wheat) HYVs. There is little hope of salvation outside that circle, notably in non-irrigated semi-arid and arid zones, which account for more than a third of the land in India. In these regions, yields are particularly low for want of fertilizers whose application is too risky and without HYVs able to grow under water stress conditions. There can thus be only one crop per year, during the rainy season, and revenue redistribution through subsidies in favour of fertilizers, water and fossil fuel-based energies (for pumping groundwater or making fertilizers) is negligible, whereas these input subsidies have become the main public incentives in favour of Indian agriculture. This subsidy system, which favours the wealthiest farmers and disregards the poorest rural communities (Chapter 6), and which also relies on low fossil fuel prices, is no longer sustainable in environmental terms (Chapter 7): in the very basins championed by the Green Revolution, groundwater reserves are being exhausted by tube wells, soils asphyxiated by overflows of free water from canals, rivers polluted by fertilizers and pesticides, and biodiversity spoiled by rice and wheat monocultures. It is hard to see how the farmers in these basins can escape from this trap, whereas their fertile soils and their dynamism once led them to build the granary of India.

The third equation, 'food security = public procurement + redistribution', was guided by two basic objectives: to secure farmers' incomes from a sharp fall in the prices of their products, and to insure the poorest citizens against a lack of commodities deemed essential for their subsistence. From these good intentions there emerged a system of minimum support prices (MSP) upstream, and a public distribution system (PDS) downstream. However, between the two, the government had to introduce 'procurement prices' in order to build-up public stocks and redistribute them via the PDS. These procurement prices were introduced at national level in 1971, but only for rice and wheat—alongside a similar system for sugar—and they were in fact the ones that secured farmers' incomes, since MSPs were set at such low levels that they very rarely led to public intervention. These procurement prices naturally encouraged farmers to grow wheat and rice whenever possible (up to 38 per cent of the total gross cropped area, i.e. more than 70 million ha in 2000 as against 55 in 1970), and they played a central role in supplying Indian households with these two basic foodstuffs. But the other side of the coin is that at the same time, other important food items like pulses or vegetables, outside the PDS, became available only at certain times of the year, or at prices beyond the reach of too many consumers. These food items supply nutrients that cereals alone cannot supply in sufficient quantities, even if their per capita consumption is high. This may provide an explanation of the present situation: despite the great achievements of the green revolution, India still accounts for a major share of the world's undernourished people, since the majority of its population lacks proteins (60 per cent), fats (50 per cent), vitamin A, and iron. In other words, the country may today be the world's leading producer of pulses, vegetables, fruit or milk, but there is some way to go before these foodstuffs are supplied to the population like cereals now are. Unless a solution is found through massive imports as is now the case for vegetable oils.

The fourth equation, 'employment = small firms', is a legacy of Gandhian thought, easily taken up by intellectuals and national leaders, but also by the small number of major industrial families who bore the establishment of a mixed economy in so far as the State bought goods from them while protecting them from foreign competition. This mixed economy was in effect an employment policy: to provide jobs for the growing working population, particularly in rural areas, it opted for modest but evenly and relatively well-distributed growth (the so-called 'Hindu growth rate') by banking on crafts, small-scale industries and small-scale trade rather than on large capitalist enterprises. From land ownership to food shops, a good many acts, licences, ceilings and taxes were introduced, which both multiplied the number of firms—along with middlemen—and, conversely, hampered their growth in terms of size. Even now, from farms to shops via mills or canning factories, it remains difficult to 'think big' in India. This 'licence raj' prevented massive population migration from rural to urban areas, and limited the development of abject poverty and violence in overcrowded slums. But here again, there is another side to the coin. With low financial capacity or drastic limitations on expansion, how can Indian firms be expected to invest in the training, expertise or equipment they need? Or in the processing, storage or distribution chains that the country currently lacks? How can they control certain upstream or downstream activities to reduce the cost of dealing with middlemen? to guarantee high, consistent product quality at a reasonable price? How, above all, can they reduce losses and wastage? This wastage is currently huge in India, as for instance for fruit and vegetables, about half of which are lost between field and stall, whereas they are still in short supply in too many Indian plates.

The fifth and last equation, 'subservience = imports + foreign capital', harks back to the *swadeshi* movement against British imperialism. The trend since then had long been to protect the domestic market against foreign competition and influence, so as to build and affirm the country's independence. The 1947 Imports and Exports Control Act and the 1955 Import Trade Control Order set out to ban imports of consumer goods, some intermediate and processed goods, and products considered 'non-essential' for a mostly poor population. In 1973, Indira Gandhi also had the FERA passed, limiting multinational share ownership in their Indian subsidiaries to 40 per cent (IBM and Coca Cola pulled out of the country a few years later). But two decades on, India's financial collapse in July 1991 and the subsequent Structural Adjustment Plan were the nail in the coffin of this closed economy (Chapter 8). However, free-market orthodoxy is still hotly debated, particularly in the agricultural sector. Reforms were launched concerning fertilizer subsidies, and so as to pinpoint the beneficiaries of the PDS more effectively, but at the same time, when the Indian Union signed the Marrakech Agreements in 1994, it hoped that article XVIII/B of the GATT would allow it to keep its many non-tariff barriers (NTBs) on agricultural imports for some considerable time. However, it was betting on the poor structural health of its balance of payments, whereas by mid-1997, its currency reserves had reached almost $30 billion, a comfortable situation partly due to the growth in agricultural exports (coffee, tea, spices, cashew nuts; fish and shellfish; basmati rice; soybean oilcake). After all sorts of incidents, India was ordered to lift all these barriers by April 2001, which it did. With the exception of a few products, however, import duties could now very well replace those NTBs, since on average, and entirely legally under WTO rules, the rate on agricultural products can be anything up to 114 per cent.

The world's second largest food market can thus continue to protect itself from outside influences. However, it is often from the inside that upheavals come. The 1991 reforms asserted the principles of a market economy in which supply responds primarily to solvent private demand rather than to state-controlled consumption. Since then, a shining Indian middle class has emerged from 'Indian Socialism' (farmers favoured by the green revolution, heads of family firms, civil servants, traders): more than 200 million people eager and able to buy consumer goods that were barely available a few years ago, like cars, two-wheelers, televisions, mobile phones or washing machines. These households are also changing their eating habits: Indian demand for meat, eggs and fish is likely to treble by 2030, when the country will probably have almost 1.4 billion inhabitants and a much more urbanized population. Demand for fruit, vegetables and milk is also likely to increase tremendously—along with that for bio-energies, bio-materials and eco-friendly foods.

Conversely, that for cereals is unlikely to be more than 40 million tonnes above 2005 production (nearly 200 million tonnes), most of this extra being to feed animals and not humans.

Indian agriculture is woefully unprepared for this change. But how can it be reorganized? In May 1999, the Indian president called for a new agricultural revolution. This is as vital for the 50 per cent of the population suffering from under-nutrition as for the other 50 per cent keen to diversify the cereal-based diet imposed by the green revolution. But how can it be done? The president's answer was that India needed to invent rather than imitate. There is no doubt about it: the disconcerting problems and questions raised by agriculture in India are not specific to the country, far from it, but because they are exacerbated by the country's high and ever-growing population density, they need to be solved there sooner than anywhere else. The Indian countryside is already full of original experiments and promising gardens. But in New Delhi, it must first be agreed that the equations of the past need to be reviewed at length if innovation is to flourish and bear all the fruits expected of it. A huge and challenging task lies ahead, but since the Indian elephant is accustomed to it, we dare to hope that we shall soon benefit from these new Indian equations. A sustainable doubly Green Revolution is required on a global level if we are to welcome nine billion inhabitants by 2050 or so, and we are all looking for the way ahead.

APPENDICES

APPENDIX 1

Two Indian Villages after the Green Revolution

There are two reasons for rounding off our book with two local case studies. The first is to provide some sort of summary of previous Chapters, given that villages and their farms are a condensed and often highly evocative version of many of the elements analysed above. The second is to pinpoint the variations in the environments surrounding Indian farms and in how they operate, and thus the difficulty of describing them, even though they are the leading players in the Indian agrifood economy. The text was first published in French in December 1997, in a special 'India' issue of the French monthly Chambres d'Agriculture.

Indian farms are not entirely unlike French farms in the 1950s: small, primarily family-run structures in which decisions are made by the head of the household, growing a range of crops—albeit dominated by cereals—as well as rearing animals. The internal complexity seen in sub-Saharan Africa as a result of the partial autonomy of women and the younger brothers is not an issue here, and India also differs from Africa in that its farmers practise complementary crop-animal operations on the same farm, which guarantees productivity: it provides animal draught and boosts soil fertility and energy production (dried dung is an excellent fuel). However, animal feed is a problem in a country where priority has always been given to feeding its very dense human population, and where incomes are often too low to buy fodder and compound feeds. India is thus 'caught between two stools': the 'crop-based civilization' of the Far East Asia, where animals are rare due to human population density, and the African system, where land pressure had remained limited until very recently.

However, can we generalize much further? Is there any such thing as a typical farm in India? As in Europe, an area similar in size, it is difficult to sum up the whole range of types in a single example. Are they mini-farms? Well, 62 per cent of farmers in 1995-6 had less than 1 ha, but farms of more than 10 ha, i.e. 1 per cent of the total number, nevertheless account for 15 per cent of the cultivated area. Traditional cropping systems? It is true that high-yielding varieties now account for slightly more than 40 per cent of cereal seed sales, and swing ploughs drawn by oxen are still the most commonly used implements, but Punjabi farmers use tractors and combine harvesters in their commercial production systems, which differ very little from those of French cereal farmers. To reflect these disparities, it thus seems more appropriate to describe two very different cases, in terms of the types of farm and of the cropping systems practised, as well as of the regional environment.

THE GREEN REVOLUTION IN MATHANA (HARYANA)[1]

Haryana, in the western Ganges plain, was the main beneficiary of the Green Revolution, along with neighbouring Punjab. By the end of the nineteenth century, these two states were already one of the most productive regions in India, and the best suited to growing high-yielding varieties in the future. The British colonial authorities had perfected the Himalayan network of diverted rivers set up in the Middle Ages, particularly in Haryana (the Western Yamuna canal was built in 1355). The area was further favoured by its proximity to Delhi, near the Great Trunk Road leading to Pakistan: capital, markets and urban influence have always been and are still easily available.

The population of Haryana, with an average density of 477 inhabitants/km^2 in 2001, is 71 per cent rural, slightly less than India as a whole. It is split between large villages, surrounded by geometric sets of fields often covering more than a hectare and an almost treeless landscape due to the extent of land clearance in the past. Mathana is one such village, with a bus stop, post office, secondary school, dispensary, market, rice mill and small shops: its 4,200 inhabitants mostly live in urban-style houses with flat concrete roofs, built around a courtyard. These houses, particularly those owned by the wealthiest villagers, are home to joint families, including uncles and grandparents, but the families are generally nuclear and the households have 'just' 6.5 members on average.

Almost all the available land, with its relatively fertile dark alluvial soil, is cultivated: there is no fallow, despite the fact that rain (less than 900 mm a year) falls only during the monsoon, in July-August. Everything is irrigated, not by the canals that fell into disuse in the 1970s, but by deep private tube wells that have been equipped with submersible pumps since 1984 so as to reach the water table, which is now as much as 24 m below the surface during the dry season. All the elements of the Green Revolution are there: large numbers of tube wells, an agricultural extension and credit network (a 'cooperative' enables farmers to buy fertilizers and phytosanitary products and repay their loans after the harvest), high-yielding varieties, and even mechanization: all the landowners have a tube well (and even two, on average, with 15-HP pumps), and all the farmers with more than 4 ha of land have a tractor (generally 28-HP). Farmers who do not own their own equipment increasingly hire harvesters,

[1]Based on dissertations for French M.Phil. in Geography and in Economics by Delphine Grandcolas and Christine Rosellini (University of Paris X, 1996).

threshers, sprayers and tractors. Overall, yields are satisfactory: 3.6 tonnes of wheat per hectare, four times more than 40 years ago. This is despite the fact that up to three crops are grown each year: rice during the monsoon (using a 60-day variety means two crops), or maize if the plot is insufficiently irrigated, and wheat during the dry season on two-thirds of the cultivated area, along with oilseeds, pulses, and Egyptian clover (*barseem, Trifolium alexandrianum*) for livestock (there is no grazing).

Dharam Pal lives on 10 ha with his two brothers (one of whom is currently away in the army), their families and a farmhand. He is one of the wealthier farmers in Mathana. When interviewed in March 1996 alongside a 1.2-ha wheat field, he explained that in November or late October, after the rice harvest, he ploughs the field four or five times with a disc plough, flattens and waters it and then goes over it another twice or three times with a Canadian cultivator. He sows his wheat in December (105 kg of WH 542 seed/ha, mixed with 150 kg of diammonium phosphate and sometimes with 75 kg of urea), using seed that he replaces every three years or so, once smut begins to appear. Three weeks later, he irrigates the field again, adding 150 kg of urea/ha, plus a weedkiller (isoproturon). After another three weeks, he waters it yet again if necessary, maybe adding 75 kg of urea/ha. He has been applying increasing amounts of fertilizer in recent years, otherwise his yields would have dropped.

In April, the wheat is harvested with a scythe, or sometimes with a hired harvester. However, harvesters cut the stems too high up, which produces less straw to feed Dharam Pal's animals, and hired labourers, whom he pays less than 250 kg of grain per hectare harvested, are in fact more cost-effective than one might think. Dharam Pal usually hopes for around four tonnes per hectare, and maybe more provided the field has not been overrun by blackgrass, which is proving increasingly herbicide-resistant. The wheat is threshed using a thresher powered by his tractor engine (over half a hectare can be threshed in a night).

Dharam Pal is one of the lucky ones: he has land and a tractor. However, he does have his problems, which are shared by all the farmers in the village and demonstrate the shortcomings of the green revolution. They can be split into four types.

(a) The small area of land available is a major handicap. Dharam Pal can expect an annual yield per hectare greater than that of many French farms, but he is still poorer than the majority of French farmers. This is obviously due to the difference in prices and subsidies between the two countries, but also due to the lack of land. The average farm size in Mathana (2.3 ha) is barely above the Indian average. There are also significant variations. Of the two-thirds of villagers who are farmers, half are agricultural labourers, working full time if they do not own land themselves, or to top up their meagre income if they do have a patch of land. Each full-time worker thus cultivates between 0.8 and 5 ha, depending on the farm.

These economic disparities roughly tally with the inequalities between castes. Scheduled Castes (Dalits) make up 30 per cent of the population in Mathana: they are generally landless and mostly live in mud huts with straw or corrugated iron roofs, rarely with electricity, grouped together in quite separate parts of the village, in contrast to the homes owned by people from the Ror or Jat castes, where the television will be on most evenings. Some Rors are indeed landless, but generally speaking, the alleged degree of religious purity is correlated with household incomes; there is a strong relation between class and caste position.

Incomes in the village vary by a factor of 1 to 20, and maybe even more if we take account of the many large landowners who have managed to dodge the legal maximum of 7.25 ha of irrigated land per family. The most shocking case is probably that of the seasonal migrants who come from Bihar or eastern Uttar Pradesh between April (wheat harvest) and July (rice transplanting). They are generally housed in huts out in the fields, and their starvation wages create competition for the local day labourers and the few farmhands still found on the largest farms.

The future looks bleak in this respect. The traditional inheritance system splits the legacy into as many shares as there are sons (just under two on average). There is also the matter of dowries: some day labourers have to come up with the equivalent of three times their annual wage when their daughters marry. Although having a son goes some way towards restoring a balance, and although these exchanges of money take place within a closed circuit, i.e. within the endogamy group, dowries are still a major blow from which some farms never recover. Lastly, and above all, agriculture is still more or less the only occupation option.

(b) Economic diversification is in effect still limited. The high proportion (by Indian standards) of non-agricultural workers here bears witness to the region's wealth: over a third of people in Mathana own a small shop or a poultry farm, or work at the rice mill or for the local bus company. It is these people who wear trousers rather than the traditional white *dhoti* (loincloth), and they often have the highest qualifications. However, less than half the villagers (two-thirds of them men) can read and write: this figure, which is even lower than the Indian average, no doubt reflects the profitability of farming (there is no need to invest in education in order to be sure of making a living). However, it is equally clearly an obstacle to the diversification of rural activities.

(c) Nor does this low level of education do anything to foster solidarity between farmers or the formation of groups that would help ensure sustainable development. Such development is now under serious threat. Between 1974 and 1994, the water table dropped by 8 m. In addition to the extra cost to agriculture of having to install ever deeper submersible pumps, it is the very principle of irrigated agriculture that is in question. Loans to sink wells and install pumps are still distributed relatively liberally, with no specified minimum distance between wells. Water is cheap, indeed free, and electricity is billed based on the power of the pumps used, rather than on actual consumption. The disappearance of irrigation canals was in fact the nail in the coffin of collective water management and marked the start of wholesale wastage.

Unlike in other villages in India, the water table in Mathana does not yet seem to be polluted, and soil salinization is not yet a problem. However, like anywhere else, against the advice of local agricultural advisers, farmers in Mathana have steadily increased the amount of chemical fertilizer they use. Moreover, weeds are proving increasingly herbicide-resistant. Organic fertilizer is not widely used, due to the energy problem: for lack of trees, cow dung is mainly used for fuel (there are piles of dried 'patties' on the edge of the village). Furthermore, mechanization is reducing the numbers of bullocks and male buffaloes. However, she-buffaloes, which are excellent milkers, are still very popular, and some farmers are beginning to rear cross-bred dairy cows, although they have not yet specialized in animal production or abandoned their crops.

(d) The viability of farming is thus less and less clear-cut. The land is still just as productive, but production costs have soared, particularly as fertilizer and electricity subsidies have been in the hot seat since the 1991 reforms. However, the government procurement prices for wheat are notoriously low: Rs. 415 per 100 kg in 1997, or around $11.60. That year, in the face of protests from farmers and the state authorities in Punjab and Haryana, and a strike by the Bharatiya Kisan Union (BKU), which boycotted sales to the government, New Delhi had to add a 'bonus' of Rs. 60 per 100 kg. However, that was not enough to pacify the protesters, particularly as at the same time, India resigned itself to importing almost 2 million tonnes for at least an equivalent price. The problem is in fact one of local overproduction, and even basmati rice is no exception.

The rice situation is so problematical that there is no local marketing circuit other than brokers, who all sell to the government: this guarantees producers an outlet, but also keeps prices down.

It is the largest farmers who have the upper hand in such situations. With anything over 7 ha sown with wheat, the net margin (income) becomes positive, by virtue of certain economies of scale. Incidentally, this figure just happens to be the legal land ownership ceiling set in Haryana, which is grist to the mill of people who would like to see the law relaxed. As these farmers have the means to take risks, they tend to grow wheat merely for their own consumption (their daring does not stretch to sacrificing their self-sufficiency in flour). They have changed their crop rotations in favour of crops that have been more profitable since the start of the yellow revolution, notably sunflower and rapeseed. They also grow more sugar cane, since they can afford to wait a year for it to mature. They sometimes even try chilli or potatoes, whereas small farmers, hampered by their need for self-sufficiency, grow wheat and rice year after year.

The future thus looks bleak for these small farmers whom the green revolution helped to make self-sufficient. The sharing of inherited land, the halt in yield growth, a shortage of non-agricultural jobs, and economic liberalization look likely to conspire to push them out of farming. Are we heading for a polarization of village life? Almost certainly. However, the process is still relatively slow-moving: smallholders are continuing to hire land to a much greater extent than they are letting out their own.

It is little consolation that the poor in Haryana are much better off than others in less developed parts of India, such as Jharkhand.

SARWAL, IN TRIBAL JHARKHAND

Bihar was already lagging behind in the nineteenth century. It was the poorest state in India, and was long overlooked by the green revolution, with steadily falling rice yields until 1974. In the central Ganges Plain, where fights over land between large landowners and the working classes cause dozens if not hundreds of deaths every year, class inequalities are compounded by caste inequalities (Dalits against higher castes). Moreover, in the mining region of the Damodar, the situation for the workers is exacerbated by the existence of a mafia backed by the political authorities.

Violence is less commonplace in what was southern Bihar, presently Jharkhand (forest country), at the northern tip of the Deccan Peninsula. However, its inhabitants are just as poor. Apart from a few isolated pockets of development, such as Ranchi or Jamshedpur, towns built on steel, this plateau 600 m above sea level is largely rural, and primarily inhabited by native groups (Adivasis). These people, known as 'tribes' in India, who were originally Animist rather than Hindu, claim to have been the country's first inhabitants: they are still concentrated in the isolated highland areas of central India, from Maharashtra to Orissa, and in the Himalayas. A range of policies has gradually been introduced to support both them and Dalits: quotas of reserved jobs in the public sector and seats in the national and state assemblies, study grants, and so on. Moreover, since 1908, it has been forbidden in Jharkhand (Chhotanagpur) to transfer tribal land to non-tribals. However, the legacy left by the area's history is continuing to make itself felt.

From the nineteenth century onwards, the zamindar system became institutionalized in Jharkhand and throughout northeastern India. Large absentee landowners of Hindu or Muslim origin levied taxes on the tribal groups, while violating their indigenous customs. The system, created by the British, in fact replaced the almost equally inegalitarian social structures set up by the Raja of Chhotanagpur. More or less forced migration to the tea estates of Assam or the mines of Bihar, and subsequently to the steelworks of Jamshedpur, added to the breakdown process of these tribal communities that Protestant missionaries had been working to convert since 1845. The regionalist movement, which has since been discredited by internal disputes and corruption, did obtain the division of the state of Bihar in 2000 and the creation of the state of Jharkhand, but it did not succeed in rejuvenating native cultures, not even that of the largest group, the Mundas.

The two neighbouring hamlets that make up the village of Sarwal are 20 km from the 8,63,000 inhabitants (2001) of Ranchi, the capital of Jharkhand, and 2 km from the nearest metalled road. Some 63 per cent of the village's inhabitants are from three Munda clans. The remainder are more or less 'tribalized' Hindus (who speak Hindi rather than Mundari): a low caste of potters, and Dalits who were initially blacksmiths or weavers. At the time of our first survey in 1984, there were 360 inhabitants, and the number of houses had quintupled since the 1910s. The houses were generally mud huts with handmade tile roofs and no windows (to keep them cool in the summer and warm in the winter, and to ward off evil spirits).

Rural population densities in the region are relatively high (more than 120 inhabitants/km^2 in 1991 around Sarwal), and land is in short supply, or in any case reasonable quality land, since nothing like all of the landscape is covered by fields. Just outside Sarwal, the 'jungle' begins; it is in fact a secondary forest of relatively small sal trees (*Shorea robusta*) in which tigers and elephants have now died out, despite official protection by the state. The remainder is a treeless, bare plateau of largely uncultivated land with granite outcrops, crossed by valleys in which rice is grown. The soils are red, sandy and acidic. In short, the environment is not really propitious to agriculture and has already been damaged by erosion and deforestation.

Of the two existing cropping systems, the less economically important but more common in spatial terms is the one practised in the highlands. Using only the monsoon (1,400 mm of rain per year), farmers generally practise three-year rotations of finger millet (ragi, *Eleusine coracana*) from which they make flatbread, traditional upland rice varieties, and black gram. They also grow some oilseeds (rapeseed/mustardseed), sometimes intercropped in the same field: these are the only traditional cash crops, but yields are very low (0.15 t/ha on average!). With rice or millet, they obtain 0.6 t/ha on average. Following the first monsoon rains in late June, fields are generally ploughed four times with a swing plough drawn by buffaloes or by yoked oxen. Swing ploughs are very fragile (and have to be replaced almost every year), and are entirely made of wood, except for the metal ploughshare, which is made by the local blacksmith. There are two types, with the heavier of the two being used in the last ploughing round for digging in. It is taboo for Munda women to touch ploughs, as legend has it that they were invented by the god Haram's wife. The seeds are sown broadcast, after fertilizing the soil in the case of millet: farmers apply between 5 and 10 t/ha of manure, which will already be dried out and leached from being stored in the open. They weed their fields by hand or with a hoe, not really taking any great care except with millet and black gram. Stick branches and decorated pots are planted in the soil to ward off evil spirits. The crop is harvested with a scythe in October or November before being threshed with a stick. In poor years, these fields do not produce anything except straw for livestock. However, farmers continue to cultivate these highland areas, as there are not enough paddy fields in the low lands to feed everyone.

The village economy relies on the cropping system practised in those low lands, as it centres on paddy, the staple food. On the horizontal terraces set up on the slopes, early varieties produce just 0.8 t/ha due to the limited amount of water (the fields are often dry from October onwards). However, in the valley bottoms with their clay soils, late paddy (which takes around five months to ripen) gives 1.4 t/ha in average, and sometimes as much as 2.2 t/ha. Yields are not always optimum, even when improved varieties are used or—even more rarely—when farmers are able to apply manure or urea. The huge variations in yield are in fact due to other factors: rainfall levels, adherence to the cropping calendar, uncontrolled grazing. Although this flooded rice growing system looks relatively sophisticated (terraces built with bunds to retain rainwater, common transplanting of seedlings), it is in fact far from perfect: the choice of seeds, of whether to transplant and of the dates of agricultural operations are often governed by constraints relating to the availability of livestock, cash and labour, or to gaps in the rains. The economic fragility of these farms hampers the cropping systems practised, as in the case of one Munda farmer in particular, who owns more than 6 ha, but is still poor as he has lost his four buffaloes to disease. He now has only two zebus, and as his children are too young to help him, he has to lease a good deal of his land to tenant farmers or sharecroppers. Yet as he is still officially classified as a 'big farmer', he cannot apply for an IRDP loan to buy animals.

After harvesting with a scythe in December or thereabouts, the farmers carry the sheaves from the fields on their backs, before using their buffaloes to thresh them. Once the women have winnowed the grain, it is tipped into large round baskets made from paddy straw rope, not forgetting to add a few drops of water so that the 'rice spirit' is not thirsty. The straw is stored in trees, away from animals (there is no risk of rain at this time of year). The women parboil and then hull the paddy as and when they need it, using foot-operated pestles whose regular beat can be heard in the village as early as five o'clock in the morning.

These low lands account for a growing proportion of the food supply (as recently as 1991, the PDS still was not operational in the region). It would seem that yields in the highlands are falling as a result of the drop in rainfall (perhaps linked to deforestation in the region), and soil fatigue due to insufficient fertilization. Organic fertilizer is in particularly short supply, due to the decreasing number of animals per farm, in turn caused by a reduction in the areas owned: like anywhere else in India, population growth and the sharing of inherited land have wreaked havoc.

The collapse of tribal social structures has also played a part, particularly the decline in solidarity which was one of the particularities of native culture, although its importance is no doubt exaggerated nowadays. One consequence of this has been the disappearance of the village herdsmen who used to look after the animals. This caste moved away as the growth in individualism was increasingly leading farmers to have their own children watch over their animals; the new system is cheaper and more flexible, but poses a threat to crops, as the young herdsmen are less vigilant. Another collective institution has also died out: the practice of impounding animals caught grazing cultivated fields, which the owner could only retrieve by paying a fine to the village council. These various factors have combined to make cultivating the highlands an increasingly risky undertaking. Red gram has almost completely disappeared from the area since 1985, as the variety that used to be grown is sown in July and is not ready for harvesting until February, by which time all the other crops have been harvested and the animals have been left to roam freely. The fact that the animals are now left to free grazing explains why the few villagers who used to grow fodder crops no longer do so, and why a second rice crop, which would theoretically be possible in the lowest-lying plots, is still rarely practised in Sarwal.

The system is thus in crisis. Although the blacksmiths' caste is the only group without land, half the farms are not self-sufficient in terms of cereals, and the situation is bound to worsen unless solutions are found soon. What are the traditional solutions? Mutual aid is one possibility, but there are increasingly few signs of it (interest-free loans, seed banks, and so on). How about paid agricultural work in the village? There are only very few farms without enough family labour for most crop management operations. The largest farm, owned by the traditional village headman, covers 14 ha, but mostly with poor, stony soils, and the old man does not have the means to pay agricultural labourers, hence he has left his land to lie fallow, which is clearly a scandal in view of the situation in the village as a whole. In any event, labour opportunities are almost non-existent during the dry season, and wages are very low: the equivalent in rupees of 4 kg of paddy for a day's harvesting (but then what more can farmers offer in view of their yields?).

Working outside the village is a more profitable option. There is a brickworks in the surrounding area, which operates during the dry season; jobs on public works projects (road building), where wages are set by the state; temporary and, for the lucky ones, full-time jobs in factories in the region, albeit only for the small number of relatively well educated villagers (over 60 per cent of people in Ranchi District were illiterate in the late 1980s). None of the villagers from Sarwal move away to work as seasonal agricultural labourers in Punjab or Haryana, but a few do sometimes decide to try their luck in Assam or Tripura, or in the big cities (Patna and Kolkata). Ironically, despite the shortage of land in the village, this often means that their land is left to lie fallow, or cultivated very extensively for want of family labour once the migrant member has moved away.

This migration is going some way towards integrating the village into the national economy, but often means that these tribals are exploited, as they are at a disadvantage when they move away from home. Local commercial activity too often develops in the same way, with unscrupulous traders exploiting the locals, as is the case with shellac, which is obtained by tapping certain sorts of trees and sold to middlemen. The lucrative sale of alcohol that the families produce by distilling leaves of mahua (*Bassia latifolia*) is more direct, through the small weekly markets in and around Sarwal, albeit unfortunately to essentially local customers: by five o'clock in the afternoon, most Mundas aged over 40 are hopelessly drunk, which is no doubt just another sign of the breakdown of village society.

Since the mid-1980s, however, there has been a profound change. Until then, only around ten farms had a beam well and grew a few vegetables, year in year out, after the monsoon crop, stray animals and water supply permitting. However, in 1982, the ASVIN programme of the French National Council for Scientific Research (CNRS) installed a solar-powered pump that uses photovoltaic energy to irrigate just under 2 ha during the dry season (the village did not have electricity until 1984, at least officially: the transformer blew during a storm and was not repaired for several months). The idea was that lending plots in the irrigated area to villagers free of charge would allow large numbers of them to benefit from the project. Unfortunately, after a few years, the owners of the irrigated land decided that they no longer wanted to lend it out during the dry season, as they had realized that they could make a profit from growing vegetables. Nevertheless, the experience does seem to have revived a degree of cooperation at the village level: farmers have begun to keep a closer watch on their animals during the dry season and to grow red gram again.

Another event served to boost the development of irrigation and increased surveillance of animals: the authorities decided to sink around 50 wells in Sarwal, as the village had become famous because of its solar-powered pump. Many were rapidly abandoned as they had not been sunk properly and collapsed (an extreme example of how the Indian development authorities generally operate), or because there was no water, or the farmers had no need of them (although they had asked for them, given that wells were free for Dalits and natives), not to mention the problem of the diesel required to run the pumps, which has been rationed in Bihar since 1989.

Nevertheless, with the solar-powered pump and these wells, market garden cropping has still increased, with some farmers even beginning to grow vegetables rather than cereals during the rainy season. The pound for stray animals was relaunched in 1991, and there is talk of engaging a new village herdsman. Vegetables are still taken to market by cart, or even by cycle rickshaw (there is no machinery at all, no tractors, not even rototillers), and the villagers have not yet managed to reach agreement on building an efficient marketing structure, but there are some reasons for optimism.

Sarwal is clearly not a case of rural destitution, just of great poverty. We could have looked at even less developed regions, but they would have seemed like another world. In effect, further south, on the edges of Madhya Pradesh and Orissa, there are still some generally tribal groups living several hours' walk from the nearest metalled road, which have been decimated by malaria and malnutrition. Their bows and arrows are of little use now, as the area's wildlife has disappeared. Their farming systems are based on slash-and-burn: between the burnt stumps, they grow maize, sorghum and peas, sown using a dibber. After two years' cultivation, the land is left to lie fallow for around ten years (although the fallow period is ever-shorter due to population growth). This is where pockets of famine in India still persist, and even if these tribal groups are not killed by hunger, alcohol and disease might finish them off.

APPENDIX 2

Exchange Rates, GDP and Production Indices

TABLE 19 : EXCHANGE RATE OF RUPEE *VIS-À-VIS* SELECTED CURRENCIES (1980-1 TO 2004-5)

	US Dollar (US $)	French Franc (FF)	Euro (€)
1980-1 (April-March)	7.909	1.800	
1981-2 (April-March)	8.968	1.570	
1982-3 (April-March)	9.666	1.425	
1983-4 (April-March)	10.340	1.299	
1984-5 (April-March)	11.889	1.301	
1985-6 (April-March)	12.235	1.491	
1986-7 (April-March)	12.778	1.929	
1987-8 (April-March)	12.966	2.203	
1988-9 (April-March)	14.482	2.370	
1989-90 (April-March)	16.649	2.680	
1990-1 (April-March)	17.943	3.387	
1991-2 (April-March)	24.474	4.299	
1992-3 (April-March)	30.649	5.790	
1993-4 (April-March)	31.366	5.463	
1994-5 (April-March)	31.399	5.855	
1995-6 (April-March)	33.450	6.749	
1996-7 (April-March)	35.500	6.767	
1997-8 (April-March)	37.165	6.239	
1998-9 (April-March)	42.071	7.211	
1999-2000 (April-March)	43.333	6.812	44.791
2000-1 (April-March)	45.684		41.483
2001-2 (April-March)	47.692		42.181
2002-3 (April-March)	48.395		48.090
2003-4 (April-March)	45.952		53.990
2004-5 (April-March)	44.932		56.513

Source: Reserve Bank of India.

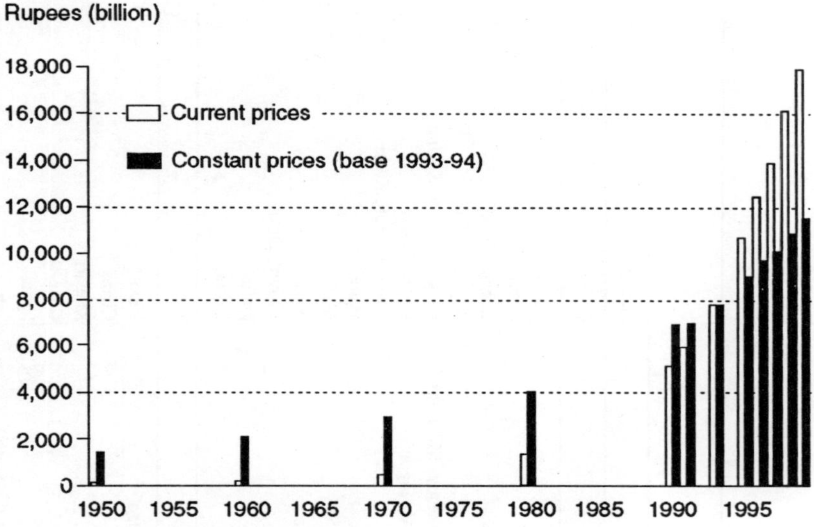

Source: Based on Economic Survey (2001).

FIGURE 39: GROWTH DOMESTIC PRODUCT (1950-1 TO 1999-2000)

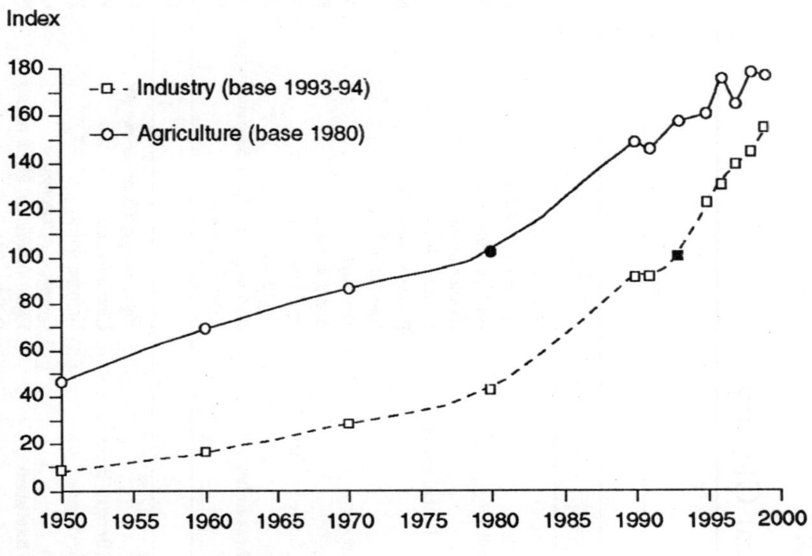

Source: Based on Economic Survey (2001).

FIGURE 40: AGRICULTURAL AND INDUSTRIAL PRODUCTION INDICES (1950-1 TO 1999-2000)

APPENDIX 3

Botanical Glossary

English	Latin	French	Hindi*
Cereals		Céréales	
Barley	*Hordeum vulgare*	Orge	Jau
Barnyard millet	*Echinochloa frumentacea*	Panic	Kutki
Common millet	*Panicum miliaceum*	Millet proso	Cheena, Barri
Finger millet	*Eleusine coracana*	Eleusine	Ragi, Mundua
Italian millet, Foxtail millet	*Setaria italica*	Millet des oiseaux, Mil à épi	Kangani, Kauni, Kakum
Kodo millet	*Paspalum scrobiculatum*	Millet kodo, Varangon	Koden, Kodra
Little millet	*Panicum milliare*	Petit mil	Sawan, Gundli, Kutki
Maize, Indian corn	*Zea mays*	Maïs	Makka
Oat	*Avena sativa*	Avoine	Jaie
Pearl millet, Spiked millet	*Pennisetum typhoideum*	Mil chandelle	Bajra
Rice, Paddy	*Oryza sativa*	Riz, Paddy	Chawal, Dhan
Sorghum, Great millet	*Andropogon sorghum, Sorghum vulgare*	Sorgho	Jowar
Wheat	*Triticum aestivum*	Blé	Gehun
Pulses		Protéagineux	Dal
Black gram	*Vigna mungo, Phaseolus mungo*	Haricot mungo	Urad
Chick pea, (Bengal) gram	*Cicer arietinum*	Pois chiche	Chana
Chickling vetch/pea	*Lathyrus sativus*	Pois carré	Khesari
Cluster bean	*Cyamopsis tetragonoloba*	-	Guar
Cow pea, White gram	*Vigna unguiculata, Vigna catjang*	Niébé	Lobia
Field bean	*Dolichos lablab*	Dolique, pois d'Egypte	Sem

French bean	*Phaseolus vulgaris*	Haricot vert	Faras bean
Green gram	*Vigna radiata, Phaseolus aureus*	Ambérique, Haricot à rayons	Mung
Horse gram	*Dolichos biflorus*	Haricot jacinthe	Kulthi
Kidney bean	*Vigna aconitifolia, Phaseolus vulgaris*	Haricot rouge	Moth, Rajma, Loba
Lentil	*Lens culimaris*	Lentille	Masur
Pea	*Pisum sativum/arvense*	Petit pois	Matar
Red gram, Pigeon pea	*Cajanus cajan*	Pois d'Angole	Tur, Arhar
Oilseeds		Oléagineux	
Castor	*Ricinus communis*	Ricin	Rehri
Groundnut, Peanut	*Arachis hypogaea*	Arachide	Kash
Linseed	*Linum usitatissimum*	Lin	Alsi
Niger	*Guizotia abyssinica*	Guizotia	Kala, Ramtil
Rapeseed/Mustard	*Brassica napus/campestris, Brassica nigra*	Colza/Moutarde	Sarson, Rai, Toria
Safflower	*Carthamus tinctorius*	Carthame	Kusum
Sesame, Gingelly	*Sesamum indicum, Sesamum orientale*	Sésame	Til
Soyabean	*Glycine max*	Soja	Soyabean
Sunflower	*Helianthus annuus*	Tournesol	Surya mukhi
Sugar crops		Cultures sucrières	
Sugar cane	*Saccharum officinarum*	Canne à sucre	Ganna
Fruits (and nuts)		Fruits (et noix)	Fal
Apple	*Malus sylvespris, Pyrus malus*	Pomme	Seb
Apricot	*Prunus armeniaca*	Abricot	Khoobani
Banana	*Musa paradisiaca*	Banane	Kela
Cashew nut	*Anacardium occidentale*	Noix de cajou	Kaju
Custard apple	*Annona squamosa*	Anone, Pomme-cannelle	Sharifa, Sitaphal
Fig	*Ficus carica*	Figue	Anjeer
Grape	*Vitis vinifera*	Raisin	Angur

(Contd.)

English	Latin	French	Hindi*
Guava	*Psidium guajava*	Goyave	Amrood
Jackfruit	*Artocarpus heterophyllus*	Jaque	Katahal
Lemon	*Citrus lemon*	Citron jaune	Nimbu
Lime	*Citrus aurantifolia*	Citron vert	Neembu
Litchi, Lychee	*Litchi chinensis*	Litchi, Lychee	Litchi
Mandarin orange	*Citrus reticulata*	Mandarine	Santara, Narangi
Mango	*Mangifera indica*	Mangue	Aam
Papaya, Pawpaw	*Carica papaya*	Papaye	Papeeta
Pineapple	*Ananas comosus*	Ananas	Ananas
Pomegranate	*Punica granatum*	Grenade	Anaar
Sapota plum	*Achras zapota*	Sapote, Sapotille	Chiku
Sweet Orange	*Citrus sinensis*	Orange douce	Melta, Mosambi
Vegetables (and tubers)		Légumes (et tubercules)	Subzi
Ash gourd	*Benincasa hispida*	Gourde (-)	Petha
Beet root	*Beta vulgaris*	Betterave	Chukandar
Bitter gourd	*Momordica charantia*	Gourde (Paroka)	Karela
Bottle gourd	*Lagenaria siceraria*	Gourde (-)	Lauki
Cabbage	*Brassica oleracea* var. *capitata*	Chou	Band gobi, Gajar
Carrot	*Daucus carota*	Carotte	Gajar
Cauliflower	*Brassica oleracea* var. *botrytis*	Chou-fleur	Phul gobi
Celery	*Apium graveolens*	Céleri	Ajmund
Cucumber	*Cucumis sativus*	Concombre	Kheera
Eggplant	*Solanum melongena*	Aubergine	Baingan, Brinjal
Lady's finger	*Hibiscus/Abelmoschus esculentus*	Gombo	Bhindi
Little gourd	*Cuccinia cordifolia*	Gourde (-)	Kundur
Muskmelon	*Cucumis melo*	Melon	Kharbooza
Onion	*Allium cepa*	Oignon	Piyaz
Pointed gourd	*Trichosanthes dioica*	Gourde (-)	Parwal, Potal

Potato	*Solanum tuberosum*	Pomme de terre	Alu
Pumpkin	*Curcurbita moschata*	Potiron	Sitaphal, Lal kaddu, Kumbhra
Radish	*Raphanus sativus*	Radis	Muli
Snake gourd	*Trichosanthes anguina*	Gourde (Patola, Kikenga)	Chachinda
Tapioca	*Manihot esculenta*	Tapioca, Manioc	Simla alu
Tomato	*Lycopersicum esculentum*	Tomate	Tamatar
Turnip	*Brassica rapa*	Navet	Shalgam
Watermelon // Round Gourd	*Cirtrullus vulgaris // fistulosus*	Pastèque	Tarbooz // Tinda
Condiments, Spices		Condiments, Epices	Massala
Anise	*Pimpinella anisum*	Anis	Sonf
Black pepper	*Piper nigrum*	Poivre gris	Kalimirch
Cardamom, Cardamum (lesser)	*Elettaria cardamomum*	Cardamome	Ellaychi
Cinnamon	*Cinnamomum zeylanicum*	Cannelle	Dalchini
Clove	*Syzygium aromaticum*	Girofle	Laung
Coriander	*Coriandrum sativum*	Coriandre	Dhania
Cumin, Caraway	*Cuminum cyminum*	Cumin	Jira
Fennel	*Foeniculum vulgare*	Fenouil	Sonf
Fenugreek	*Trigonella foenum graecum*	Fenugrec	Methi
Garlic	*Allium sativum*	Ail	Lahsan
Ginger	*Zingiber officinale*	Gingembre	Adrak
Nutmeg (Mace)	*Myristica fragrans*	Muscade (Macis)	Jaiphal (Javithri)
Pistachio	*Pistacia vera*	Pistache	Pista
Red pepper, Chilli	*Capsicum frutescens*	Piment rouge	Lalmirch
Saffron	*Crocus sativus*	Safran	Kesar, Zaffran
Turmeric	*Curcuma longa*	Curcuma, Safran des Indes	Haldi
Drugs, Stimulants		Drogues, Stimulants	
Betel leaves	*Piper betle*	Feuille de bétel	Paan
Betel nut, Arecanut	*Areca catechu*	Noix d'arec	Supari

(Contd.)

English	Latin	French	Hindi*
Coffee	*Coffea spp.*	Café	Kafi
Indian hemp	*Cannabis sativa*	Chanvre indien, Cannabis	Bhang, Ganja
Opium, Poppy	*Papaver somniferum*	Opium	Afeem
Tea	*Camellia* spp.	Thé	Chai
Tobacco	*Nicotiana tabacum, Nicotiana rusticà*	Tabac	Tambaku
Fibres		Fibres	
Cotton	*Gossypium* spp.	Coton	Kapas
Jute	*Corchorus* spp.	Jute	Shada, Tosha pat
Sunhemp	*Crotalaria juncea*	Chanvre	Sann
Miscellaneous plants		Plantes diverses	
Coconut palm	*Cocos nucifera*	Cocotier	Nariyal
Hevea	*Hevea brasiliensis*	Hévéa	Rabbar
Neem tree	*Azadirachta indica, Malia azadirachta*	Margousier	Neem
Palm-kernel	*Elaeis guineensis*	Palmiste, Palmier à huile	-
Palmyra palm	*Borassus flabellifer*	Rônier	Tar, Tola
Tamarind	*Tamarindus indica*	Tamarin	Imli, Tentul
-	*Actinodaphne hookeri*	-	Pisa
-	*Amoora rohituka*	-	Rayana
-	*Argemone mexicana*	Chardon marbré	Argemone
-	*Butea monosperma*	-	Palas
-	*Calophyllum inophyllum*	Galba	Undi
-	*Calotropis spp.*	Arbre de soie	Akra
-	*Ceiba pentandra // Bombax ceiba*	Kapokier, Fromager, Mapou	Kapok // Simul
-	*Celastrus paniculatus*	-	Malkanguni
-	*Cleome icosandra/viscosa*	Collant, Mouzambé jaune	Hurhur
-	*Diploknema butyracea*		Phulwara
-	*Garcinia indica*	-	Kokum

-	*Garcinia morella*	-	Tamal
-	*Hydnocarpus spp.*	-	Maroti
-	*Jatropha curcas*	Médecinier	Ratanjyoti
-	*Litsea glutinosa*	-	Chirandi
-	*Madhuca indica/latifolia*	-	Mahua
-	*Mallotus philippinensis*	-	Kamala
-	*Mesua ferrea*	-	Nahor
-	*Pongamia pinnata*	-	Karanja
-	*Salvadora spp.*	-	Khakan-pilu
-	*Schleichera oleosa / trijunga*	-	Kusum
-	*Shorea robusta*	-	Sal
-	*Sterculia foetida*	-	Pinari
-	*Terminalia belerica*	-	Baheda
-	*Vateria indica*	-	Dhupa
-	*Vernonia anthelmintica*	Tabac à jacot, Grande violette	Somraji
-	*Xanthium strumarium*	Gros cousin	Gokhru

Note: * Sometimes in another Indian language. See the book *Nutritive Value of Indian Food* (National Institute of Nutrition, Hyderabad, 1995, p. 156) for a much more detailed list of the various names given to plants in India.

Sourcs: *Agricultural Statistics at a Glance,* New Delhi: Ministry of Agriculture, 2000, p. 172;
Fournet, J., *Flore illustrée des phanérogames de Guadeloupe et de Martinique*, Paris: INRA, 1978, p. 1654;
Handbook of Agriculture, New Delhi: Indian Council of Agricultural Research, 1980, p. 1303;
Kamath, M.G., *Dictionary of Indian Agriculture,* New Delhi: Allied Publishers, 1972, p. 607;
Nutritive Value of Indian Food, Hyderabad, National Institute of Nutrition, 1995, p. 156.

APPENDIX 4

Maps of Principal Crops (1980–2)

CEREALS

Main cereals

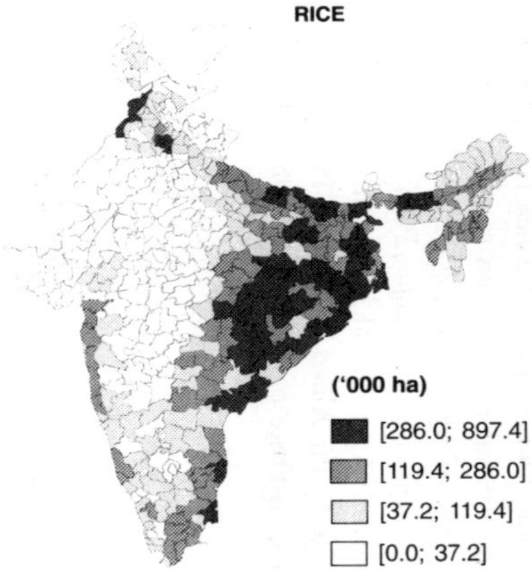

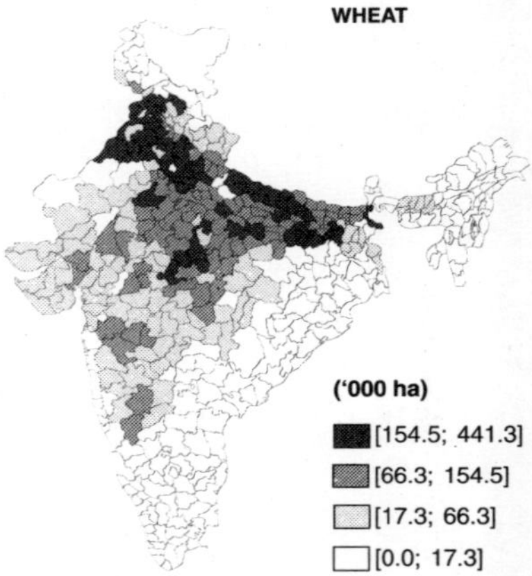

Coarse cereals

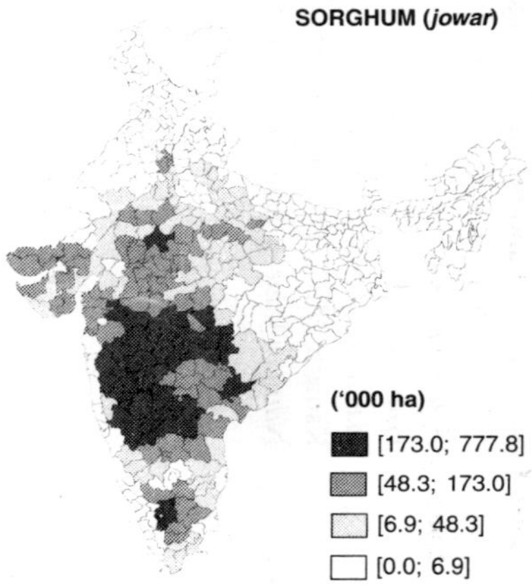

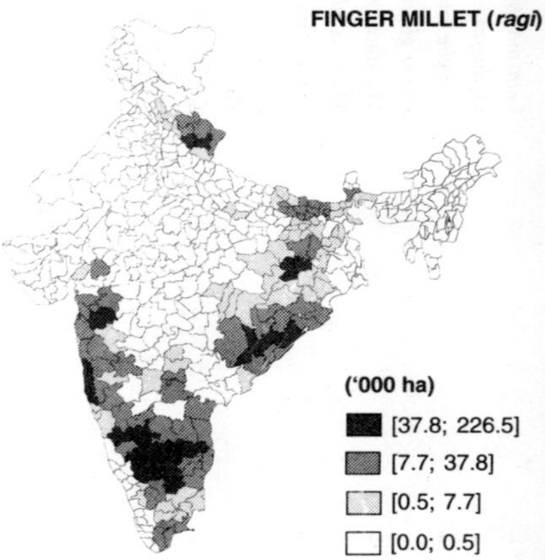

CEREALS (contd.)

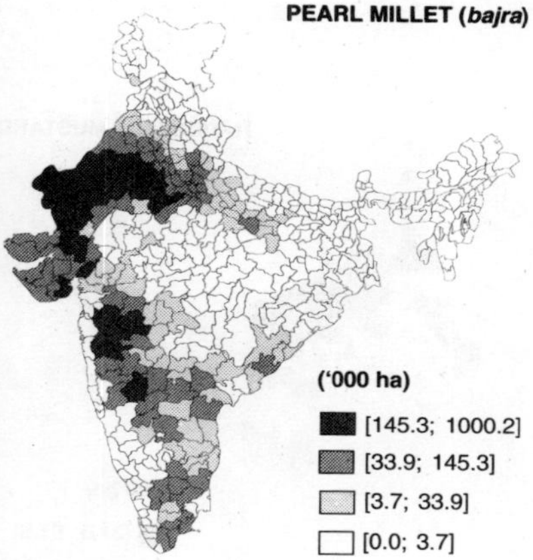

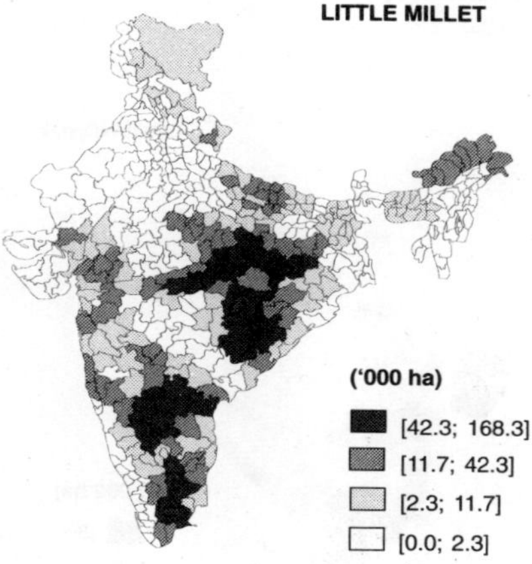

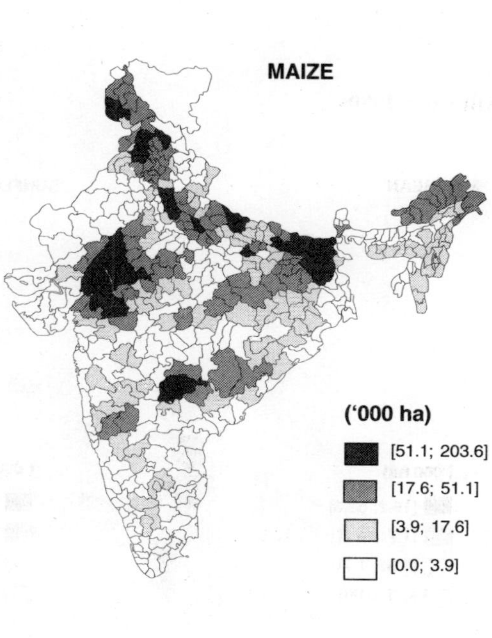

OILSEEDS

Main crops

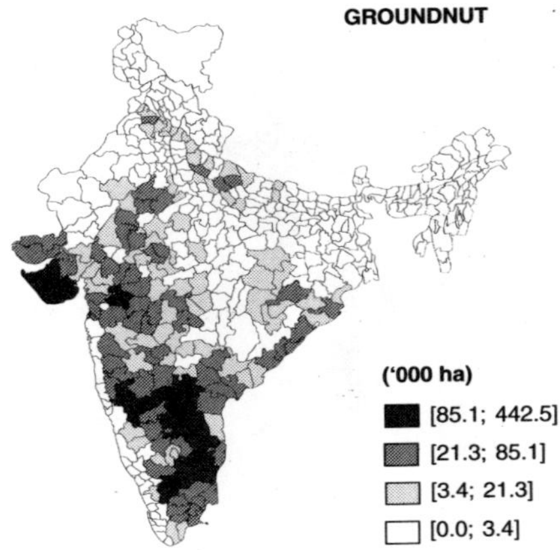

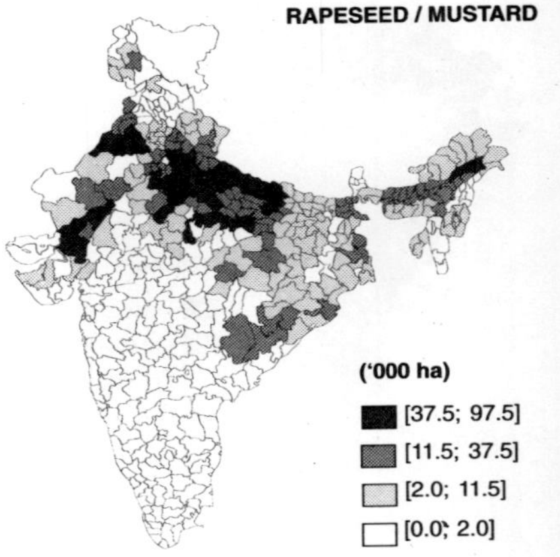

Crops with a steep growth since 1980s

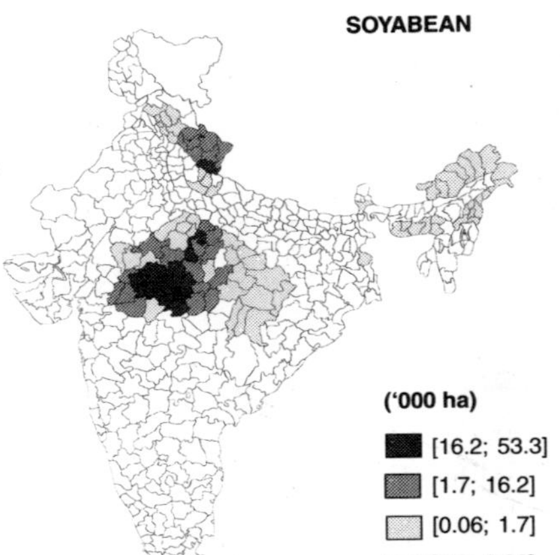

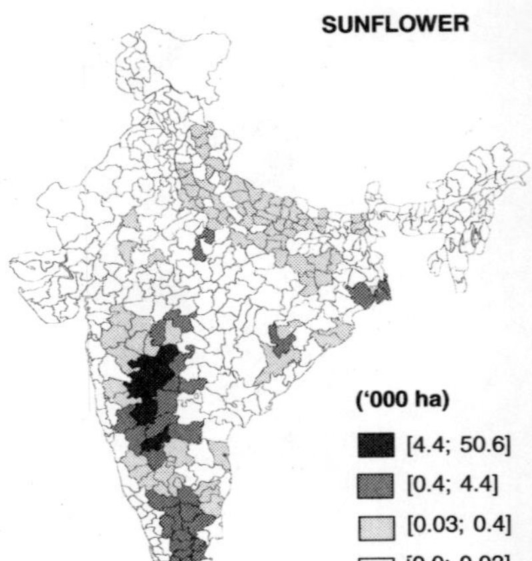

OILSEEDS (contd.)

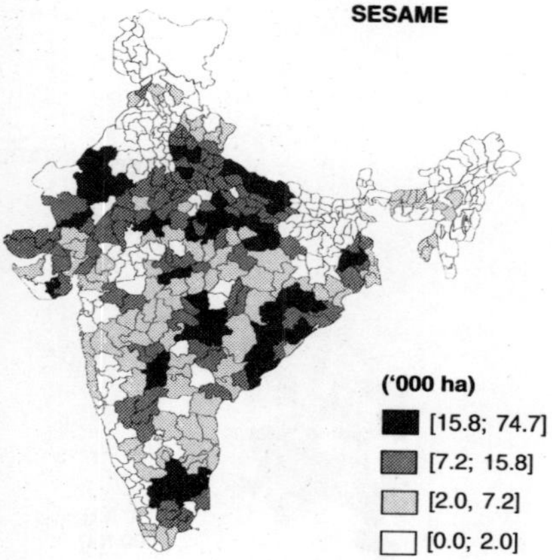

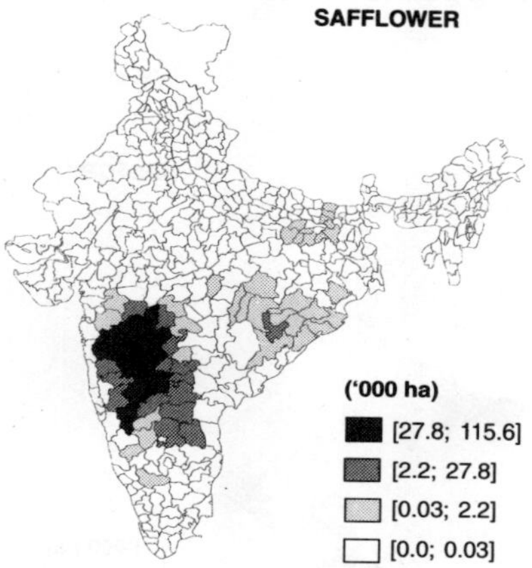

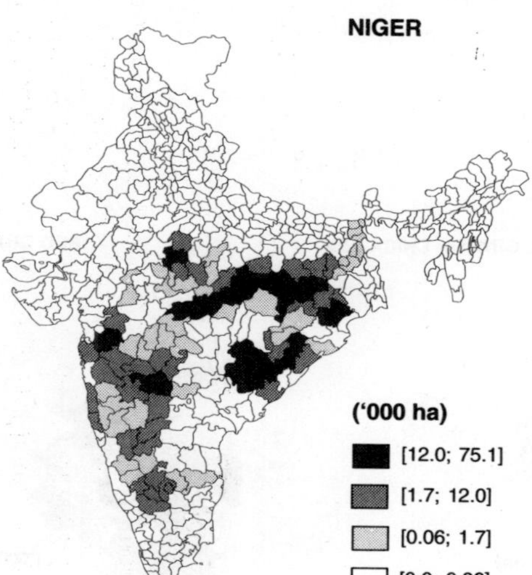

OILSEEDS (contd.)

Non-edible oilseeds

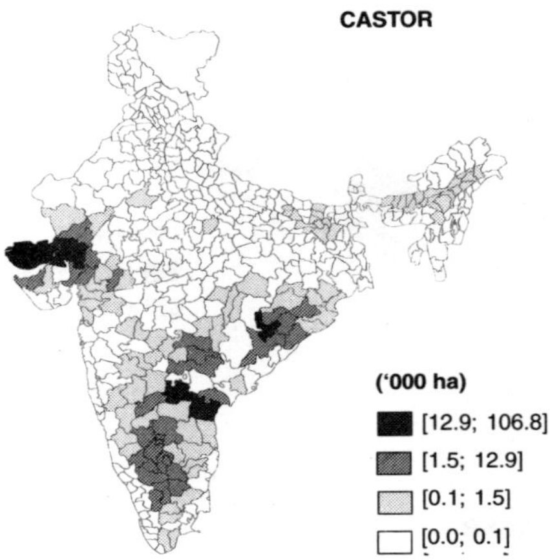

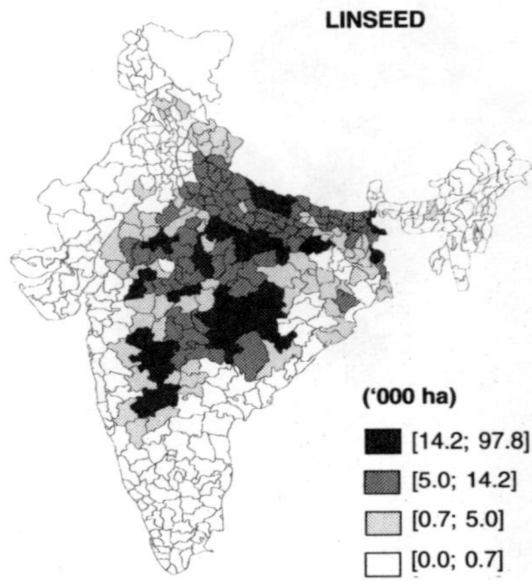

PULSES

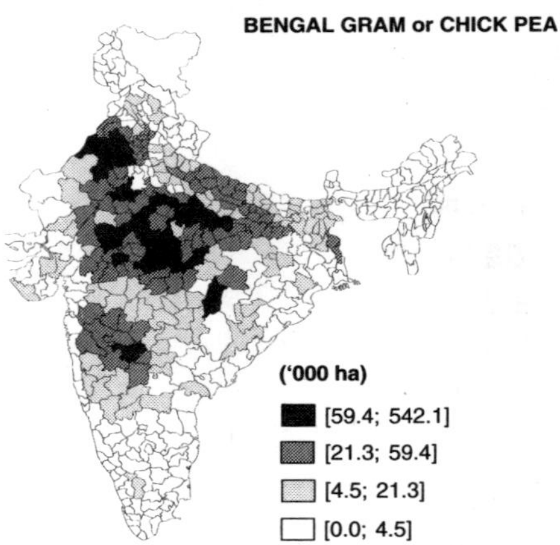

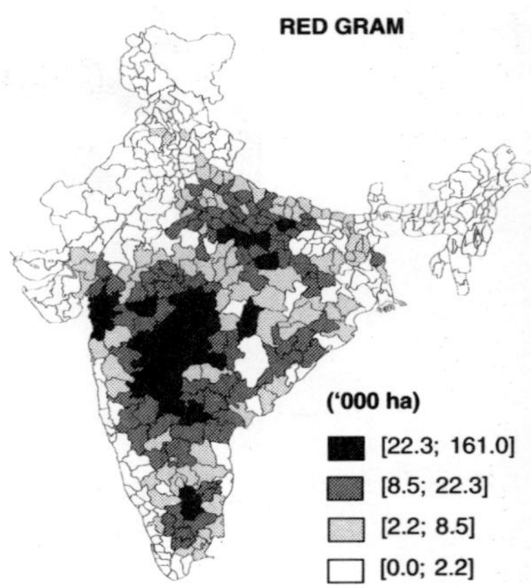

PULSES (contd.)

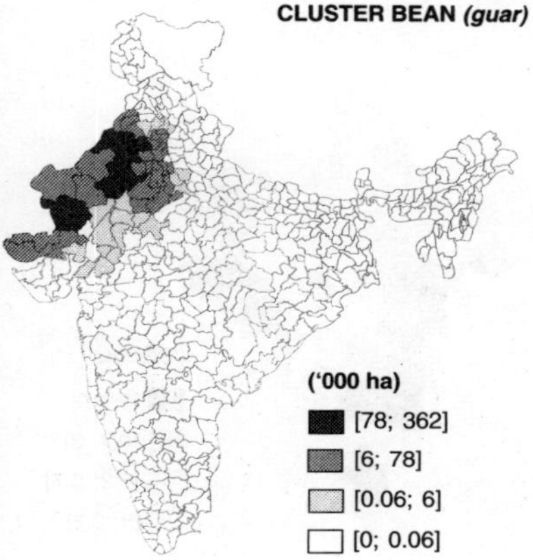

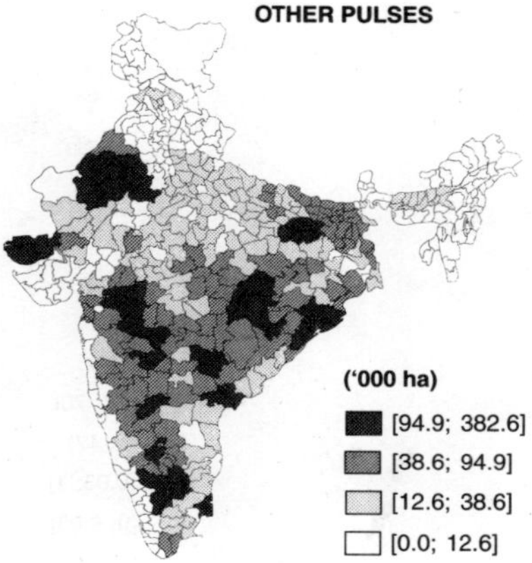

VEGETABLES AND FRUIT

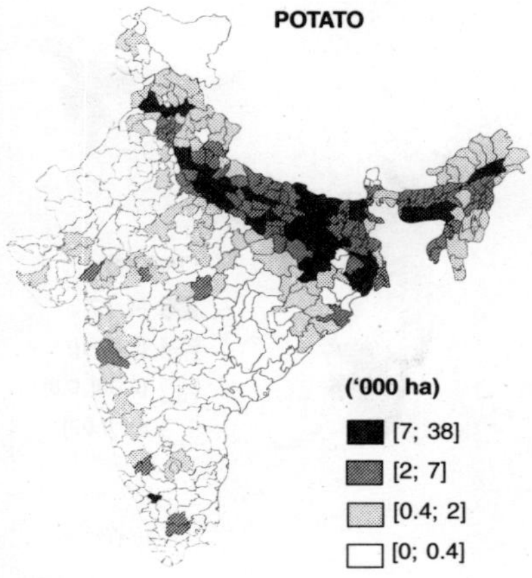

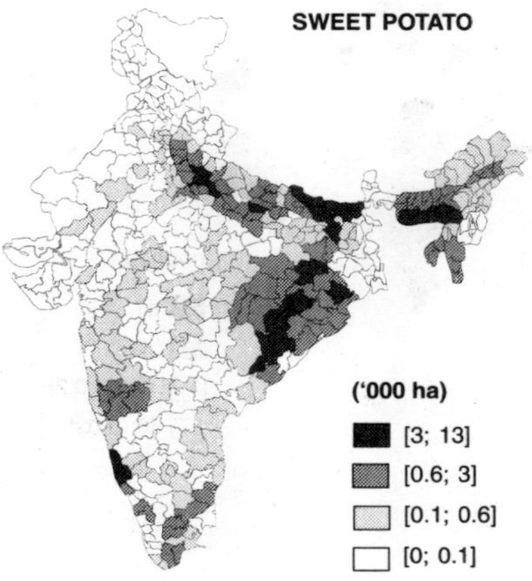

VEGETABLES AND FRUIT (contd.)

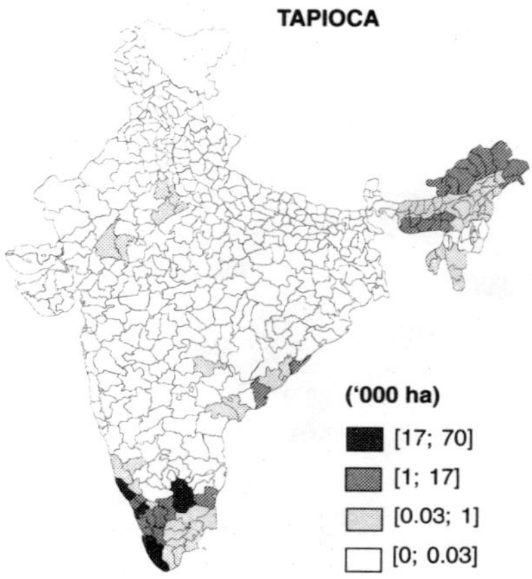

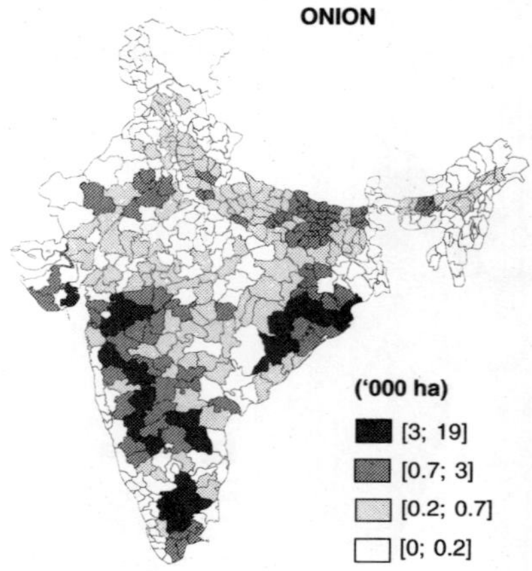

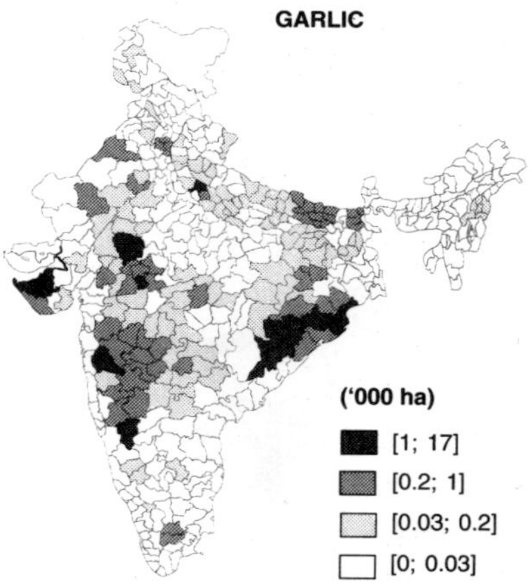

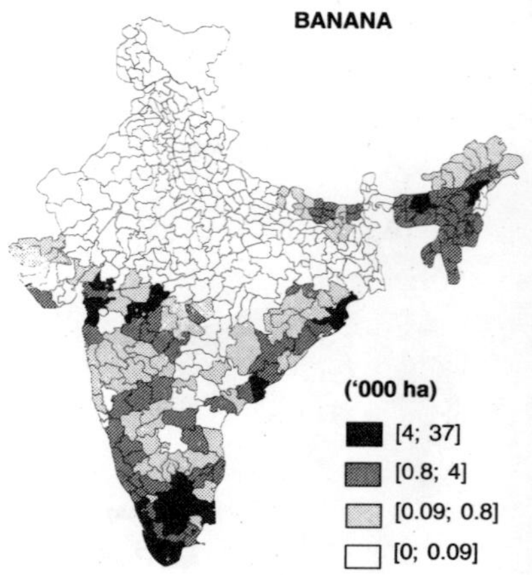

NUTS, SPICES, CONDIMENTS

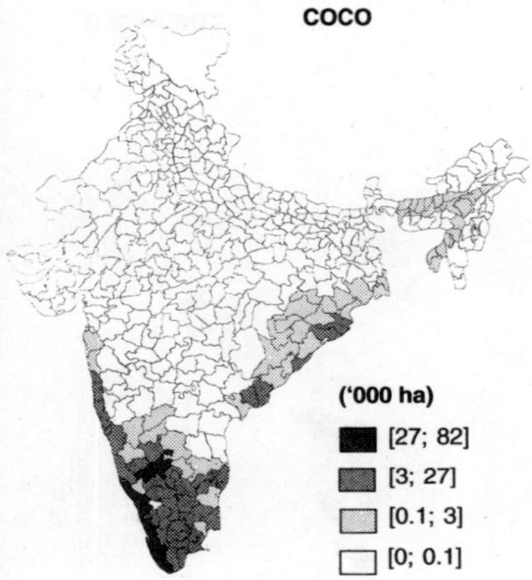

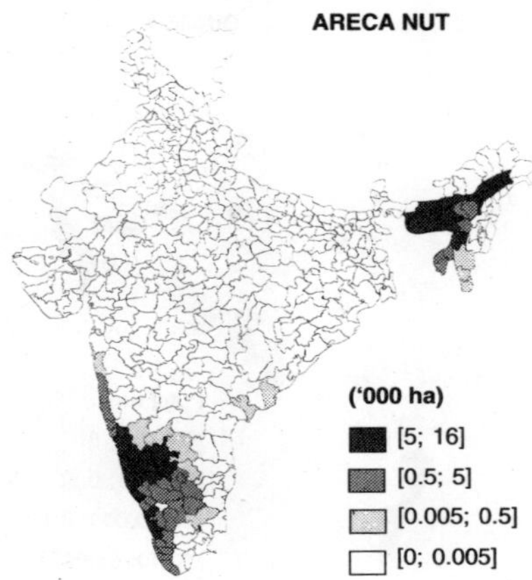

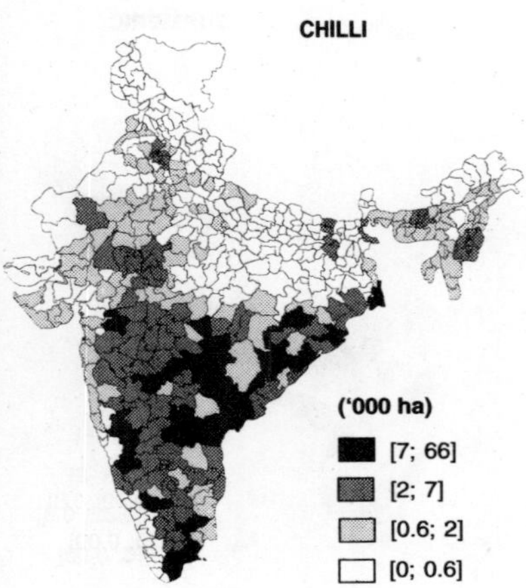

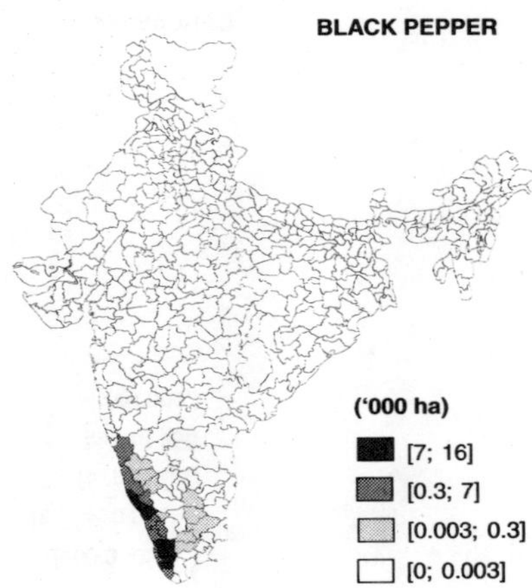

NUTS, SPICES, CONDIMENTS (contd.)

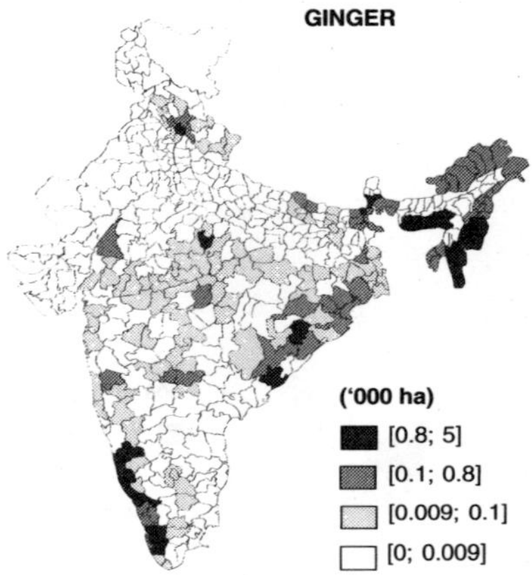

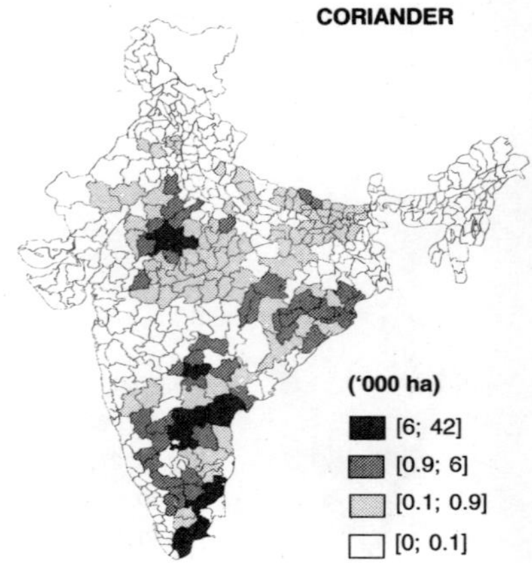

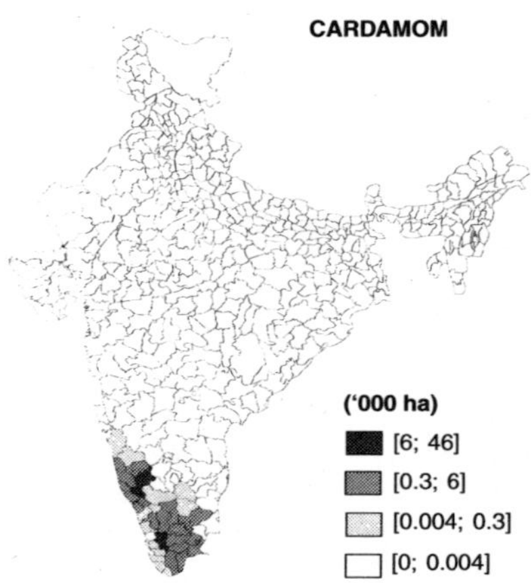

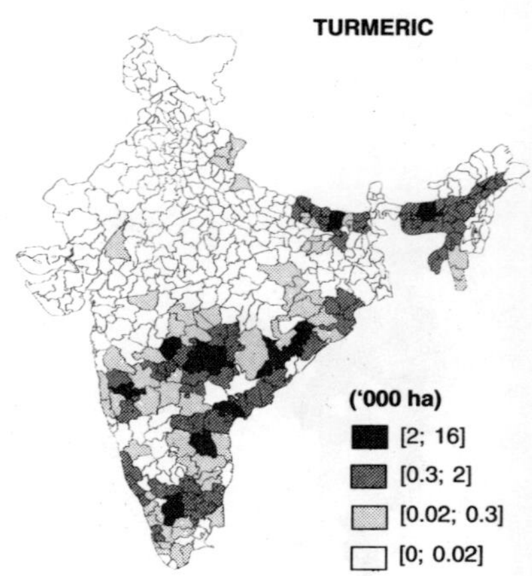

FIBRES

COTTON

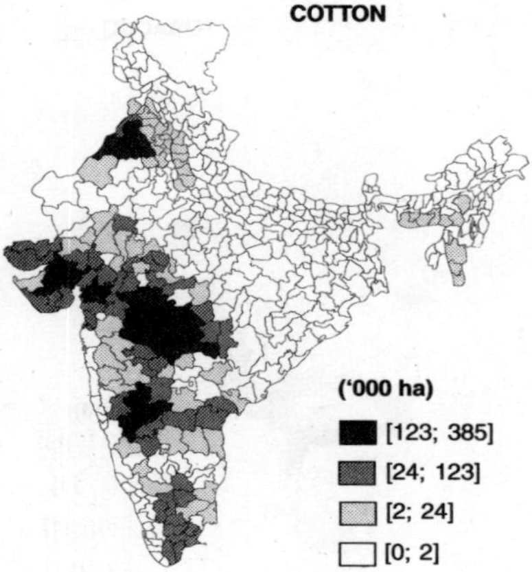

SUNHEMP

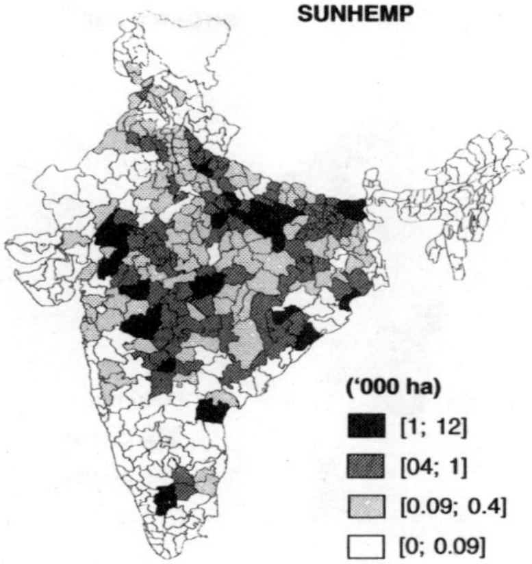

JUTE

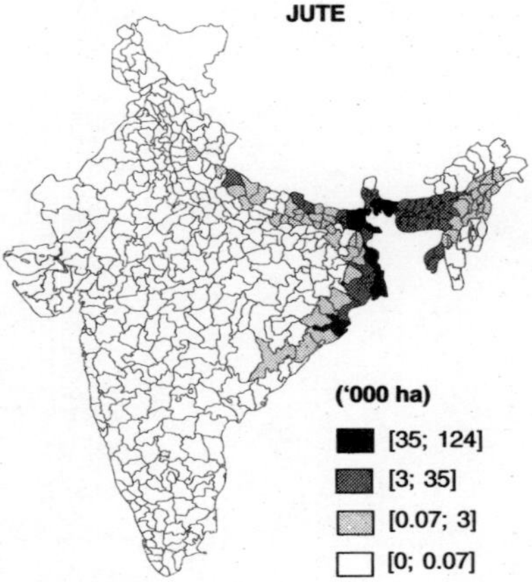

MESTA

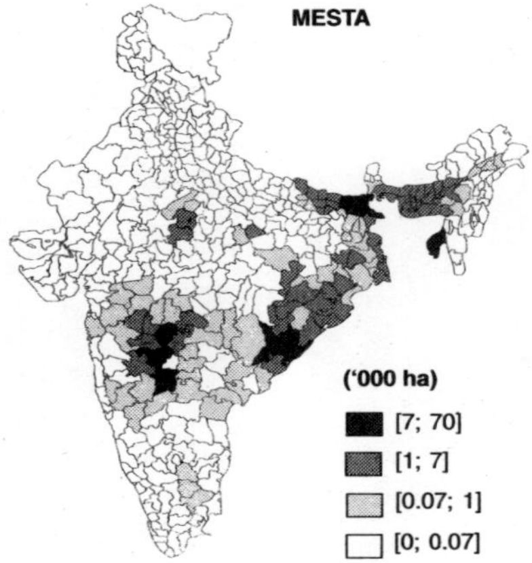

OTHERS

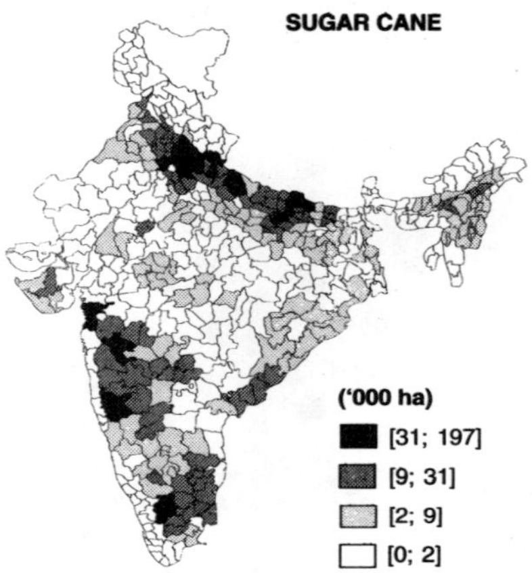
SUGAR CANE
('000 ha)
[31; 197]
[9; 31]
[2; 9]
[0; 2]

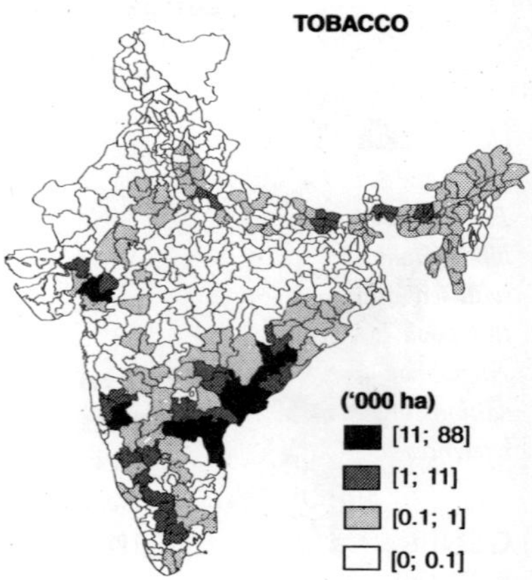
TOBACCO
('000 ha)
[11; 88]
[1; 11]
[0.1; 1]
[0; 0.1]

Bibliography

Except numerous articles published in Economic and Political Weekly, *this bibliography brings together most of the references used for writing this book, along with few other useful documents. The original bibliography of the French version of this book has been maintained to a large extent in order to give the Indian and Anglophone readerships some specifically French perspectives. However, when English editions of some French books were existing, they have been cited instead, and some references have been updated.*

GENERAL ISSUES (GEOGRAPHY, HISTORY, RELIGION, PHILOSOPHY, POLITICS, SOCIETY, ETC.)

Bernard, J.A., *Le pouvoir et la puissance*, Paris: Fayard,1985.

Centre de Sciences Humaines, New Delhi: a set of papers now available on internet (http://www.csh-delhi.com)

Deliège R., *Le système des castes*, Que sais-je?, Paris: Presses Universitaires de France, 1993.

Drèze, J. and A. Sen. (eds.), *India: Development and Participation*, New Delhi: Oxford University Press, 2002.

Dorin, B. (ed.), *The Indian Entrepreneur: A Sociological Profile of Businessmen and Their Practices*, New Delhi: Manohar, 2003.

Dumont, L., *Homo Hierarchicus: The Caste System and Its Implications*, New Delhi: Vedam Books, 1998.

Durand-Dastès, F., *Géographie de l'Inde*, Que sais-je?, Paris: Presses Universitaires de France, 1997.

Durand-Dastès, F. and G. Mutin (eds.), *Afrique du Nord. Moyen Orient. Monde indien*, Paris, Paris: Géographie Universelle, Belin-Reclus, 1995.

Encyclopaedia Universalis, CD Rom.

Etienne, G., *Inde-Chine. Le match du XXIème siècle*, Paris: Editions de Science-Po, 1998.

French Institute of Pondicherry: a set of papers now available on internet. (http://www.ifpindia.org)

Filliozat, J., *Les philosophies de l'Inde*, Que sais-je?, Paris: Presses Universitaires de France, 1998.

Heuzé, G., *Entre émeutes et mafias: l'Inde dans la mondialisation*, Paris: L'Harmattan, 1996.

Jaffrelot, C. (ed.), *L'Inde contemporaine de 1950 à nos jours*, Paris: Fayard, 1996.

Landy, F., *L'Union Indienne. Une géographie*, Paris: Editions du Temps, 2001.

Lardinois, R., *Miroir de l'Inde: études indiennes en sciences sociales*, Paris: Editions de la Maison des Sciences de l'Homme, 1989.

Racine, J.-L., 'Climat et politique en Union indienne', *Hérodote*, 39, Paris, 1985.

Markovits, C. (ed.), *A History of Modern India 1480-1950*, London: Anthem Press, 2002.

Mazars, G., *La médecine de l'Inde*, Que sais-je?, Paris: Presses Universitaires de France, 1995.

Ministry of Information and Broadcasting, *India*, New Delhi, annual issues.

Robinson, F. (ed.), *The Cambridge Encyclopedia of India, Pakistan, Bangladesh, Sri Lanka, Nepal, Bhutan and the Maldives*, New York: Cambridge University Press, 1989.

Sorman, G., *Le génie de l'Inde*, Paris: Fayard, 2000.

Vidal, D., G. Tarabout and E. Meyer (eds.), *Violences et non-violences en Inde*, Paris: Editions de l'Ecole des Hautes Etudes en Sciences Sociales, 1995.

Viramma, J. and J.L. Racine, *Viramma: Life of a Dalit*, New Delhi: Social Sciences Press, 2000.

Zins, M.-J., *Inde. Un destin démocratique*, Paris: La Documentation Française, 1999.

STATISTICS

Bansil, P.C., *Agricultural Statistical Compendium*, New Delhi: Techno Economic Research Institute, 2 vols., 1992.

Centre for Monitoring Indian Economy, *Agriculture*, New Delhi, annual issues.

Centre for Monitoring Indian Economy, *TRADES*, New Delhi, digital database.

Census of India, various publications (http://www.censusindia.net).

Chandhok, H.L. (The Policy Group), *India Database: The Economy: Annual Time Series Data*, vol. 2, New Delhi: Living Media India, 1990.

Economic and Political Research Foundation, *National Accounts of India: 1950-51 to 1996-97*, Mumbai, 1999, CD Rom.

Food and Agriculture Organization, *Food Balance Sheets* (http://faostat.fao.org/default.aspx).

Datanet India, *Indiaagristat* (http://www.indiaagristat.com).

Marine Products Export Development Authority (http://www.mpeda.com).

Ministry of Agriculture, *Agricultural Statistics at a Glance*, New Delhi, annual issues (http://agricoop.nic.in/Agristatistics.htm).

Ministry of Agriculture, *Livestock Censuses* (http://www.dahd.nic.in/census.htm).

Ministry of Agriculture, *Cost of Cultivation of Principal Crops in India*, New Delhi, various issues.

Ministry of Finance, *Economic Survey*, New Delhi, annual issues (http://indiabudget.nic.in).

Ministry of Finance, *Weekly Retail/Wholesale Prices*, New Delhi (http://goidirectory.nic.in/fministry.htm).

Ministry of Industry, *Wholesale Price Index*, New Delhi (http://eaindustry.nic.in).

National Horticulture Board, Gurgaon, annual publications.

National Informatic Centre (http://www.nic.in): a gateway for all government websites, in particular *Indiaimage* (http://indiaimage.nic.in/).

National Sample Survey Organisation, *Consumer Expenditure*, annual and quinquennial publications (http://www.mospi.nic.in).

Reserve Bank of India, *Report on Currency and Finance,* Mumbai, annual issues (http://www.rbi.org.in/scripts/BS_ViewPublicationReport.aspx).

Tata Services Limited, *Statistical Outline of India*, Mumbai, annual issues.

UNCTAD, *Trade Analysis and Information System*, Geneva, CD Roms. (http://r0.unctad.org/trains_new/index.shtm).

World Bank, *World Development Report*, Washington D.C., annual issues (http://www.worldbank.org/wdr).

ECONOMY, AGRICULTURE

Ambassade de France en Inde, Mission Economique et Financière, New Delhi, occasional publications (http://www.missioneco.org/Inde).

Audinet, P., *L'état entrepreneur en Inde et au Brésil: économie du sucre et de l'éthanol*, Paris: L'Harmattan, 1998.

Bansil, P.C. and P.N. Bhat, 'Poultry Development in India: Perspectives and Approaches', *Indian Journal of Animal Production*, XXVIII, 5, New Delhi, 1996.

Bhalla, G.S. and G. Singh, *Indian Agriculture: Four Decades of Development*, New Delhi: Sage, 2001.

Bhalla, G.S., J.L. Racine and F. Landy (eds.), *WTO and Agriculture. Perspectives from France and India*, Paris: Maison des Sciences de l'Homme, 2001.

Brass, T. (ed.), *New Farmers' Movements in India*, Ilford: Frank Cass, 1995.

Chambard, J.L., *Atlas d'un village indien*, Paris: Mouton Editions, Ecole des Hautes Etudes en Sciences Sociales, 1980.

Dandekar, V.M., *The Indian Economy 1947-92. Agriculture* (vol. 1), New Delhi: Sage, 1994.

Dorin, B. and T. Jullien (eds.), *Agricultural Incentives in India: Past Trends and Prospective Paths towards Sustainable Development*, New Delhi: Manohar, 2004.

Dorin, B., 'Globalization and Self-sufficiency: A Tentative Revolution in Oilseeds', in F. Landy and B. Chaudhuri (eds.), *Globalization and Local Development in India,* New Delhi: Manohar, 2004.

——,'Food Policy and Nutritional Security: The Unequal Access to Lipids in India', *Economic and Political Weekly*, XXXIV, Mumbai, 26 June 1999, pp. 1709-17.

——, B., 'L'économie oléifère de l'Union Indienne. Evaluation d'une stratégie d'autonomie', Ph.D. thesis (Economics), University of Montpellier I, 1994 (mimeo).

Economic and Political Weekly, Mumbai, weekly journal (http://www.epw.org.in)

Etienne, G., *Rural Change in South Asia*, Delhi: Vikas, 1995.

French Embassy in India, Mission Economique et Financière, New Delhi, various publications (www.missioneco.org/Inde).

Frontline, fortnightly journal (http://www.frontline.in).

Indian Council of Agricultural Research, *Handbook of Indian Agriculture*, New Delhi, 1980 (rpt. 2005).

Indian Journal of Agricultural Economics, Mumbai, quarterly journal.

Indira Gandhi Institute of Development Research, *India Development Report*, New Delhi: Oxford University Press, various issues.

Lachaier, P., *Firmes et entreprises en Inde*, Paris: EFEO-IFP-Karthala, 2000.

Landy, F., *Paysans de l'Inde du Sud. Le choix et la contrainte*, Paris: IFP, Karthala, 1994.

Mazoyer, M. and L. Roudart, *Histoire des agricultures du monde*, Paris: Seuil, 1997.

Ministry of Science, *Land Resource Atlas of India*, New Delhi: Government of India, 1986.

National Council of Applied Economic Research, *India Human Development Report*, New Delhi: Oxford University Press, 1999.

——, *The Great Indian Market*, New Delhi, 2005 (http://www.ncaer. org).

Pouchepadass, J., *Champaran and Gandhi: Planters, Peasants and Gandhian Politics*, New Delhi: Oxford University Press, 1999.

Pursell, G. and A. Gupta, *Trade Policies and Incentives in Indian Agriculture: Sugar and Sugarcane*, Policy Research Working Paper 1953, World Bank, Washington D.C., 1998.

Rao, V.M. and H.G. Hanumappa, 'Marginalisation Process in Agriculture: Indicators, Outlook and Policy Implications', *Economic and Political Weekly*, 25 December 1999, pp. A133-8.

Sarkar, G.K., *Agriculture and Rural Transformation in India,* Kolkata: Oxford University Press, 1995.

Sathyamurthy, T.V. (ed.), *Industry and Agriculture in India since Independence*, New Delhi: Oxford University Press, 1995.

Sengupta, D., D. Chakraborty and P. Banerjee, *Beyond the Transition Phase of WTO: An Indian Perspective on Emerging Issues*, New Delhi: Academic Foundation-CSH, 2006.

Singh, J., *Agricultural Development in South Asia*, New Delhi: National Book Organisation, 1997.

Singhal, V., *Indian Agriculture 1999*, New Delhi: Indian Economic Data Research Centre.

The Economic Times, daily newspaper (http:// economictimes.indiatimes.com).

The Hindu, daily newspaper and other publications (www.hinduonnet.com).

The Hindu, *Survey of Indian Agriculture*, Chennai, annual issues.

Thorner, D. (ed.), *Ecological and Agrarian Regions of South Asia: Circa 1930*, Karachi: Oxford University Press, 1996.

Vaidyanathan, A., 'India's Agricultural Development Policy', *Economic and Political Weekly*, 13 May 2000, pp. 1735-41.

World Bank, *Implications of the Uruguay Round Agreement for South Asia: The Case of Agriculture*, South Asia Rural Development Series, New Delhi: Allied Publishers, 1999.

——, *Indian Livestock Sector Review: Enhancing Growth and Development*, South Asia Rural Development Series, New Delhi: Allied Publishers, 1999.

——, *The Indian Oilseed Complex: Capturing Market Opportunities*, South Asia Rural Development Series, New Delhi: Allied Publishers, 1999.

World Trade Organization, *Quantitative Restrictions on Imports of Agricultural, Textile and Industrial Products*, Report of the Panel, WT/DS90/R, April, Geneva, 1999 (http://www.wto.org/english/tratop_e/dispu_e/90r.pdf).

FOOD, FOOD POLICY

Acharya, K.C.S., *Food Security System of India: Evolution of the Buffer Stocking Policy and its Evaluation*, New Delhi: Concept, 1983.

Asthana, M.D. and P. Medrano (eds.), *Towards Hunger Free India: Agenda and Imperatives*, New Delhi: Manohar-WFP, 2001.

Centre Français du Commerce Extérieur, *Inde: le marché des produits alimentaires (épicerie, produits frais, boissons) - Réseaux commerciaux des industriels, comportements d'achat des ménages*, Paris, 1997.

Chopra, R.N., *Evolution of Food Policy in India*, New Delhi: Macmillan India, 1981.

Drèze, J., A. Sen and A. Hussain, *The Political Economy of Hunger*, New Delhi: Oxford University Press, 1995.

Gopalan, C., B.V. Rama Sastri and S.C. Balasubramanian, *Nutritive Value of Indian Foods*, Indian Council of Medical Research (New Delhi), National Institute of Nutrition (Hyderabad), 1995.

International Food Policy Research Institute, Washington, various papers (http://www.ifpri.org).

Krishnaji, N. and T.N. Krishnan (eds.), *Public Support for Food Security: The Public Distribution System in India*, New Delhi: Sage, 2000.

Paroda, R.S. and P. Kumar, 'Food Production and Demand Projections for South Asian Countries: Policy Implications for Indian Agriculture', in B. Dorin and T. Jullien (eds.), *Agricultural Incentives in India: Past Trends and Prospective Paths towards Sustainable Development*, New Delhi: Manohar, 2004, pp. 223-79.

Landy, F., *Feeding India: The Spatial Parameters of Food Grain Policy*, New Delhi: Manohar, 2009.

——, *Fertilizers, Structural Adjustment and Food Policy*, Pondy Papers in Social Sciences, 25, Pondicherry: Institut Français de Pondichéry, 1997.

McKinsey & Company, *Food & Agriculture Integrated Development Action: Modernising the Indian Food Chain*, New Delhi: McKinsey & Company, 1997.

Mahias, M.-C., *Délivrance et convivialité*, Paris: Editions de la Maison des Sciences de l'Homme, 1985.

Malassis, L. and M. Padilla, *Economie agro-alimentaire*, III, *L'économie mondiale*, Paris: Cujas, 1986.

Mooij, J., *Food Policy and the Indian State: The Public Distribution System in South India*, New Delhi: Oxford University Press, 1999.

Padilla, M., *Les politiques alimentaires*, Paris: Cujas, 1996.

Rabobank International, *Food and Agribusiness in India*, Utrecht: Rabobank International, 1996.

——, *Food and Agribusiness in India—1999 update*, Utrecht: Rabobank International, 1999.

Radhakrishna, R. and K. Subbarao, *India's Public Distribution System: A National and International Perspective*, Discussion Paper, 380, World Bank, Washington D.C., 1996.

Rao, C.H.H., *Agriculture, Food Security, Poverty and Environment*, New Delhi: Oxford University Press, 2005.

Swaminathan, M., *Weakening Welfare: The Public Distribution of Food in India*, New Delhi: Left Word, 2000.

ENVIRONMENT, ECOLOGY, INTELLECTUAL PROPERTY

Agarwal, A. and S. Narain, *Dying Wisdom: Rise, Fall and Potential of India's Traditional Water Harvesting Systems*, New Delhi: Centre for Science and Environment, 1997.

Centre for Science and Environment, *The Citizens' Fifth Report*, CSE, 1999.

Centre for Science and Environment, *Down to Earth*, New Delhi, weekly journal (www.downtoearth.org.in).

European Patent Office, various papers (http://ec.espacenet.com).

Institute of Intellectual Property Development, various papers (http://www.iprindia.org).

Pachauri, R.K. and P.V. Sridharan, *Looking Back to Think Ahead: GREEN India 2047*, New Delhi: Tata Energy Research Institute, 1998.

Pionetti, C., *Semences et savoirs en Inde: Diversités en peril. Enquête sur la biodiversité agricole*, Editions Cultures Croisées, Foundation Charles Léopold Mayer pour le Progès de l'Homme, 1998.

Shiva, V. and G. Bedi (eds.), *Sustainable Agriculture and Food Security: The Impact of Globalisation*, New Delhi: Sage, 2002.

Swaminathan, M.S., *Sustainable Agriculture*, Delhi: Konark, 1996, 2 vols.

Index

Abad, 146
Abattoirs, 136
Affirmative action, 33
Agarwal, Anil 188
Agricultural authorities, 36
Agricultural policy, 199
Agrifood policy, 126
Aid – Dependence on aid, 155; Food aid, 154; Social aid, 153; Support of rural entrepreneurs, 156
Alcohol, 64
Al-Kabeer, 136, 146
Allana, 136, 146
Amalgam, 146
AMS, 207
Amul, 101
Anand, 101
Animal feed, 142
Animal husbandry, 132
APEDA, 126
Aquaculture, 143, 145
Areca, 46
Aryans, 32
Aviculture, 137
Ayurvedic medicine, 43

BAIF, 3
Bakeries, 99
Banks, 91, 92
Beedis, 56
Biodiversity, 185, 196
Biscuit factories, 99
BKU, 40
Blocks, 35
Brahmins, 32
Breeding, 132
British trade, 67
Brooke Bond Lipton, 51
Bureaucracy, 111, 155
Butter, 118

CAD, 79
Cadbury, 54
Calories, 164
Canal irrigation, 79, 175
CARI, 137
Cashew, 46
Castes, 32, 42
Castlerock, 146
Cattle, 132
CBD, 192
Centralism, 33, 160
Cereals, 66, 86, 95, 209
Chapattis, 41
Chicken, 141
Chirag & Co., 146, 147
Chutneys, 125
CIP, 88
Climate, 26
Cocoa, 54
Coconut, 118
Coffee, 52
Condiments, 44
Cooperatives, 63, 82, 84, 101
Corruption, 111, 158
Cotton, 56, 74, 118, 189, 209
CPI, 203
Credit, 89
CTC tea, 50
Customs duty, 224
CWC, 79, 85

Dalits, 32
Decentralization, 33
Deforestation, 180

Development authorities, 35
Dal, 41
Dispute with the United States, 222
Districts, 34
Dravidians, 32
DWCRA, 151

EAS, 152
Eggs, 138
Electricity, 182
Environmentalists, 176, 188
Erosion, 179
Europe, 218
Exports, 58, 137, 158, 215, 216

Famine, 67
Farmers' movements, 39
Farms, 38
Fats, 166
Fauna, 29
FCI, 85
Fertilizers, 74, 94, 96, 183
Fish, 143
Fishing, 144
Flora, 29
Flowers, 131
Food, 41
Food corporations, 85
Food for work, 152
Food projections, 225
Food security, 169
Food grains, 86, 96, 97, 99
Forest, 180
FPS, 88
Fresh products, 125
Fruit, 121, 125
Fuel, 182
Futures markets, 205

GATT, 206
Geography, 23
Gandhi, Mahatma, 57, 68, 149
Gandhi, Rajiv, 112, 201
Ghee, 118
Glaxo, 108
GMO, 73, 189
Godrej, 115, 128
Greenhouse gases, 185
Groundnut, 116
Grow More Food campaign, 68
Gur, 59, 62

Haryana, 240
Hind Industries, 136
Hindu growth rate, 149
Hindus, 32
Hindustan Lever, 52, 115
Horticulture, 121
HYV, 71, 96

IARI, 70
ICAR, 36, 71
ICDS, 153, 156
IFFCO, 75
Import barriers, 219
Imports, 68, 76, 86, 110, 116, 117, 158, 215, 216, 221
Indo-Gangetic Plain, 26
Indus Valley, 66
Instant Socialism, 161
Intellectual property, 194
IRDP, 151, 155
Irrigation, 78, 96, 174
ITC, 55, 115

Jatis, 32
JGSY, 152
Jharkhand, 244
JRY, 152, 156

Kaveri, 174
Khadi, 56
Khandsari, 59, 62
Kharif, 27
Kissan, 128
KRIBHCO, 75
Krishna, 174
KRRS, 40, 188
Kurien, V., 101
KVIC, 56
KVKs, 36

Land, 36
Legumes, 98

Liberalization, 106, 198
Livestock, 132
Losses, 123

Mahyco, 72
Mandals, 35
Marico, 115
Market access, 219
Marketing chain, 123
Mauryan Empire, 66
MDMS, 153
Meat, 134, 141
Mechanization, 94
Microfinance, 92
Middle classes, 201
Milk, 101
Millet, 29, 41, 73, 74
Mills, 99
MIO, 113
MIS, 84
Mixed economy, 198
Monsanto, 73
MPEDA, 143
MPPO, 106
MSP, 58, 84
Mushrooms, 130
Muslims, 32
MWS, 80

NABARD, 91
NAFED, 84
Narmada, 173
Natural resources, 147, 171
NDDB, 101, 107, 113, 124
NECC, 137
Neem, 190
Nestlé, 52, 108, 128
NREGS, 152
NSAP, 153
NSC, 71
NTB, 222
Nutrition, 161
Nuts, 44

OGL, 219
Oilseeds, 109
Onions, 129
Operation Flood, 102
Over-grazing, 180

PACS, 90
Panchayats, 35
PAP, 150
Pastoral nomadism, 134
Patents, 190, 191, 194
PDS, 88, 154, 157, 158, 160, 186
Peninsular India, 26
Pepsi, 128
Pesticides, 94, 183
Pickles, 125
Pioneer, 73
Pitroda, Sam, 112
PL 480, 68, 154
Planning, 68
Plantations, 44, 47
Pollution, 183
Population, 29, 96
Populism, 157
Potatoes, 129
Poultry, 137
Poverty, 149, 161
Poverty Alleviation Programmes, 150
Prawn exports, 145
Preserves, 125
Price – Central Issue Price, 88; Minimum Support Price, 58, 84; Procurement Price, 58, 84; Retention Price, 77; Statutory Minimum Price, 60
Prices, 203
Primary Agricultural Credit Societies, 90
ProAgro, 72
Productivity, 93, 228
Protein, 167
Public Distribution System, 88
Pulses, 96, 98, 209

Quantitative restrictions, 222

Rabi, 27
Rallis, 73
Rapeseed/mustard, 116
RBI, 91